H.D.

Donna Krolik Hollenberg

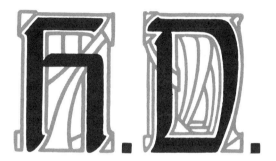

THE POETICS OF CHILDBIRTH
AND CREATIVITY

Northeastern University Press
BOSTON

Northeastern University Press

Library of Congress Cataloging-in-Publication Data

Hollenberg, Donna Krolik.
H.D. : the poetics of childbirth and creativity / Donna Krolik Hollenberg.
p.   cm.
Includes bibliographical references (p.   ) and index.
ISBN 1-55553-104-0 : $25.00
1. H. D. (Hilda Doolittle), 1886–1961—Criticism and interpretation.
2. Creativity in literature.   3. Childbirth in literature.   I. Title.
PS3507.0726Z74   1991
811'.52—dc20   91-10588
                                                        CIP

Designed by Ann Twombly

This book was composed in Cheltenham by focus/graphics in St. Louis, Mo. It was printed and bound by The Maple Press in York, Pennsylvania. The paper is Sebago Antique, an acid-free sheet.

Manufactured in the United States of America

95 94 93 92 91   5 4 3 2 1

To my mother
— and in memory of my father

Contents

Contents

Acknowledgments

I have had generous support—from institutions, colleagues, friends, and family—in the writing of this book. The Simmons College Fund for Research enabled many essential trips to the Beinecke Rare Book and Manuscript Library. For excellent bibliographic advice and warm hospitality, I am indebted to Louis H. Silverstein, who catalogued H.D.'s papers and continues to be an invaluable source of information. In particular I wish to thank him for allowing me to draw upon his extensive *H.D. Chronology*. I also wish to thank Susan Stanford Friedman, Adalaide Morris, Jeanne Kerblat Houghton, and Rosamund Rosenmeier for sharing their research in progress with me.

My work benefited enormously from the thoughtful critiques of Susan Gubar and Elizabeth Ammons, who read the whole manuscript at key junctures in its composition. I am also very grateful to Ann Cobb, Jill Bloom, Bette Mandl, and David Cavitch for their careful readings of chapters at various stages of completion. Jerome Gans also made important comments along the way that clarified my thinking. Further, I wish to acknowledge, with thanks, the dedicated labor of the editorial staff at Northeastern University Press: Deborah Kops, Ann Twombly, Maggie Carr, and Emily McKeigue.

This book is dedicated to my parents, Albert and Sheila Krolik. However, my children, Ilana and David Hollenberg, and my husband, Leonard Rubin, deserve as much gratitude. Without their encouragement, humor, and love, it would not have been completed.

Grateful acknowledgment is also made to New Directions Publishing Corporation for permission to quote from the following copyrighted works of H.D.: *Bid Me to Live [A Madrigal]* (Copyright © 1960 by Norman Holmes Pearson); *Collected Poems 1912–1944* (Copyright 1925 by Hilda Doolittle, Copyright © 1957, 1969 by Norman Holmes Pearson, Copyright © 1982 by the Estate of H.D., Copyright © 1983 by Perdita Schaffner); *End to Torment: A Memoir of Ezra Pound* (Copyright © 1979 by New Directions Publishing Corporation); *The Gift* (Copyright © 1969, 1982 by the Estate of Hilda Doolittle, Copyright © 1988 by Perdita Schaffner); *Hedylus* (Copyright © 1928, 1980 by the Estate of Hilda Doolittle); *Helen in Egypt* (Copyright © 1961 by Norman Holmes Pearson); *Hermetic Definition* (Copyright © 1958, 1959, 1961, 1969, 1972 by Norman Holmes Pearson); *HERmione* (Copyright © 1981 by the Estate of Hilda Doolittle, Copyright 1981 by Perdita Schaffner); *Ion* (Copyright © 1937 by Hilda Aldington, Copyright © 1986 by Perdita Schaffner); *Tribute to Freud* (Copyright © 1956, 1974 by Norman Holmes Pearson); *Trilogy* (Copyright © 1973 by Norman Holmes Pearson) (*Tribute to the Angels*, Copyright 1945 by Oxford University Press, Copyright renewed 1973 by Norman Holmes Pearson; *The Walls Do Not Fall*, Copyright 1944 by Oxford University Press, Copyright renewed 1972 by Norman Holmes Pearson; *The Flowering of the Rod*, Copyright 1946 by Oxford University Press); *Trilogy* (Copyright © 1973 by Norman Holmes Pearson); "Vale Ave" in *New Directions in Prose and Poetry* 44 (Copyright © 1982 by New Directions Publishing Corporation). All previously unpublished letters and manuscripts not currently in print are used by permission of New Directions Publishing Corporation, agents for H.D.'s daughter, Perdita Schaffner (Copyright © 1986 by Perdita Schaffner).

Guide to Abbreviations

"Advent"   "Advent," in *Tribute to Freud* (Boston: David R. Godine, 1974)
BAR   *By Avon River* (New York: Macmillan, 1949)
BML   *Bid Me to Live [A Madrigal]* (Redding Ridge, Conn.: Black Swan Books, 1983)
CF   *Compassionate Friendship*, unpublished ms. in Beinecke Library
CP   *Collected Poems, 1912–1944*, ed. Louis Martz (New York: New Directions, 1983)
ET   *End to Torment: A Memoir of Ezra Pound* (New York: New Directions, 1979)
FA   *Fields of Asphodel*, unpublished ms. at the Beinecke Library
G   *The Gift* (New York: New Directions, 1982)
H   *HERmione* (New York: New Directions, 1981)
"HA"   "Helios and Athene," in *Extended Outlooks: The Iowa Review Collection of Contemporary Women Writers*, ed. Jane Cooper et al. (New York: Collier, 1982)
"HD"   "Hermetic Definition," in *Hermetic Definition* (New York: New Directions, 1972)
HD   *Hermetic Definition* (New York: New Directions, 1972)
HE   *Helen in Egypt* (New York: New Directions, 1961)

Hed	*Hedylus* (Redding Ridge, Conn.: Black Swan Books, 1980)
I	Euripides, *Ion*, trans. with notes by H.D. (Boston: Houghton Mifflin, 1937)
MM	*Magic Mirror*, unpublished ms. at the Beinecke Library
MR	*Magic Ring*, unpublished ms. at the Beinecke Library
Notes on Greek Poets	*Notes on Euripides, Pausanias, and Greek Lyric Poets*, unpublished ms. at the Beinecke Library
NTV	*Notes on Thought and Vision & The Wise Sappho* (San Francisco: City Lights, 1982)
P	*Palimpsest* (Carbondale: Southern Illinois Press, 1968)
PIT	*Paint It Today*, unpublished ms. at the Beinecke Library
"S"	"Sagesse," in *Hermetic Definition* (New York: New Directions, 1972)
"Sketch"	Perdita Schaffner, "Sketch of H.D.: The Egyptian Cat," in H.D., *Hedylus* (Redding Ridge, Conn.: Black Swan Books, 1980)
Some Notes	*Some Notes on Recent Writing*, unpublished ms. at the Beinecke Library
Sword	*The Sword Went Out to Sea*, unpublished ms. at the Beinecke Library
T	*Trilogy* (New York: New Directions, 1973)
TF	*Tribute to Freud* (Boston: David R. Godine, 1974)
TT	*Thorn Thicket*, unpublished ms. at the Beinecke Library
"VA"	"Vale Ave," in *New Directions 44*, ed. James Laughlin (New York: New Directions, 1982)
"WL"	"Winter Love," in *Hermetic Definition* (New York: New Directions, 1972)
WW	*Within the Walls*, unpublished ms. at the Beinecke Library

Chronology

1886	Birth of H.D. (Hilda Doolittle) on September 10 in Bethlehem, Pennsylvania, to Charles Leander Doolittle, professor of astronomy at Lehigh University, and Helen Wolle Doolittle, a teacher of music and art at the Moravian Seminary.
1886–1895	Lives in Bethlehem; attends Moravian schools and assimilates Moravian history, culture, and religion; moves to Upper Darby, outside of Philadelphia, in 1895; father becomes professor of astronomy at the University of Pennsylvania and director of the Flower Observatory.
1901	Meets Ezra Pound, a student at the University of Pennsylvania.
1905–1908	Becomes engaged, then disengaged to Pound, who nurtures her reading and encourages her writing ambition; attends Bryn Mawr College as a day student for three semesters; withdraws, possibly because of ill health, failing grades, involvement with Pound.
1910	Meets Frances Josepha Gregg, a student at the Pennsylvania Academy of Fine Arts; lives in Greenwich Village, where she attempts to earn living as a writer.
1911	Sails to Europe with Frances Gregg and her mother, Julia Gregg; spends summer in Paris with the Greggs, then resides in London where Pound has settled; intro-

duced to the literary and cultural circles frequented by Pound; meets Richard Aldington, who often accompanies her on trips to Europe.

1912   Pound edits three of H.D.'s poems in accordance with evolving Imagist principles and adds "Imagiste" to H.D.'s initials as part of her signature.

1913   First known publication of poems in *Poetry*; marries Richard Aldington on October 18 in London; meets John Cournos, whom she will show early prose fiction manuscripts.

1914   *Des Imagistes: An Anthology* published; includes poems by H.D., Aldington, Pound, and others; begins friendship with D. H. Lawrence, with whom she exchanges manuscripts.

1915   Birth of stillborn daughter on May 21, after the sinking of the *Lusitania* on May 7; choruses from *The Iphigeneia in Aulis of Euripides* (translation) published.

1916   *Sea Garden* (poems) published; Aldington enlists as a private in the British Army in May and is sent to France in December; H.D. begins translating Euripides' play *Ion*.

1918   Goes to live with Cecil Gray in Cornwall; becomes pregnant there and later acknowledges Gray as the father of her child; meets Bryher (Annie Winifred Ellerman) on July 17 in Cornwall; returns to London in mid-August; H.D.'s brother, Gilbert Doolittle, is killed in action in France on September 25.

1919   Contracts the war influenza and later credits Bryher with saving her life; H.D.'s father dies on March 2 in Pennsylvania; H.D. gives birth to a daughter, Frances Perdita, on March 31 in London; registers the child as Aldington's on May 6, against Aldington's wishes; goes to Cornwall and the Scilly Islands with Bryher in June and July; has "jelly-fish" and "bell-jar" experiences described in *Notes on Thought and Vision* (essay).

1920	Travels to Greece and Corfu with Bryher from February through April, accompanied by Havelock Ellis; meets Peter Rodeck on the ship; has writing-on-the-wall experience in Corfu; writes "Helios and Athene" (poem).
1921	Through 1946, alternates residences between Territet and Burrier-La-Tour, Switzerland, where she lives with Bryher, and London, where she usually maintains her own flat; Bryher marries Robert McAlmon in New York.
1921–1922	Writes the novels *Fields of Asphodel* and *Paint It Today*; *Hymen* (poems) published in 1921.
1923	Travels with her mother and Bryher to Egypt by way of Italy from January through February; itinerary includes Luxor, Karnak, and a cruise down the Nile.
1924	*Heliodora and Other Poems* published.
1925	*Collected Poems of H.D.* published; interest begins to deepen in psychoanalysis, astrology, numerology, and tarot.
1926	*Palimpsest* (novel) published; meets Kenneth Macpherson.
1927	Lives in a ménage in Switzerland with Macpherson, Bryher, and Perdita until 1932; H.D.'s mother dies on March 1; Bryher divorces McAlmon in June and marries Macpherson in September; H.D. writes the novel *HERmione*.
1928	*Hedylus* (novel) published; H.D. has abortion in Berlin; Bryher and Macpherson adopt Perdita in May.
1930	Stars with Paul Robeson in *Borderline*, a film produced by Macpherson in Switzerland.
1931–1932	*Red Roses for Bronze* (poems) published; undergoes psychoanalytic treatment, first with Mary Chadwick, in London, then with Hanns Sachs, Bryher's analyst; begins writing the poems she later titles "The Dead Priestess Speaks," which she works on through 1938.

1933	In analysis with Freud in Vienna from March 1 through June 12.
1934	Has a brief but severe breakdown in August after hearing of the death of J. J. Van der Leeuw, whose hour with Freud preceded hers; returns to Vienna to complete her analysis with Freud, beginning October 31 and ending on December 2.
1937	Initiates divorce proceedings, at Aldington's request; Euripides' *Ion* (translation) published.
1938	Divorce decree comes through.
1939	Returns to London from Switzerland; remains there during World War II with Bryher until May 1946, with occasional trips to the English countryside; begins writing the *roman à clef Bid Me to Live [A Madrigal]*.
1940–1941	Writes *Within the Walls* (sketches).
1941	Begins writing *The Gift* (autobiography), which she works on until 1943; begins period of intensified interest in spiritualism; joins the Society for Psychical Research; meets Arthur Bhaduri in 1941 and participates in regular séances with him; meets and attends spiritualist lectures by Lord Hugh Dowding; is influenced by Dowding's reports of communications through mediums with dead RAF pilots and believes she receives messages from these airmen.
1942–1944	Writes *The Walls Do Not Fall, Tribute to the Angels,* and *The Flowering of the Rod,* which are published as three individual volumes in 1944–1946.
1944	Writes *Writing On the Wall* (memoir), later published as *Tribute to Freud.*
1946	Suffers a major breakdown brought on by ill health, the strain of World War II, her feelings of rejection by Dowding; taken to Seehof, Privat Klinik Brunner, Kusnacht, near Zurich.
1946	Begins writing the sequence of novels beginning with *The Sword Went Out to Sea.*

1948–1949   Reviews, rewrites, and polishes unpublished manuscripts during what she refers to as her "sabbatical
year"; writes *Notes on Recent Writing*, an essay on
major themes and patterns in her work, at Norman
Holmes Pearson's request. (Her title is "H.D. by
Delia Alton."); *By Avon River* (poetry and essay)
published in 1949.

1949–1951   Finishes writing *Bid Me to Live [A Madrigal]*;
Perdita, who has settled in America, marries John
Schaffner; Perdita bears first child, Valentine, in
1951.

1952–1954   Writes *Helen in Egypt* (lyric epic); undergoes operation for abdominal intestinal occlusions at the Clinique
Cecil in Lausanne in 1953; moves to Klinik Brunner in
Kusnacht, where she stays until 1954; meets and enters
psychoanalytical consultation with Dr. Erich Heydt,
who regards her as his colleague and friend; Perdita's
second child, Nicholas, born in 1953.

1955   Writes *Compassionate Friendship* (memoir) and *Magic
Mirror* (novel).

1956   Falls and breaks hip at Klinik Brunner; resides there
most of the time until her death; *Tribute to Freud*
published; Perdita bears third child, Elizabeth Bryher.

1957   Writes "Vale Ave" (poem) and "Sagesse" (poem);
writes *Hirslanden Notebooks* (journal).

1958   Writes *End to Torment* (memoir).

1959   Writes "Winter Love" (poem).

1960   *Bid Me to Live [A Madrigal]* published; becomes the
first woman to receive the Award of Merit Medal for
Poetry from the American Academy of Arts and
Letters; accepts the award in person and meets St. John
Perse at the ceremony; meets Lionel Durand and grants
him an interview for *Newsweek*; begins writing the
poem "Hermetic Definition"; writes the journal *Thorn
Ticket*; Perdita's fourth child, Timothy, born.

1961   *Helen in Egypt* published; suffers a stroke in June; dies on September 27; ashes are flown to Bethlehem where they are interred in the family plot in Nisky Hill Cemetery.

1972   *Hermetic Definition* published, includes title poem, "Sagesse," and "Winter Love."

1973   *Trilogy* published, which includes *The Walls Do Not Fall, Tribute to the Angels,* and *The Flowering of the Rod.*

H.D.

Introduction

Gender, Creativity, and H.D.'s Use
of the Childbirth Metaphor

*Patriarchal thought has limited female biology to its own
narrow specifications. The feminist vision has recoiled
from female biology for these reasons; it will, I believe,
come to view our physicality as a resource, rather than a
destiny. In order to live a fully human life we require not
only control of our bodies (though control is a
prerequisite); we must touch the unity and resonance of
our physicality, our bond with the natural order, the
corporeal ground of our intelligence.*[1]

—Adrienne Rich

NOT THE LEAST of the reasons that H.D. sought help from
Sigmund Freud in the mid-1930s was a growing feeling of dissatisfaction with her work. "I have never been completely satisfied with any of
my books, published or unpublished," she wrote in the journal she
kept during her analysis.[2] Though the "crystalline" polish of her early
imagist verse had been critically acclaimed, she felt that its content had
been misunderstood and trivialized; and she blamed herself, in part,
for adhering to a poetic mode based on a strategy of self-effacement.[3]
Neither was she satisfied with the direction of her early fiction. Soon
after World War I, in such unpublished novels as *Fields of Asphodel,*

3

Paint It Today, and the discarded *Niké*, she had tried to tell the story of her artistic survival; but embarrassed by the self-revelation in these accounts, she soon turned to such disguised "historical or classic reconstructions" as *Palimpsest* and *Hedylus* ("Advent," 148).

H.D. felt frustrated at failing to represent adequately her real subject, the threat to her psychological integrity arising from her trauma in pregnancy during the war, and the birth of her second child as the symbol of a regenerated poetic identity and worldview. As she put it, alluding to the zodiac to disclaim responsibility for associating writing with maternity: "I have tried to write the story or the novel of my war experience, my first, still-born child and the second, born so fortunately, with *Leo* rising in the vernal equinox, *Aries* or the Ram" ("Advent," 147). As if complying with a cultural myth that denigrated women's intellectual achievement as inherently contradictory to normal female experience, she spoke of her books as if they were stillborn children for which she is at fault as a mother:

> My books are not so much still-born as born from the detached intellect. Someone spoke of *Hedylus* as being "hallucinated writing."
>
> Yet if I become more "human" I seem to lose my sense of direction, or my prose style. The poetry is another matter. Yes the poems are satisfactory but unlike most poets of my acquaintance (and I have known many) I am no longer interested in a poem once it is written, projected, or materialized. There is a feeling that it is only a *part* of myself there. ("Advent," 149)

In these passages, when H.D. connects her frustrated achievement as a writer with her two wartime pregnancies, she uses the childbirth metaphor to encode a problem of self-concept and voice that was exacerbated for her by traumatic events in which birth and death intersected in her experience. Typically the childbirth metaphor smoothly links artistic creativity with elements of the procreative process, that is, with conception, gestation, birth, and nurture. Prevalent in everyday speech and a stock figure in literature, it usually appears in a context that masks the historical incompatibility between procreation and intellectual pursuit, not in a context that expresses the psychic fragmentation we find in the passage quoted above.

The traumatic events in her life are as follows. A year before the publication of *Sea Garden* (1916), her first book of poems, H.D.'s first child was stillborn, a loss that deepened her sense of anomalousness as a woman poet and contributed to the breakdown of her marriage. Her second child, born out of wedlock in 1919, survived despite her own near death from double pneumonia and the deaths, during her pregnancy, of her brother and her father. She came through this second set of losses with the help of another woman writer who became a life-long companion. Not surprisingly, this protracted trauma coincident with the beginning of her artistic career formed the nexus of what she termed her "personal hieroglyph," the meanings of which she would spend a lifetime decoding.

The connection between H.D.'s view of these events and her evolving figuration of the relationship between motherhood and creativity is the subject of this study. I argue here that H.D.'s response to her trauma in pregnancy during the war, which she reinterpreted throughout her life, was a central motif in her self-representation and her poetics; these evolved in tandem. That is, H.D.'s troubled motherhood influenced all of her aesthetic choices, those of persona, genre, and theme, as well as of structure and form. However, though initially a source of personal conflict and artistic inhibition, it did not always reflect so painful a sense of alienation as in the 1930s. Rather, as H.D. explored the psychological and social consequences of woman's role as nurturer, her maternal experience inspired uniquely female images of creativity that countermanded an androcentric myth of language built upon women's subordination and silence. Eventually, H.D.'s attempt to accurately represent this experience led to a theory of poetic inspiration that recognized and critiqued the centrality of the mother-child dyad in the inner life of all artists, and to a theme of the child through which she mediated the crippling dichotomies of gender.

In the chapters that follow, I delineate three stages in the development of this poetic vision. Self-divided at the beginning of her career, H.D. tried to rid herself of her troubling personal story by writing a series of autobiographical novels that revealed the tension between creativity and procreation she was experiencing. At the same time she utilized a poetics of concision and objectivity, writing terse, "imagist" poems that encoded her loss and her emotional conflict in a mode that became increasingly unsatisfying.

In the middle of her career, during World War II and its aftermath, she used her analysis with Freud (1933–34) to integrate her experience as a mother and a poet. In the autobiographical writing of this period, which employs the associational methods of psychoanalysis, she reconstructed her personal past and connected her poetic gifts with a reassessed matrilineage. Then she used this new perspective in her innovative long poems to deconstruct two central western images of women: that of the Madonna in the "holy family," the sanctified mother of a male child who embodies the Word, and that of Helen of Troy, whose independent sexuality is blamed for causing the Trojan War. Also in this period she began to use the symbol of the child both to suggest the human potential to re-create the self and to critique the institution of motherhood.

Finally, when she was a grandmother, H.D.'s life-long preoccupation with the meanings and contexts of motherhood revitalized the childbirth metaphor. In her last texts she confidently reclaimed the analogy between reproductive and linguistic generativity for women writers, simultaneously illuminating and revising cultural inequities that had been previously concealed. In her hands, a cliché grown mute in repetition became a linguistic harbinger of new awareness, and thus a potential instrument of social change.

Besides its personal importance, H.D.'s evolving use of the childbirth metaphor has enormous ideological and historical resonance. In the second passage quoted above, H.D.'s dissatisfaction with books "born from the detached intellect," combined with fear of losing her artistic direction if she becomes more "human," suggests a dilemma peculiar not only to her but to the whole tradition of women artists who have felt fragmented and depersonalized upon confronting the cultural inequity the childbirth metaphor masks. In ordinary usage the process of giving birth appears prototypical of power in our culture. Its implied equivalency with intellectual creativity is evident in the many words — such as *conceive*, *fertile*, or *barren* — that refer to the mind as well as to the body. But in fact the imaginative equation implied by the birth metaphor as it has been used by men — the easy connection between procreation and self-realization — has been problematic for women writers because it is based on a harmony that has been disallowed in women's lives.

Historically, reproductive sex differences have formed the cornerstone of a sexual division of labor that has excluded the vast majority of women from serious intellectual pursuit by limiting their opportunities: men wrote books, women bore children. Because of the internalization of this culturally enforced opposition, the womb, biologically a source of power, has been turned against women with damaging psychological effects — even when they did gain the opportunity to create. Thus, when women writers have employed the analogy often drawn between artistic creativity and procreation, they have found themselves in a painful double bind. On the one hand, bearing a child is charged with feelings of self-cauterization and alienation from the public world.[4] On the other, the substitution of art for children, perceived as being at the expense of a literal child, is felt to be transgressive.[5]

How the silence of women in history has contributed to the woman writer's quarrel with the childbirth metaphor becomes clearer when we consider the way metaphor works. As linguistic theorists tell us, metaphor is a trope that places into juxtaposition two terms that are thought of as both similar and dissimilar. One of these terms will be continuous with the topic of discourse or context; the other will be discontinuous. Because the context establishes the moral perspective that prefigures response, the continuous term is favored.[6] However, commonplace knowledge of the discontinuous term and its semantic domain governs the aptness of the metaphor, and when such knowledge is merely perfunctory, the metaphor becomes an ornamental cliché.[7]

The relevance of this dynamic to the childbirth metaphor is as follows. In the past the childbirth metaphor has been used mainly by

7

men (whose role in procreation is relatively limited). Therefore the context of its use was usually intellectual creativity, and the experience of birth was represented from the male point of view. Although the metaphor seemed to equate the two domains, associations with the (male) mind were privileged over associations with the (female) body. Thus, male use of the metaphor, in Susan Friedman's words, intensified "difference and collision" of the two terms, covertly affirming the traditional cultural separation of creativity and procreation.[8]

Since metaphors provide access to the basic premises and values of a society, H.D.'s anxious use of the birth metaphor underscores a related cultural distortion. Her association of her creativity with "the detached intellect"—something divorced from the fullness of her experience—reminds us that to the extent that we do have a philosophy of birth in western culture, it has either depreciated or coopted woman's part. Some have attributed this phenomenon to man's unconscious fear and envy of women's sexual and reproductive powers, to "male womb envy."[9] As Mary O'Brien has written, "man the procreator, by virtue of his need to mediate his alienation from procreation, is essentially man the creator."[10] The ideologies and institutional forms he has created—such as the domination of the male seed, marriage, and paternity—serve to mediate the contradictions in male reproductive consciousness. For example, in classical times Plato consciously transferred the dynamics of procreation to creative intellectual intercourse between men; in the *Timaeus* the "reality of maternity as opposed to the ideality of paternity is simply inverted and motherhood becomes passively abstract while male creative inspiration becomes a potent and regenerative force."[11] Similarly, Christian religious symbolism has rendered maternity passive and even virginal, blatantly reversing natural fact, while it has attributed divine agency to paternity.

This privileging of paternity, with its glorification of male sexuality at the expense of female, has had profound repercussions for the female imagination. As Sandra Gilbert and Susan Gubar have written, literary women have long been inhibited by "male metaphors of literary creation" that depend upon the "patriarchal etiology that

8

defines a Father God as the only creator of all things."[12] By representing the pen as a metaphorical penis, male writers have privileged the one moment in the procreative process in which men are necessary. Thus they have distorted consciousness of this process to serve their own interests, simultaneously denying women the psychological authority to create.

The other side of the coin, the male writer's appropriation of female moments of procreation to legitimize the birth of his "brain children" has been equally inhibiting to women writers—because this has been accomplished at the expense of women's maternal subjectivity. Throughout the androcentric Judeo-Christian tradition, women's procreativity has served as a symbol for human qualities men are ambivalent about: particularly emotion and intuition, which (like childbirth) have been perceived as mindless and uncontrolled. Therefore, although the associations with childbirth vary in given historical periods, reflecting positive or negative views of these qualities, they all reify male bias and, at worst, misogyny.

For example, Elizabeth Sacks attributes the popularity of the birth metaphor in the English Renaissance to a number of causes, some of them psychological. She suggests that male womb envy may have had a particularly important impact on the national subconscious during this period, during which writers witnessed both the "dynastic crises" that plagued Henry VIII and Queen Elizabeth's barren reign.[13] This hidden agenda may have underlain the male Renaissance poets' extensive incorporation of the neo-Platonic concept of two routes to immortality—through one's child and through one's art—into their own poetic ideal.

Similarly, Terry Castle has argued that the childbirth metaphor was abundant during both the Enlightenment and the Romantic era—but with opposite meanings that reflected the larger aesthetic values of these periods. Satirists like John Dryden and Alexander Pope, who privileged (male) reason and purpose, used the trope as a "negative model for the work of the bad artist," whereas the Romantic poets, reaffirming the (female) values of spontaneity, feeling, and intuition, used it to celebrate the organic nature of poetic genius.[14] Further, in such nineteenth-century novels as *Anna Karenina* and *The Scarlet Letter*, in which "fallen women" suffer in childbirth and bear daughters instead of sons, male writers used the childbirth metaphor to show the tragic results of the "improper" exercise of female sexuality. Such plots thereby validated marriage and motherhood, institutions that ensured the continued confinement of women to the domestic sphere, just as they were beginning to battle for the right to enter all areas of public life.[15]

As women became increasingly successful in the battle for social change, simultaneously creating a powerful female literary tradition, male writers devised a variety of defensive strategies to defuse their anxiety at what they increasingly perceived as an unwelcome encroachment on their turf.[16] Not surprisingly, the childbirth metaphor was one of them. For example, in his novels *Women in Love* (1920) and *Aaron's Rod* (1922) D. H. Lawrence characterizes women artists who reject traditional female roles as vicious and miserable in their envy of men's freedom. In James Joyce's *Ulysses* (1922) the maternity hospital where Mrs. Purefoy suffers in childbirth is also the locus of Bloom's fertilizing encounter with the embryonic Stephen, an encounter that produces the rival birth of one of Joyce's most dazzling linguistic feats — a sequence of stylistic parodies of English literature organized in nine parts to correspond with the nine months of gestation.[17]

Because the childbirth metaphor, as it has been used by men, perpetuates both the split between mind and body and women's confinement to the domestic sphere, it has not been a comfortable vehicle for women writers. Capable of both creation and procreation but feeling the two at odds, they have used it mainly to express an anxiety of female authorship that has tragically reinforced the opposition of body and mind, private and public, implicit in the male tradition. For example, through the birth metaphor women writers have proffered disparaging attitudes toward their own creative abilities, such as those of the Puritan poet Anne Bradstreet, who addresses her book (published by her brother-in-law) as "Thou ill-formed offspring of my feeble brain, / Who after birth didst by my side remain / Till snatched from thence by friends, less wise than true."[18] Or they have proffered tragic views of birth, like that of Mary Shelley in *Frankenstein* (1818), where the monster formed in the "workshop of filthy creation" reveals Shelley's own horror at female generativity.[19] Or they have depicted the conflict between creativity and procreation as a deadly no-win situation, as Olive Schreiner did in *The Story of an African Farm* (1883), where her artist-heroine Lyndall dies after giving birth to a dead baby.

However, H.D. was concerned with the birth metaphor at an extremely significant moment in history, a time when the declining infant and maternal mortality rate and the mass acceptance of contraception had begun to bring about a fundamental change in our social institutions. Her artistic maturity coincided with the sexual revolution in Europe and America in the 1920s, a movement rooted in socialism and feminism that led to women's demands for reproductive self-determination.[20] The freedom for women to choose parenthood was a historical development as significant as the discovery of physiological paternity; it created a transformation in human consciousness of our relations with the natural world. Thus, in the twentieth century the female writer's use of the birth metaphor, besides reflecting a recoil from the trap of biology as social destiny, began to perform another, more subversive, function.

For although metaphors provide access to the prevailing values of a society, they can also subvert the status quo by changing our perception of the relationship between categories of thought.[21] Freed from the biological imperative to procreate, women writers in the twentieth century began to exploit rather than decry their double birthing potential. In their hands the context of the metaphor became *either* creativity or procreation, and the semantic terms bidirectional. They began to engage the two topics simultaneously, allowing each to provide the discontinuous term for the other. By deliberately confounding the literal (childbirth) with the figurative (creativity), they blurred the distinction between life and art, suggesting the philosophical basis for a new pattern of social organization.

This ambivalence of perspective is evident in the passages from H.D.'s journal quoted above. For although the predominant emotion

11

expressed there is anxiety, H.D. does try to connect her progress as a writer with the birth of her two children: the first stillborn, and the second "born so fortunately, with *Leo* rising in the vernal equinox." These words allude not only to biographical facts but also to imaginative strategies in H.D.'s work that place her in a tradition established by such contemporaries as Dorothy Richardson, Katherine Mansfield, Virginia Woolf, and Willa Cather, women who wrote *kunstlerromans* in which the childbearing process, newly valorized, is an important subtext in their self-definition as artists. As Susan Gubar has argued, using Katherine Mansfield as a prototype, these writers wrote novels in which the artist-heroines call into question the identification of artistry with the autonomy of sons by utilizing several imaginative strategies that reconciled their writing with their rearing as daughters. They created "a revisionary domestic mythology" that reconstructed the degradation of their domestic reality, a fantasy of "a woman's language" that countered the distortion of female experience in male language, and an "erotics of mother and child" that explored the mother-daughter bond as "a release from the solipsism of individual consciousness."[22]

Similarly, most of H.D.'s early fiction may be read as forms of the bildungsroman or *kunstlerroman* in which the procreative process serves as subtext. As I argue in chapter 2, in *Fields of Asphodel* (1921–22), *Paint It Today* (1921), and *HERmione* (1927, published in 1981), and (more covertly) in other early prose fiction, H.D. depicts nascent artist-heroines who struggle with precisely this tension between procreation and self-realization, and she invents comparable defensive strategies to restructure it. Also, in her later *kunstlerroman*, the autobiographical novel *Bid Me to Live* (1948, published in 1960), the heroine (H.D.) experiences the inner permission to write freely (after a devastating loss in childbirth) as an imagined rebuttal to the phallocentric views of an absent male writer (D. H. Lawrence) about the source of creativity.

However, in her early *kunstlerromans* H.D. did not complete the imaginative leap that would enable the innovative uses of the childbirth metaphor in her late poetry. As her early lyrics suggest, in the more intimate form of poetry she remained caught in a struggle against self-denial, a problem I analyze in chapter 3. She accomplished this breakthrough in a different genre—one with goals more commensurate with poetry than with fiction—in an autobiography of her childhood, *The Gift* (1941–43, published in 1982). Here she adopted, for the first time, the twice-removed psychological perspective that would inform the critique of woman's role as nurturer evident in her long poems *Trilogy*, *Helen in Egypt*, and the volume *Hermetic Definition*. Though this book is dedicated to her mother, in it H.D. attributes her "gift" of vision, which enabled her to withstand the war's destruction, to the Moravian mysticism and peace-loving communal ideal passed on to her by her maternal grandmother.

It is not surprising that H.D. achieved an important innovation in poetic form after she wrote an autobiography of her childhood. Richard Coe informs us that this genre differs subtly from both standard autobiography and the *kunstlerroman*.[23] It differs from standard autobiography because inner, symbolic truth is substituted for factual accuracy. (The subject of the "Childhood" is the author's former self-as-child, a state of mind qualitatively different from an adult's, which requires the creation of a convincing alternative world.) The "Childhood" also differs from the *kunstlerroman*, a form of fiction. Instead of a plot, there is a pattern endowed retrospectively with significance, which affects or reveals the narrator-subject (not the surrounding characters), and which ends when the immature self is conscious of its transformation into the mature self who narrates the earlier experience. Relatively speaking, the *kunstlerroman* ultimately subordinates the self to the judgment of the world, whereas, in Coe's words, "the Childhood imposes its own standards, judging and frequently condemning the world in terms of the self."[24]

As I show more fully in chapter 4, the liberating impact of this genre on H.D.'s poetry is apparent when we relate the form of *The Gift* to the psychological "story" of *Trilogy*. Fortified by her analysis with Freud, during which she had retrieved valuable, repressed childhood memories, H.D. makes the relation between childhood and adult consciousness central to the narrative structure of *The Gift*. She employs the perspective of an imaginal child (the child reconceived by an adult self) to re-create the childhood world that shaped her awareness as a poet. By privileging her position as granddaughter in that world, she aligns self-creation and procreation with less ambivalence than before. The achievement of this psychological distance enables the deconstruction of the myth of the "holy family" evident in *Trilogy*.

Begun in London during the Blitz, a year before the first volume of *Trilogy*, H.D.'s portrait of herself-as-child in *The Gift* anticipates the appearance of the symbolic child in her late poetry. Like the Romantic poets, who proclaimed the value of imagination and sensibility in a world given over increasingly to abstracted intellect and the machine, H.D. employs the symbol of the child in her late work to express her dissatisfaction with those social forces that would denature humanity. Like Blake and Wordsworth, she employs the symbolic child as an agent in her quest for psychological insight and vision, alluding not only to an offspring but to an adult's potential for growth.[25]

However, unlike the Romantic poets, who exaggerated the innocence, unworldliness, and freedom of the child, an idealization of childhood that also pervaded much of Victorian writing, H.D. was more interested in psychological realism.[26] Like Freud (and those contemporaries who were influenced by his ideas), she was concerned with infancy and childhood as periods that the adult may study to understand the development of identity. She viewed the nurture of the child as part of a larger procreative process that was itself socially constructed.

H.D. did not agree with all of Freud's theories, however. In particular, she realized that his view of psychosexual development was androcentric; it did not recognize fully enough the effect of socialization upon gender identity and gender role.[27] (According to Freud, the successful resolution of the Oedipus complex—for which boys are the prototype—requires the boy to repress his childish dependency on his mother and to internalize the paternal authority that demanded this of him, with its emphasis on autonomy and renunciation.) Besides doubting its relevance to women, H.D. realized that Freud's oedipal model purported to speak for nature rather than for history: it assumed the inevitability of domination and gender difference. H.D. questioned whether this model reflected a social system conducive to human growth and creativity. Anticipating the critique of such contemporary theorists as Jessica Benjamin, she saw that Freud's oedipal drama reproduced on the psychological level a "fusion of autonomy and authority uniquely suited to the epoch of liberal capitalism."[28] She had inherited a communal ideal from her Moravian ancestors, who organized their community like an extended family of "brothers" and "sisters," and she had created an alternative nuclear family, which accommodated both her bisexuality and her dual roles of poet-mother. Thus, she questioned both the sufficiency of the patriarchal family script and the social system that produced it.[29] She felt free to create her own cultural myth—one that, Adalaide Morris maintains, placed her in opposition to the gender roles prevalent in a capitalist economy.[30]

Like D. H. Lawrence, who coined the phrase "child consciousness" to describe the child's pristine mental state before it is thwarted by the family and social education, H.D. also used this phrase to refer to an eternal well-spring of human potential.[31] In *By Avon River* (1949), her prose tribute to Shakespeare, she elaborated on Lawrence's ideas. Instead of valorizing the ideal of autonomy that he endorsed, a view of psychological differentiation that assumes an unhealthy symbiosis of mother and child, she believed that mutual recognition and interdependence informed the psychic lives of creative individuals. As I show in chapter 5, she used the phrase "child-consciousness" to connect her own creative renewal after World War II with an appraisal of the continuing role of the mother-child bond in the fertile imaginative life of Shakespeare, the literary father of the whole English-speaking world.

Later, H.D. used this insight—of the pivotal intrapsychic power of the first bond—to critique the institutions of romantic love and motherhood, related elements of a patriarchal gender system that perpetuates the subordination of women in order to guarantee social stability, with devastating results for everyone. As I show in chapter 6, in her lyric epic *Helen in Egypt* she exposes the self-destructive psychodynamics that devolve from unequal gender roles. Internalized in early childhood, these gender roles form the basis for patterns of domination and submission in both the personal and political spheres. Using the symbolic child as a neutral interlocutor, she shows, from the inside, the connection between patriarchal socialization, the warrior ethos, and the exploitation of women.

Finally, having worked through the conflict between motherhood and authorship, and having dramatized its relation to androcentric cultural myth, in her last volume of poetry, *Hermetic Definition*, H.D. uses the childbirth metaphor to underscore and mediate this false dichotomy. Here she celebrates the double-birthing potential she had earlier decried. In her last poem, which I analyze in chapter 7, the trimesters of pregnancy provide a tropological analogue to the poet's final project: the mysterious creation of a poem-child through which she integrates and transcends the finality of death. Thus H.D. adduces gestation and nurture as paradigms for creativity in order to restate the themes and values of a previously muted femininity.

1

"Serpent and Thistle"

The Emotional Charge around the Child

IN *Tribute to Freud*, the memoir written during World War II in the
period of artistic breakthrough following her analysis, H.D. describes
an important dream she discussed with Freud. She points out the
phallocentrism of his interpretation of it, and she suggests the disagreement with his theories that came to underlie her mature view of
the source of her creativity. In the "dream of the Princess," as they
called the woman in the dream, H.D. watches anxiously at the foot of
the steps as a regal Egyptian lady in a saffron robe slowly descends a
marble staircase to a river on which floats a shallow basket containing
a baby: "The Princess must find the baby. I know that she will find
this child. I know that the baby will be protected and sheltered by her
and that is all that matters."[1]

This dream-image reminded H.D. of the Paul Gustave Doré
illustration "Moses in the Bulrushes" in the family Bible of her
childhood, yet it had "nothing in common with this except the subject"
of finding the child (*TF*, 37). Of course Freud knew the Doré picture
too, and he suggested that she may have wished to be the baby Moses
in fantasy, the "male founder of a new religion" (*TF*, 37). Delicately
suggesting her disagreement with the penis-envy theory behind this
interpretation, H.D. both refuses Freud's view and transmutes it,
attributing to him a more suitable alternative: perhaps she is Moses'
sister Miriam, half-concealed in the rushes.

Continuing to reflect upon the implications of her dream, H.D. then points out that "any amateur dabbler with the theories of psychoanalysis" can reconstruct the motive or "repressed psychic urge" that projected it, finding its root in the oedipal scenario that results from the patriarchal "family romance": "the little girl with her doll in her father's study" (*TF*, 38). However, her interpretation underscores the cultural origins of this psychic construct, rather than its prescriptive value. Here H.D. anticipates sociologist Nancy Chodorow, who regards the Oedipus complex as a problematic product of the patriarchal system where the mother is the sole caretaker.[2] Like Chodorow's ideas, H.D.'s account implies that the social organization of gender, already evident in the unconscious imagery of childhood, is a crucial factor in the reproduction of mothering and male domination. Having come to her father's study "to be alone or to be alone with him" because her brother is not interested in her "doll-family games," the little girl's gender identity emerges from and is embedded in the theory of reality reflected in a "recognized religious pattern" that infantilizes women:

> *Father*, aloof, distant, the provider, the protector—but a little un-get-at-able, a little too far away and giant-like in proportion, a little chilly withal; *Mother*, a virgin, the Virgin, that is an untouched child, adoring, with faith, building a dream, and the dream is symbolized by the third member of the trinity, the *Child*, the doll in her arms. (*TF*, 38)

Grateful to Freud for enabling her to project this dream of a Princess and a child, to revive "the child in [her]" that she thought had died, and thereby to experience psychological growth, H.D. continues to use the associational method she learned from him—but to a different end. Freud had suggested that H.D.'s trip to Greece after the traumatic events of World War I represented a flight from the reality of her troubled domestic situation, and that her visions at Corfu represented an unconscious "desire for union with [her] mother. . . . a flight from a flight" (*TF*, 44). In a radical reinterpretation of these visions (which I describe in a later chapter), she divests Freud's

18

diagnosis, megalomania, of its judgmental quality, claiming that the series of light-pictures she saw projected on her hotel bedroom wall had the same clarity and authenticity as the Princess dream and were thus a "sort of half-way state between ordinary dream and the vision of those who . . . we must call psychics or clairvoyants" (*TF*, 41). Thus she amplifies his interpretation of her visions to include not only the ego's defensive response to trauma in childbirth but also the possibility of prophetic power in poetry.

Written twenty-four years after the trip to Corfu and ten years after her analysis, H.D.'s account of her visions in *Tribute to Freud* is poised and deliberate. In her early work, however, she could not successfully integrate her experience as a poet and a mother. Rather, her first aesthetic statements, like her early poetry and prose fiction, bear eloquent witness to the emotional conflicts that preoccupied her after her trauma in childbirth during World War I.

Two paradigmatic texts, in which we see H.D.'s first attempts to articulate a theory of creativity based on the emotional issues arising from her trauma in childbirth, are *Notes on Thought and Vision* (1919) and "Helios and Athene" (1920). In *Notes on Thought and Vision* H.D. gives the physical experience of childbirth metaphysical dimensions: she claims "womb vision" and focuses on the mother-child dyad as the psychic structure underlying creativity. Similarly, the prose-poem "Helios and Athene" extends male myths of creativity to include female experience. A meditation upon the statue of Athene Parthenos, this early poem reveals H.D.'s concerns about psychic integrity and boundary ambiguity, concerns that devolved from her recent pregnancies.

Although neither the childbirth metaphor nor the symbol of the child per se appears in H.D.'s work until after her creative renascence in World War II, a range of meaning and emotion associated with childbirth is evident from the beginning of her career. In *Notes on Thought and Vision*, the cryptic document in which she sets down her earliest thoughts about creativity, H.D. writes that she is "concerned chiefly with the mental process that is in some form or other the complement of the life process."[3] H.D. wrote the *Notes* in 1919 while recuperating on the Scilly Islands with her devoted friend Bryher (Winifred Ellerman) just two months after she had given birth to her daughter, Frances Perdita, after a near fatal second pregnancy in the course of which she lost most of the significant men in her life. Just a few years before that, in 1915, when she was beginning to establish herself as an artist, she suffered a painful stillbirth at the end of her first pregnancy, brought on, she felt, when her young British husband (the poet Richard Aldington) abruptly broke the news of the sinking of the *Lusitania*. In the aftermath of the stillbirth she saw her marriage break down as Aldington turned increasingly to other women for sexual satisfaction because H.D. was afraid to become pregnant again. Confused and depressed, H.D. went to live temporarily with a supportive male friend, Cecil Gray, and became pregnant (by him) a second time, miraculously surviving double pneumonia to give birth to her daughter despite medical predictions that they could not both live.

H.D.'s emotional state during this second pregnancy was further complicated by the shock of her brother Gilbert's death in action, which was followed shortly by the death of her father, who was grief-stricken by his son's death. Also, she felt repudiated by such key members of her literary circle as D. H. Lawrence and Ezra Pound, who sided with Aldington in the breach that ensued after he refused responsibility for the child. (Aldington threatened to sue H.D. for adultery if she registered the child in his name.)[4] H.D. was pregnant and critically ill when Bryher found her in a cold wartime pension. She arranged for proper medical care and saw H.D. through her second delivery, promising to shelter and cherish her child and to take her to her beloved Greece when she recovered.

As these facts suggest, H.D. began to explore the imaginative implications of childbirth at a psychological turning point. In the company of the woman who had mothered her and the child she had just borne, she experienced a moment of breakdown or breakthrough during which the physical reality of childbirth acquired suprapersonal, metaphysical dimensions. Later she called it the "'jelly-fish' experience of double-ego," in which she felt insulated from "the war disaster" by two separate bell jars, one over her head, the other over her body ("Advent," 116). In her description of this experience (written during her analysis), H.D. conveys its resemblance to the "oceanic feeling" of boundlessness that Freud thought was a form of nostalgia for the time when the ego did not seem distinct from the external world: when the infant was nursing at her mother's breast.[5] H.D.'s account also emphasizes Bryher's support in what could have been a frightening collapse:

> There were palm-trees, coral-plants, misambeanthum, opened like water-lillies the length of the grey walls; the sort of fibrous under-water leaf and these open sea-flowers gave one the impression of being submerged.
>
> We were in the little room that Bryher had taken for her study when I felt this impulse to "let go" into a sort of balloon, or diving bell . . . that seemed to hover over me. . . . When I tried to explain this to Bryher and told her it might be something sinister or dangerous, she said, "No, no it is the most wonderful thing I ever heard of. Let it come." . . . There was, I explained to Bryher, a second globe or bell jar rising as it were from my feet. I was enclosed. I felt I was safe but seeing things as through water. I felt the double globe come and go and I could have dismissed it at once and probably would have if I had been alone. It was being with Bryher that projected the fantasy. ("Advent," 130)

In *Notes on Thought and Vision* H.D.'s explanation of the source of creativity is derived from this experience. She proposes a schema that divides the self into "body, mind, and over-mind," and she asserts that creative men and women experience dream and vision as the product of an "over-mind," a supernormal mental state in which consciousness is experienced physically. In her case this over-mind takes on the figurative attributes of a pregnant uterus; it is like a gelatinous sac or cap upon her forehead, "fluid yet with definite body, contained in a definite space . . . like a closed sea-plant, jelly-fish or anemone," into which thoughts pass, along tubular tentacles, like "fish swimming into clear water" (*NTV*, 20). Though both sexes experience it, "it was before the birth of [her] child that the jelly-fish consciousness seemed to come definitely into the field or realm of the intellect or brain" (*NTV*, 20). Though she first realized it in her head, she is able just as well to visualize this consciousness "centered in the love-region of the body or placed like a foetus in the body" (*NTV*, 19). Both centers of consciousness, the womb and the brain, are equally important.

Though H.D.'s overheated language in these *Notes* — their rather crude literalness — reflects her psychological strain after the birth of her child, their defensive quality may also be a response to the prejudices against intellectual women still current in this period. When H.D. asserts that "the brain and the womb are both centres of consciousness equally important," she controverts the brain-uterus competition, current in Victorian medical circles, which was based on the theory that women's reproductive functions diverted creative energy from the brain and vice versa: that every mental effort of the pregnant woman could deprive her unborn child of some vital nutrient.[6] H.D. had Havelock Ellis in mind as the interpreter of the "psychological data" recorded in these *Notes*, she wrote later, but she was disappointed in his lack of sympathy (*TF*, 130). She had begun to read Ellis's *Studies in the Psychology of Sex* in Devon after her stillbirth, when she began to question the adequacy of her relationship with Aldington, and she had consulted Ellis during the emotional upheaval of her second pregnancy. Interested in the connection between sexuality and creativity, and in pregnancy as a state of heightened nervous impressionability, Ellis nevertheless distinguished between sexuality's primary reproductive function and a secondary spiritual function of "furthering the higher mental and emotional processes."[7] Drawing upon her recent pregnancy and the "jelly-fish experience of double ego," H.D.'s theory reconnects the physiological and spiritual functions that Ellis separated.[8]

Further, anticipating such contemporary psychoanalytical theorists as Heinz Kohut, H.D.'s focus on the mother-child dyad, which precedes the oedipal stage, leads to a view of psychic structure and creativity that privileges recognition by a loved other, not prohibition and separation.[9] She believed that though we approach the visionary state through the intellect, in this state our intellect utilizes its receptive capacity for empathy, not its analytical faculty. "There is no great art period without great lovers," she writes (*NTV*, 21). Through sympathy of thought, the minds of lovers merge, creating the "over-mind" or jelly-fish that is placed over and about the brain. Similarly, the love-region, excited by the beauty of the loved one, takes on its character of "womb-brain" (if its energy is not dissipated in physical relation), which she pictures as a jelly-fish in the body (*NTV*, 22). The "love-mind" and the "over-mind" are like the two lenses of an opera glass that, when properly adjusted, bring the world of vision and of art into focus. This world of vision is one of "eternal, changeless ideas that [the artist] had grown aware of, dramas already conceived that he had watched; memory is the mother, begetter of all drama, idea, music, science or song" (*NTV*, 23).

Just as great works of art are a product of the world of "over-mind consciousness," so the aim of ancient sacred rituals, such as the Eleusinian mysteries, was to bring the initiate through the desires of the body, through the sensitivities of the intellect, to a realm of mystical consciousness in which these merged and were transcended, wherein even fear of death was subsumed to an awareness of the continuity of life. In the mysteries at Eleusis, both male and female initiates participated in the mourning mother's "finding again" of her lost daughter who had given birth among the fires of Hades. According to H.D., the mystery of Demeter, the Earth Mother, was such that the body of the initiate became "one with the earth, as his soul had become one with the seeds enclosed in the earth" (*NTV*, 52). Or, in Carl Kerenyi's fuller explanation, the meaning of Persephone's birth-in-death was not the unique, original beginning of all things, but continuity in an uninterrupted sequence of births:

> In the identity of the mother and daughter, the eternally child-bearing mother manifests herself as an eternal being, and it is into her being and her destiny that the celebrants enter. The child is a sign that the duration is more than individual; that it is continuity and continual rebirth in one's offspring.[10]

Through the reassertion of the mother-child bond in her second experience of childbirth, H.D. had moved into a realm of consciousness in which feelings of self-division and alienation gave way to a sense of organic wholeness, in which loss and fear of death were circumscribed by paradisal vision. As Albert Gelpi informs us, "H.D.'s signet was the thistle and the serpent, not separate and antagonistic, but paired."[11] This image first came to her in a dream when she was eighteen or nineteen, and Pound tried unsuccessfully to interpret it for her then. When she went to Paris in 1911, H.D. was amazed to find a signet ring engraved with the thistle and the serpent awaiting her in the Louvre; but it was not until 1919 on the Scillys that she began to understand what it symbolized. As she wrote in her *Notes*, the thistle is life accepted in the knowledge of "pain and despair"; the serpent represents the "world of vision," or of "death to the stings of life" in priestly cults throughout the world. In her personal language, however, she called "this serpent a jelly-fish" (*NTV*, 40). Under its aegis, by means of "womb vision," she had begun to integrate her art with her life as a woman.

H.D.'s "womb vision" on the Scillys was followed within the next year by another haunting supernormal episode that was related to this first experience of double ego. Not surprisingly, it occurred in connection with her coveted trip to Greece, the land she associated with her artistic aspirations. In February 1920 H.D. sailed with Bryher and Havelock Ellis for Piraeus, leaving Perdita behind in a London nursery. She later commented on her extremely shaky emotional state during that voyage: "This spring of 1920 held for me many unresolved terrors, perils, heartaches, dangers, physical as well as spiritual or intellectual. If I had been maladjusted or even mildly deranged, it would have been no small wonder" (*TF*, 41). On board the *Borodino* she had a minor flirtation with a witty, worldly architect, Peter Van Eck (Peter Rodeck), who sat beside her at dinner ("Advent," 159). Though superficially unimportant, the flirtation became imaginatively significant when it gave rise to a vivid, dreamlike meeting with a sympathetic, perfected double of Van Eck, who

24

shared with her a vision of dolphins leaping in rhythmic order from a serene and perfectly patterned sea ("Advent," 158).

This encounter with the mysterious "Man on the boat" occurred after a stormy day at sea during which she had felt temporarily youthful and renewed while trudging around the deck with Bryher and Havelock Ellis. In *Magic Ring* (1943–44), her diary of séances with the medium Arthur Bhaduri, H.D. claimed that this vision of Van Eck represented the way in which part of her shattered self, her ego, met the accumulated shocks of the World War I years. Momentarily transported out of historical time into a mythic dimension, she felt that she and Van Eck were like "Helios and a diminished edition of his half-sister" (Artemis).[12] She was singularly blessed, she believed, by the vision of dolphins, because they were the sea animals revered by the Greeks as "uterine beasts," symbols of generation sacred to Apollo.[13] Her mysterious companion's assurance that he loved her despite the earlier circumstances of her distress in London absolved her of survivor guilt: "all at once the burden of mortality—the albatross—fell off into the sea" (*MR*, 162).

I discuss this meeting with the "Man on the boat" more fully in a later chapter, when I explain H.D.'s creative use of her analysis with Freud. Here I would simply point out that it formed part of the emotional context of her second aesthetic statement, the prose-poem "Helios and Athene" (1920). Written in Athens, just before the journey past Delphi to Corfu, this poem is the "meditative preparation" for the visions of spiritual ascendancy and artistic triumph H.D. had on Corfu.[14] It contains images similar to those in her account of the latter, but here the images appear in a configuration that reveals H.D.'s emotional conflicts during the journey more than her spiritual triumph. Also, unlike the tightly controlled, "crystalline" verse that precedes and immediately follows it, this poem's long prose lines suggest heretical, anti-imagist models. In Adalaide Morris's words: "'Helios and Athene' is not an objective formulation of perception: it is impassioned mythology and history, biography and psychology, aesthetics, epistemology, and metaphysics."[15]

If in *Notes on Thought and Vision* H.D. attempted to articulate the connection between creativity and procreativity from the psychological perspective of the mother-creator, in "Helios and Athene" she writes from the position of the daughter-creator. Consequently, fears of merging become paramount. H.D. must have been deeply moved by the reproduction of Phidias's giant gold and ivory statue of Athene Parthenos in the Athens Museum, for her four-part sequence explores the psychological condition of being "one-in-herself" that is represented by this virgin goddess who holds a winged victory, her own soul, upon the palm of her left hand. As she prepared to journey from Athens toward Delphi, H.D. considered the relation of Helios to Athene, that is, the part the ancient Greek sun-god, embodiment of potentially destructive male energy, played in Athene's spiritual triumph. In keeping with her signet of serpent and thistle, she found the central clue to lie in the goddess's relation to the serpent at her right hand: the serpent in Phidias's statue "does not crouch at Athene's feet. / The serpent lifts a proud head under the shelter of her shield."[16]

To H.D., Athene's protection of this age-old symbol of fertility and chthonic power meant Phidias's acknowledgment of ancient maternal associations hidden behind the conventional image of the martial maiden, who sprang full-grown from her father Zeus' head, according to later Greek myth. In the first section of the poem H.D. keeps faith with these hidden maternal associations: she connects the serpent with Athene's nurturance of Helios' son Ion (the first Ionian), and she reminds us that serpents were inscribed upon the altar of Demeter at Eleusis. The Eleusinian initiate, protected by love of Athene, entered into a womblike "black cave, the retreat of snakes," before his or her psychic rebirth. Further, Athene's stature as "guardian of children, patron of the city," proponent of civilization, is contingent on our understanding that when "Helios the god slays the serpent, he slays in reality not so much the serpent, as fear of the serpent" ("HA," 150).

H.D.'s statement that Helios slays "not so much the serpent, as fear of the serpent" deliberately countervails misogynist accounts of the Delphic oracle's mythic origin. Classical historians inform us that

Apollo's killing of the Python, a female serpent who guarded access to the sacred springs at the earth's center, was an act that celebrated the emergence of a repressive male-oriented religion.[17] H.D. intuited this act's symbolic connection with the wish of Athenian men (whose childhoods were dominated by women) to cut the umbilicus, or break emotional ties with the mother, in order to achieve spiritual independence and superiority. (Compare the close association between the *omphalos*, the navel of the earth, and the serpent that guarded it.) As H.D. traveled toward Apollo's shrine, she carefully replaced him in her thoughts with the more archaic Helios, or the assignation Phoebus (meaning brilliant), to represent the "essential male principle."

Mindful that Greek philosophers preempted the dynamic of procreation to explain intellectual intercourse between men, H.D. devotes her contemplation of Athene Parthenos in the poem's second section to inspiring a "new standard" to set beside the "naked Greek, the youth in athletic contest," that is the conventional Apollonian ideal of beauty and divinity. Because great works of art have the power to intercede between us and "the gods," she asserts that rapt concentration on such masterpieces as Phidias's statue can produce a new approach to "Hellenic literature and art":

> The mind, in its effort to disregard the truth,
> has built up through the centuries, a mass of polyglot
> literature explanatory of Grecian myth and culture.
>
> But the time has come for men and women of
> intelligence to build up a new standard, a new
> approach to Hellenic literature and art. ("HA," 152)

Invoking the Furies' subterranean, serpentine associations and their function as goddesses of retributive justice, she admonishes: "Let daemons possess us! Let us terrify like / Erinyes, the whole tribe of academic Grecians!" ("HA," 152).

In the poem's third section the Athene Parthenos exemplifies the perfect balance of potentially destructive instinctual heat (Helios) and dazzling intellect (Athene). H.D. asserts that Delphi and Athens, the serpent and the silver olive leaf, gain strength from each other here through "interdependence of hatred" ("HA," 153). Phidias's statue reflects an internal state of creative tension in which neither loses. A snake goddess, Athene Parthenos reclaims the "demoniac" power appropriated by Apollo; filled from within, she stands unconquerable. In the first three sections of the poem H.D.'s focus on the hidden aspects of the serpent allows her to acknowledge a connection with the mother without losing any of the power associated with the male. Here she anticipates the interpretation of such contemporary theorists as Philip Slater. According to Slater, the phallic aspects of the snake (based on its capacity for erection) are less salient and resonant than its female qualities: its power to encircle; its capacity to shed its skin (which provoked fantasies of immortality and rebirth); its yawning jaws that allow it to devour and envelop. (The snake swallowing its prey is a mirror image of the pregnant woman who will expel the fetus.) A bisexual symbol, the serpent is involved in the emotional and cultural issue of expressing or transcending sexual differentiation. Also, the ubiquity of this symbol in classical myth reveals that in the representation of ancient deities the dichotomies that dominate our current thinking (creation and destruction, birth and death, male and female) were conjoined. Further, because its female qualities are most salient, the snake is primarily an "oral-narcissistic symbol" rather than an oedipal one. In Slater's words:

> it is the most common symbol of boundary-ambiguity. It appears in connection with the boundary between life and death, consciousness and unconsciousness, male and female, and so on. Devouring and being devoured are associated with it, dying and being born, and everything that has to do with the edges of the body or with changes in its shape (pregnancy).[18]

In the poem's last section, though H.D. switches from the serpent on the statue's right to the winged Niké in her other hand, her concerns about sexual differentiation and merging with the mother continue to be evident. H.D. suggests that though the Apollonian ideal may appear to favor men, Greek art approaches Athene (and woman) indirectly: "The greatest Athenians of the greatest period / were initiates of the Eleusinian mysteries" ("HA," 154). Since it is associated with Demeter as well as Helios, with the female "cavern or grot in the earth" as well as the "creative power and passion of the male" ("HA," 154), the serpent comes to represent the restored balance of the two forces within the initiate's psyche. H.D. switches to the winged Niké in Athene's left hand to describe the spiritual transcendence that results from the "surrender to neither, the merging and welding of both, the conquering in herself of each element" ("HA," 154). In this image of Athene masculine and feminine merge: "the softness and tenderness of the mother" with "the creative power of the male" ("HA," 154). The winged Niké is the symbol of this "double conquest and double power" ("HA," 154). Like the virgin forest that is especially fruitful because it has taken life into itself and transformed it, "Athene, the maiden, Parthanos, is doubly passionate" ("HA," 154).

It is not surprising that these early works document the excitation of long-buried, unresolved feelings. Despite significant advances in birth technology and contraception in the twentieth century, for many women pregnancy remains a psychological turning point during which the issues of previous developmental phases are revived.[19] In H.D.'s case, old conflicts around affiliation and autonomy and around nurturance and achievement were reopened. For though she chose to become pregnant a second time and survived wartime pneumonia with her child intact, H.D. nevertheless continued to find psychological affiliation with the role of mother problematic. We see this difficulty in her reversion to the perspective of daughter in "Helios and Athene." In her vacillation between the psychological positions of mother and daughter in these two works, H.D.'s early attempts to articulate a theory of creativity based on her maternal experience correspond with the narrative strategies of other modernist women writers who, Marianne Hirsch has written, take a "liminal position between maternal/female and paternal/male affiliations."[20]

Moreover, it is not surprising that H.D. was preoccupied with the mythological symbol of the serpent at this time in her life;

psychoanalysts emphasize that the relationship between mother and child centers on oral and alimentary psychological issues, fantasies, and modes of relating for both mother and infant.[21] In both *Notes on Thought and Vision* and "Helios and Athene" H.D. relies on mythic invocation to aid her speculation about the creative process that complements the life process, a method she will continue to use. In both, the achievement of an integrated self-image and the connection of motherhood with creativity are a struggle. Yet, though they contain contradictions that reveal H.D.'s psychological strain, these works contain the beginnings of a theory of creativity based on female reproductive consciousness.

2

~~

Creativity and Procreativity in H.D.'s Early Prose Fiction

H.D.'s DAUGHTER has provided a poignant introduction to the way in which the conflict between motherhood and authorship informed H.D.'s self-conception. In an elegant essay written after she had borne and raised four children, Perdita Schaffner reflects upon the ironies connected with a tiny, turquoise Egyptian cat (now an inherited treasure) that H.D. bought in the 1920s, wore around her neck on a velvet ribbon, and frequently used as a mantra. Like H.D., whose nickname was "Kat," the cat has "aristocratic" features, and it, too, is a mother: "Between her front paws, pressed against her chest, she guards a microscopic replica, her kitten."[1] Remembering how H.D. used to point out the affinity between cat and kitten to her, Schaffner considers the painful discrepancy between an ideal of motherhood that H.D. wished to reconcile with her work and the incessant reality of child care that threatened to impinge upon it:

> H.D. was hardly an archetypal mother, nor would one expect her to be. At the time, I really didn't expect or know anything otherwise. We lived in Switzerland with her friend Bryher, isolated from the world. Visitors came by from time to time; mostly writers, adults only. I never consorted with other children, other families, other mothers. So, for all I knew, everybody's mother was a poet; a tall figure of striking beauty, with fine bone

structure and haunting grey eyes; and frequently overwrought, off in the clouds, or sequestered in a room, not to be disturbed on any account.

She was intensely maternal — on an esoteric plane. She venerated the concept of motherhood, but was unprepared for its interruptions. She flinched at sudden noise, and fled from chaos. Mercifully for her, she was well-buffered. We had a staff, almost a bodyguard. I could always be removed. *"Madame est nerveuse; viens ma petite!"* Or Bryher would step in and marshal me off. "Your mother's very nervous today." Every day, it seemed. So, fair enough, that's the way it was. A mother was someone who wrote poetry and was very nervous. And who walked alone and sat alone. And was capable of overwhelming affection, but on her own time and terms, preferably out of doors. ("Sketch," 143–44)

John Cournos's less sympathetic account of H.D.'s conflict in the early years is also telling. H.D.'s confidant during World War I and its aftermath, Cournos knew how difficult it was for her to integrate her work with her personal life. In his novel *Miranda Masters*, which is based on the marriage of H.D. and Richard Aldington, Cournos depicts the psychological pain Miranda (H.D.) suffers because of the incompatibility between her dedication to poetry and conventional womanly duties.[2] Though Miranda regards herself as a poet equal to her husband and tries to think of her poems as her children, an earlier stillbirth creates such feelings of inadequacy and guilt that her marriage is threatened. Unable to withstand the pressure to conform, she becomes pregnant a second time.

Because he was a fledgling novelist himself, H.D. sent Cournos some of her early prose fiction manuscripts, explaining on one occasion (after he had commented negatively) that she did not consider all of this prose to be art. Rather, she thought it a form of exorcism, a way of clearing space for her poetry by getting rid of a troubling personal story: "I do not put my personal self into my poems. But my personal self has got between me and my real self, my artist personality."[3] Although she considered them unfinished, H.D.'s then unpublished autobiographical novels — *Fields of Asphodel, Paint It*

Today, and *HERmione*—clearly reveal the emotional issues that preoccupied her after her traumatic wartime pregnancies, issues that she encoded in her published novels *Palimpsest* (1926) and *Hedylus* (1928) and in her imagist poetry.[4]

Since a woman reexperiences herself as a cared-for child when she becomes a mother, her identification with her own mother often revives issues from her childhood that have remained unresolved.[5] H.D.'s trauma in pregnancy bound up this identification and increased her anxiety about the mother's role in a male-dominated society. Thus the reconciliation of motherly virtue with intellectual achievement, unavailable to most women when H.D. was a child, became of paramount importance to her identity as a woman writer. In her early novels she invented competing imaginative strategies to accomplish this reconciliation, both of which revealed instead the social and emotional constraints that inhibited it. On one hand, she associated writing with virgin birth or parthenogenesis, a strategy that tacitly acknowledged the power and safety of the patriarchy. On the other, in an effort to divorce mothering from heterosexual women's subordination, she associated writing with lesbian love. Neither strategy satisfied her.

Begun after her second successful delivery (1919) with *Paint It Today* (1921) and *Fields of Asphodel* (1921–22), followed by *HERmione* (1927), the unpublished autobiographical novels present retrospective, overlapping versions of the following sequence from H.D.'s postadolescence to her early adulthood: withdrawal from Bryn Mawr in 1906; engagement to Ezra Pound and competing attraction to Frances Gregg; voyage to Europe with Gregg and Gregg's mother in 1911; first publication as "H.D. Imagiste" in 1913 under Pound's aegis; marriage to Richard Aldington in 1913; first child stillborn in 1915; Aldington's enlistment in the British army in 1916; the failure of her marriage and the dissolution of the Imagist circle in 1917–18; second pregnancy during respite in Cornwall with Cecil Gray, deaths of brother and father, and meeting with Bryher in 1918; wartime pneumonia, rescue by Bryher, and birth of Frances Perdita in 1919; dispute over Perdita's paternity and vacation in the Scillys with Bryher in 1919; voyage to Greece with Bryher in 1920.

H.D. returned obsessively to these events, writing different versions that emphasized or downplayed one part or another in an effort to work through the revived conflicts they engendered. In the first two of these novels, *Fields of Asphodel* and *Paint It Today*, she depicts the debilitating effect of rigidly defined sex roles on the psyche of an aspiring woman poet. She shows how anxiety, first about marriage, then about the feared incompatibility between motherhood and authorship, threatens her heroine's integrity and self-esteem and results in rebellious reparation. In both, a fantasy of parthenogenesis obviates the part in procreation played by men so that childbirth is reclaimed for the female as a paradigm for intellectual creativity. But though both novels cover the same biographical sequence, *Fields of Asphodel* emphasizes the effect of the heroine's marriage and pregnancies on her self-conception, whereas *Paint It Today* makes an idealized lesbian relationship the more significant context for the achievement of her identity as an artist.

Though both manuscripts are dated 1921, *Fields of Asphodel* seems earlier because of the greater literalness of its story line. With the exception of the deaths of her brother and father, which are not included, it accurately chronicles the chief events in H.D.'s life from the time she left America until after the birth of her daughter. At the center of the manuscript, dividing it into two parts, is the heroine's stillbirth, an event so distressful that it results in her personal collapse and the breakdown of her marriage. However, an idealized, illegitimate second pregnancy, which is associated with a renewed interest in writing, compensates for this loss; it provides the titular reference to Elysium, the abode of the blessed after death.

The first part of *Fields of Asphodel* begins with Hermione's voyage away from proper turn-of-the-century Philadelphia to Europe, an exhilarating passage she associates with her wish to write. This voyage with her friend Fayne Rabb (Frances Gregg) and Fayne's mother is not without conflict, however; it both stimulates her artistic aspirations and provokes criticism and fear of the fate of those exceptional women in history who defied conventional sex-role expectations. For example, when they visit Rouen, birthplace of Joan of Arc, Hermione considers the risks her own unconventional ambitions could incur. Like herself and Fayne Rabb, Joan of Arc had had "visions"; for this she had been burned at the stake as a witch and a heretic: "They had trapped her, a girl who was a boy, and they would always do that. . . . This was the warning."[6]

First Rouen and then the Louvre in Paris become scenes of potential rebellion as Hermione thinks further about the mythology of women proffered by institutionalized Christianity. A painting of the Madonna and Child first elicits criticism of the discrepancy between the enshrinement of Mary in Christian art and the diminishment of a real mother's social authority: "Are you really a mother and would you really understand? I always think the most awful thing in the world to be would be the mother of God" (*FA*, I, 19). But this defiance is quickly inhibited by remembrance of her own mother Eugenia, who had come to Paris on her honeymoon and whose difference from herself makes Hermione feel guilty and ashamed: "Such a good little Eugenia with a bustle and her hair caught with a diamond arrow (I have the picture somewhere). . . . I'm not good" (*FA*, I, 38).

Besides such instances of conflicted rebellion against the conventional female role, *Fields of Asphodel* also depicts the overwhelming social pressure on a young woman to marry. Hermione's hope that her friendship with Fayne would support her writing and allow her to avoid marriage is soon dashed when Fayne returns to America at her mother's insistence. Then when Fayne marries and George Lowndes (Ezra Pound), Hermione's former fiancé, also becomes engaged to another woman, Hermione feels completely alone. Unsure of herself amid the sophisticated European avant-garde and afraid of the specter of spinsterhood, she turns to a sympathetic young English poet, Jerrold Darrington (Richard Aldington), for companionship and encouragement. Hoping that theirs will be a relationship between two equals, two poets, she cannot resist the automatic identity and social acceptance that marriage confers: "Marry whom? Look well, Mrs. Darrington. Nobody making faces because she was miss—

miss—hit or miss. She was damn sick of it. Quaint. She was a quaint person. . . . Well, she wouldn't be quaint . . . hit or miss. Mrs. Jerrold Darrington, a person. A person" (FA, I, 128).

The novel's second part begins after Hermione, now married, returns home after the delivery of a stillborn child. Though she was briefly able to function satisfactorily as both a married woman and a poet, holding the two disparate sides of her identity in a delicate balance, this traumatic event shatters that tenuous inner equilibrium. Courageously explicit about the components of her grief, Asphodel shows how it is complicated and intensified by guilt over her earlier ambivalence during the pregnancy, feelings that she felt were unspeakable in view of society's expectations that she readily accept the self-sacrifice that the institution of motherhood required. She cannot talk now about the dead baby with Jerrold, because earlier she had felt in a state of confused power or powerlessness. Pregnancy had been a time of "deadly cruxifiction [sic] . . . when her flaming mind beat up and she found she was caught . . . like a wild bird in bird-lime" (FA, II, 12). Her husband did not know this, and he could surely never have understood her dread of confinement or her anger at the cultural stereotypes associated with pregnancy:

> Noone had known this. Noone would ever know it for there were no words to tell it in. How tell it? You can't say this, this . . . but men will say O she was a coward, a woman who refused her womanhood. No, she hadn't. But take a man with a flaming mind and ask him to do this. Ask him to sit in a dark cellar and no books . . . but you mustn't. You can't. Women can't speak and clever women don't have children. So if a clever woman does speak, she must be mad. She is mad. She wouldn't have had a baby if she hadn't been. (FA, II, 12)

Because of this ambivalence, Hermione feels responsible for the death and severed from the maternal side of herself, her womanhood at risk. She experiences the death of the fetus as an injury to her sense of self on two levels. First, its death represents a loss of that part of herself that is the adequate woman, the sufficient mother.[7] Second, because in the process of maternal-infant bonding she identified with her child as well as with her mother, the baby's premature death means the loss of hope.[8] Specifically, Hermione conflates her child's stillbirth with the earlier loss of her girlhood soulmate, who represents that part of herself that she has associated with the wish to write. She insists that in addition to the baby, "Someone, something got—killed" (*FA*, II, 2).

Remembering the gunfire that sounded around her in the nursing home, Hermione attempts to justify and ennoble her suffering in childbirth by giving it apocalyptic dimensions. She compares herself to soldiers dying in battle to bring forth a new era: "The world was caught as she had been caught. The whole world was breaking and breaking for some new spirit" (*FA*, II, 18). But this identification with male heroism is inevitably self-destructive because it involves a disavowal of her female sexual identity. Neglected and criticized by the nursing home staff because her husband is not yet in uniform, she retaliates in a gesture that can only increase her psychic pain: "The guns had made her one in her suffering with men-men-men. She had not suffered ignobly like a woman, a bird with wings caught, for she was alone and women were not left alone to suffer" (*FA*, II, 13). Such suppression of her personal grief in deference to the public devastation leaves her feeling shattered: "People now didn't call her Dryad. She had been Dryad in the old days before the earth had opened and left part on one side, part on the other" (*FA*, II, 18). Furthermore, the death of the child leads to the death of the marriage. Understandably afraid of another pregnancy, Hermione rebuffs Jerrold's physical over-tures. Then, because she feels inadequate and depressed, she condones his affair with another woman and leaves the war hysteria of London.

H.D. describes Hermione's affair with Cyril Vane (Cecil Gray), the friend who takes her to his country home in Cornwall to rest and to write poetry, as an idealized compensation for this extreme emotional distress: "Trampled flowers smell sweet. . . . Hysteria suppressed goes to the head like wine and you make pictures, patterns" (*FA*, II, 59). Exempt from the war because of heart trouble, Vane seems 1860-ish to her, then associated with Egypt, a "honeyed lotus." She is revitalized by his tenderness and begins to associate Cornwall with personal and artistic regeneration based upon idealized adulterous love, which could free her from the threat of sexual subordination implicit in marriage:

> She was in two parts. Part of her had got out, was out, was herself, the gold gauze, the untrampled winged thing, the spirit, if you will or . . . the mere careless nymph, the careless lover, the faithless wife. The faithless wife had wings of gauze and now she knew better what love was, for Cyril Vane was tall and gentle and not heavy and not domineering like her husband. . . . She had poise here, power. She was reestablished. (*FA*, II, 81)

Seeking an ethical context for this new experience, Hermione finds an alternative to the ethos of war, which she felt had caused her earlier psychic death, in the Druid altars around her in Cornwall. The remains of an ancient Celtic religion that worshiped a fertility goddess, these altars make her feel like Cassandra, an inviolate priestess ringed with inspired madness, instead of the abandoned wife Penelope. Indeed, H.D.'s account of Hermione's second conception in this magical setting stresses its importance to her as a virgin birth, a divinely ordained reparation for the narcissistic injury caused by her first loss. Hermione does not understand why God asks this second pregnancy of her, only that she had felt in "the dark subconscious an abyss of unimaginable terror, the pain, the disappointment, the utter horror of the last thing" (*FA*, II, 92).

In keeping with its importance as a virgin birth, Hermione's second conception also has a marked parthenogenetic quality, thereby excluding men who could make her feel vulnerable. Alone in her room, she thinks about her compelling wish to develop her own genius and remembers ancient Druid veneration of the sun as a fertility symbol. She contemplates the many layers of experience (England at war, her earlier personal loss) and welcomes a swallow flying outside her open window as an omen of God's will. A symbol of artistic annunciation, this swallow is associated less with biological conception than with her need to incorporate an omnipotent idealization of herself:

Body now with clean hands, having lain all day on the rocks, having floated across the aquamarine surface of the tide pool . . . are you ready for its welcoming? . . . God had prepared the answer as he had prepared the question in her own mind. God was the answer and the question. God was the lover and the beloved. God was the union of God with God. "If a swallow flies straight in now, without hesitation, just in here to me, I'll have it." (*FA*, II, 91)

Nor is Hermione very concerned about either her husband's or her lover's response to this pregnancy. The welcoming of this child is of some category other than "sheer, crass experience." It has nothing to do with logic or love, but with a wish for psychic reintegration, for an unconflicted conception of herself as both mother and creator:

It wasn't because of Cyril Vane that she had stooped and swept the hard small blue thing from the floor, sweeping it up, its little crab claws sticking like insect claws to a dark leaf. She picked up the little creature from the floor and images blend here. Undine, Morgan le Fay, some Florentine madonna, some nymph whose beauty had been violated on some Delphic shelf. She was good and bad and remote and impossible. You don't go off to Cornwall and have babies. You see the manifest impossibility of the thing? (*FA*, II, 93)

The self-division she had felt because of discordant conventional female imagery was healed now by something greater, by a lover that "made one's soul at one, that loved Morgan le Fay, Undine, and the Madonna alike" (*FA*, II, 94).

The magical quality of Hermione's second conception also resounds with buried association to the death of H.D.'s father, though her reaction to news of his death is not explicitly fictionalized here. Hermione's sense that the Cornwall coast is a ledge of enchantment, where her sorceress self is discovered by a "god watching the sunrise" who sends his bird, "the sound of a child's voice crying," is remarkably like H.D.'s account of a dream she had when she was critically ill before her second delivery, in which she calls upon her father for comfort as she faces the possibility of death in childbirth:

> I was a girl at a mountain-spring and the gigantic river-god was waiting for me. I was drifting on. The river-god had the qualities of old Dr. Ellis — who was not so old then, but . . . had the appearance of Deity. God-the-father? My own father was dying or dead; I only heard of this weeks later, after I had moved into St. Faith's. I would go to him. But chiefly, I clutched a school exercise book. What did I write? Dog-wood trees, . . . the great river, American poetry, roughed out, scribbled. My arms were cold. This was February or early March 1919.[9]

H.D.'s account of this dream clarifies the regressed emotional dynamic behind the artistic "annunciation" she describes in her novel. Though she appears to exalt the female position in the depiction of her second conception, when she imagines herself to be a divine priestess in the service of a god, such an idealization of father (God-the-father) also shows that she is struggling with a regressive pull to a devalued oedipal mother. The death of H.D.'s father during her second pregnancy must have further bound up this idealization; in her dream she associates personal and artistic survival with joining him. But since this idealization cannot occur without the repression of her aggression in relation to him (aggression operative in achievement), she feels a specifically feminine form of guilt attached to her artistic aspirations.[10] She trivializes her writing, describing her poems as scribbles in a school exercise book.

As if in response to the idealization implicit here, Hermione is contemptuous of both her husband and her lover as potential fathers. She chooses to raise the child herself, then with another woman, despite the social cost. H.D. describes this choice in the defiant but self-deprecating language of a subversive women's tradition of witchcraft: "Morgan le Fay you must summon your magic, become mere scheming wizard, witch for you must be assured that this . . . thing that is God's, this thing that is the child of some sun-daemon will be looked after" (*FA*, II, 98).

Unable to free herself from the psychological position of devalued mother, she sees herself as marginal, the vessel of a god.

A stylized "etching" of a modern woman's spiritual crisis, *Paint It Today* also begins by deploring the devitalization of an adventurous young girl by her traditional acculturation. But this time H.D. focuses on how friendship between women can provide an antidote to this denigrating heterosexual script. The only girl in a large family of boys, Midget DeFreddie feels isolated. The chief hunger of her childhood is for a spirited twin sister, visualized with "curious desperate yearning as a very little sister, a baby sister."[11] Later associated with nascent artistic ambitions, this desire is finally satisfied when, having failed out of college, she is drifting "hurt and baffled" out of a relationship with an "irreverent male youth." At an afternoon soiree she meets "the girl Josepha," also a fledgling poet, whose friendship reinvigorates her with the possibility of "another state of emotional life or being" and a new kind of poetry (*PIT*, I, 15). In language that suggests the minimalist technique of her early imagist lyrics, H.D. writes that Midget and Josepha found an alternative to the poetry of masculinist power: not "large, epic pictures," not "the tragic legions of set lines that felt like black armies with terrific force and mechanical set action, paralyzing, or broke like a black sea to baffle and to crush," but "songs that cut like swallow-wing the high untainted ether" (*PIT*, I, 12).

Their sisterhood is short-lived, however. For though the two travel together to Europe with Josepha's mother, the latter's insistence that her daughter return with her to America leads to Josepha's marriage. Betrayed and confused by her friend's behavior (they had both disavowed marriage), Midget then also feels intense pressure to conform. Angry at her own mother's favorable opinion of Josepha's decision, she wishes desperately to break from her parents and stay in London but is unable to express her deep dissatisfaction with the "tyranny" of social convention. Self-expression becomes associated with fear of devastating hurt and reprisal:

A fear possessed her that suddenly she might find words to this speech, that she might shout or sing those words, and that they would break, those good and simple people, shrivelled to ash, before her utterance, or that they might seize her, somehow tear the fiery sandals from her feet and bind her down forever. (*PIT*, I, 13)

More explicitly than before, H.D. outlines the intrapsychic nature of her heroine's dilemma, showing how the sexual division of labor in which women nurture and men create results in a sexual division of psychic organization that is fragmenting. Midget's wish to differentiate herself from her mother, aggravated by internalized sex-role stereotypes, sets off a matricidal fantasy that only increases her suffering. In order to protect herself from her mother's power over her, which she associates with emotional dependency, she idealizes her father, whom she associates with creative accomplishment. She compares herself with the Orestes of Greek tragedy:

"Your mother has betrayed your father" spoke the present to Orestes. "Your mother, your mother, your mother," the present said to Midget, "has betrayed, or would betray, through the clutch and tyranny of the emotion, your father, the mind in you, the jewel the king, your father gave you as your birth-right. Look" said the present, "and choose. Here is the knife, slay your mother. She has betrayed or would betray the gift." (*PIT*, IV, 15)

But Midget's soul also remembers her mother's many kindnesses. Recognizing the inadequacy of her fantasy yet unable to rid herself of it, she is stalemated and soon after decides to marry.

As in *Fields of Asphodel*, the heart of *Paint It Today* involves the heroine's complicated reaction to pregnancy, but this time it is her friend who has the baby, while she develops a new mode of perception that allows her to disown the anxiety associated with it. In a central chapter titled "Snow and Ash" H.D. sketches the dark clouds of wartime, when "Time had the world by the throat" and there was no love left except love of duty, love of sacrifice (*PIT*, V, 1). Soon after Midget's marriage London goes up in flames, and she feels estranged from her soldier-husband, who returns from France "with the smell of gas in his breath . . . the stench of death in his clothes" (*PIT*, V, 3). In the midst of this marital unhappiness, her friend Josepha writes from America that she is pregnant, provoking in Midget deep anxiety about the possible loss of self that motherhood may entail. Midget responds:

> Has the maid of Delos [Artemis] departed from you now that you have your baby? I feel something has departed from the world now that you have your baby. I don't know what has departed. Things look black now everywhere. I look into blackness when I close my eyes. There was beauty inside before I had your letter. Now the beauty inside is one with the black without. (*PIT*, V, 18)

In this version of her own story, H.D. transfers the self-doubt and guilt she felt following her stillbirth to Midget's response to her friend's pregnancy. In an attempt to convey emotional truth more accurately, she splits off her heroine's fears about motherhood from her artistic ambition, adducing a paradigm of imaginative parthenogenesis to account for the latter. For Midget prefaces her troubled response to Josepha's pregnancy with the description of a dream-lover she is cultivating as an alternative inseminating force. An imaginary figure who allows her to disown her fears of self-sacrifice, he understands her wish to write and validates the two women's mutual affirmation and ambition. H.D. chooses lines from Poe's "Helen," the poem she associated with her father's love for her mother, to convey Midget's wish to regain identification with her mother's strength through her friendship with Josepha, despite the latter's pregnancy. Midget writes to Josepha:

> When my lover wrote, "thy hyacinth hair, thy classic face," he was thinking of you when, that day, the morning and evening star sang. When he wrote, "Ah Psyche, from the regions which," he was thinking of me when I stand with my clothes off and admire myself, turned half sideways in the glass. (*PIT*, V, 15)

Cultivation of this incubus is related to a "new trick of seeing" that Midget has developed. Not altogether a good trick, because it "shut[s] her out from life" (*PIT*, V, 5), it nevertheless is a mode of spiritual and artistic survival. In a striking depiction of psychic numbing, which illuminates the "white world" motif in her volume *Hymen* and foreshadows the shell and pearl imagery of *Trilogy*, H.D. depicts the defensive quality of Midget's perception:

> Snow and ash, you might have said the trick was. Not the pearl
> reflecting all minute and vivid landscapes, tiny, tiny, surfaces,
> colour of bean-flower or faint tint of thistle. Not the pearl; sanity,
> life, salvation. It was not a good trick of dreaming. But what can
> you ask of life hurling the very heart and passion and beauty of
> itself high, high above, to perish as it will or drift to far distances,
> transformed to rain or subtle weight of ether? (*PIT*, V, 6)

In the remaining chapters of *Paint It Today*, H.D. focuses on Midget's convalescence after the war and her rededication to writing, effected by a more satisfying lesbian relationship that includes a veiled allusion to the welcoming of a child. Intrinsic to this renewal is an alter ego Althea, with whom she takes a liberating canoe trip (probably based on H.D.'s trip to the Scillys with Bryher) during which she rediscovers the sensible, visible world. Midget's marriage seems "remote and unbelievable" compared with this relationship, and her earlier sisterhood with Josepha ghostly and unreal. For the most compelling reality of her new life is an embryonic being, part self, part other, that bears an unmistakable likeness to a newborn baby. In the following passage Midget's wonder at what she has produced overrides her fear of her own procreative power (proof of her femininity), a step toward personal integration and ownership of her creativity:

> A small amber-coloured being crept into Midget's life, a crea-
> ture unbelievable. . . . A creature, white as a camelia, amber
> as a honey-bee, black as a gypsy's baby. White and black, amber
> and camelia white, not to be believed yet easily proved existant
> by cupping its firm black head in the hollow of a hand and

44

watching it laugh, clutching with a humming-bird's claw. I have seen it with my own eyes the creature. I know it exists. (*PIT*, VIII, 16)

Set before her trip to Europe and her wartime pregnancies, H.D.'s novel *HERmione* touches again upon the intrapsychic conflict between creativity and procreativity, this time by exploring a gifted daughter's difficulty in associating her mother with her creative power despite the desire to do so. Completed shortly after H.D.'s mother's death, it shows more incisively how the social organization of gender produces this difficulty, and it attempts to find a solution to the daughter's problem of feeling insufficiently mothered in the alternative of lesbian love.[12] Again H.D. takes as her persona young Hermione Gart, deliberately evoking both Helen of Troy's daughter and, more pointedly this time, the unjustly maligned mother of Shakespeare's *The Winter's Tale*. Home with her family after having failed out of a science program in college, Hermione is desperately trying to define herself: "Her mind still trod its round. I am Her Gart, my name is Her Gart. I am going round and round in circles."[13] Since the "biological-mathematical definition of the universe" represented by her father Carl and her older brother Burton has failed her, she turns to her mother for one more satisfying (*H*, 6). But even though Eugenia's suggestion that she "go on writing" is pertinent, it is not empowering. A self-effacing, subordinated woman who knits in the dark because her husband prefers the light concentrated in his corner of the room, Eugenia has "no midwife power" to help her daughter out of an emotional bog (*H*, 80).

Nor does the example of her sister-in-law Minnie provide a desirable alternative. Though married to Hermione's brilliant older brother, Minnie shares none of his intellectual excitement. Already enfeebled by recurrent headaches, she spends her energy nagging her mother-in-law about domestic trivia. Though Hermione is enjoined by her mother to include Minnie in the family circle, she finds her an association to avoid. Even Minnie's use of the word *father* causes Hermione anxiety. Her true sister, a kindred spirit, would be adventurous, "fleet-footed": "If her father was also the father to . . . this thing, then the half of her, the twin-self sister would be forever blighted" (*H*, 16).

Indeed, Hermione's need to free herself from the culturally prescribed domestic confinement exemplified by her mother's life ("Gart and the formula"), in conflict with her nascent recognition of her mother's fundamental potency, constitutes the complex web of feeling upon which the plot is built. Eugenia's picture is "set square in the middle" of Hermione's desk, between the small red Temple Shakespeare and the matching blue copy of the *Mahabharata*, with its exercises for meditation: She must reenvision the significance of Her (the novel's original title) in order to be inspired.

Hermione is able to reenvision her mother as a source of creative power only when she separates the experience of childbirth from the context of nineteenth- and early twentieth-century assumptions about women's passivity. When a thunderstorm reminds her of the triumphant circumstances of Hermione's birth, Eugenia forgets her subordinate role for a moment. She remembers that though her husband had been afraid during her delivery that the doctor would be unable to come in time because of the storm, she herself had been unafraid and had preferred to deliver the child unassisted. When Hermione articulates more fully to herself her mother's unimpeded connection with the lifeforce, daughter and mother share a moment of profound intimacy:

> *The morning stars sang together.* Words of Eugenia had more power than textbooks, than geometry, than all of Carl Gart and brilliant "Bertie Gart" as people called him. Bertrand wasn't brilliant, not like mama. Carl Gart wasn't brilliant like Eugenia. "Then the doctor came. But she was such a dear nurse, so much better than the doctor, she was like a mother to me. . . ."
> Demeter (such a dear nurse) lifting the tired shoulders of a young Eugenia had driven the wind back, back . . . the house was sitting on its haunches. (*H*, 89–90)

But these shared moments are rare. Thus Hermione's struggle toward individuation takes place in relation to two peers, and to a choice between conventional heterosexual romance and lesbian "sis-ter-love."[14] George Lowndes, a talented male poet (Ezra Pound), wants to marry her and take her to Europe, but their engagement is broken by Hermione's fascination with Fayne Rabb (Frances Gregg), a literary young woman who shares her visionary capacity. In part 1 H.D. focuses on Hermione's affection for George, for certainly marriage was one solution to the problems of separation and individu-ation. Though her parents disapproved of him because he was the subject of scandal and could not support her financially, an alliance with George would at least mean escape from the cloying atmosphere of Gart Grange to a more sophisticated life in Europe: "She wanted George as a child wants a doll, whose other dolls are broken. She wanted George as a little girl wants to put her hair up or to wear long skirts" (*H*, 63).

But though Hermione attempts to place their courtship within the liberating green world of Shakespearean comedy (her Rosalind to his Orlando), George's behavior reminds her that the Pennsylvania woods around Gart Grange are not the Forest of Arden, but more likely the "forest primeval":

> It was the forest primeval, it was not the forest of Arden. George almost made it the forest of Arden. If at that moment George had made it the forest of Arden, Hermione out of Shakespeare would have been again Hermione out of Shakespeare but this time Hermione from *The Winter's Tale* (who later froze into a statue) would have been Rosalind with sleek, deer-limbs and a green forester's cap with one upright darting hawk quill. Almost, Oh almost, almost this is the Forest of Arden. But not quite. (*H*, 66)

At about the same time that George returns from Italy and proposes marriage, Hermione receives an invitation from a Bryn Mawr classmate to a literary soiree where she meets Fayne Rabb, a young woman to whom she is powerfully attracted. The girl's "wild eyes" and more adventurous literary tastes distinguish her from

47

Hermione's other unimaginative female acquaintances, and she recognizes a kindred spirit. As Hermione drifts into an engagement with George, because she is not strong enough to refuse him, the memory of this meeting is both stimulating and disquieting.

Uncomfortable with the wedding plans, Hermione associates her predicament with the situation of a boy in a neighboring forest whose leg was trapped and bleeding. She feels that an adventurous, "masculine," preadolescent side of herself is being similarly wounded. Lines from Swinburne's poetry, first introduced by George, resonate anew when his mother admiringly calls her Undine, referring to her trousseau's predominant blue-green color. Hermione mentally rejects this allusion to Undine or to the Little Mermaid who "sold her sea-inheritance for feet" and replaces it with an allusion to Swinburne's poem "Itylus": "I may for a bit let go, give in, but it won't be forever . . . she heard the boy screaming and knew the woodpath was dyed red because of . . . not Undine, not any Mermaid. The woodpath was dyed red because of . . . because of . . . *Itylus*" (*H*, 121).

When Eugenia chides her again for disparaging Minnie, Hermione's discontent at the conventional married woman's self-sacrifice and isolation is heightened by an intense longing for adventure and spiritual companionship that women like her sister-in-law cannot provide. After Fayne's entry, a refrain from Swinburne's "Itylus" recurs throughout the novel: "*O Sister, my sister, O fleet sweet swallow.*" A sorrowful poem about the bond between sisters following the rape of one and the other's sacrifice of her son Itylus in revenge, it no doubt evoked H.D.'s gratitude for Bryher's rescue during her second delivery. Hermione cites in particular Philomela's poignant refusal to forget her sister Procne's terrible sacrifice, an act of devotion Hermione associates with her love for Fayne:

> '*The sound of a child's voice crying yet,*
> *Who has remembered me, who has forgotten,*
> *Thou hast forgotten, O summer swallow*
> *But the world will end*' . . . the world will end . . .
> the world will end . . . '*when I forget.*' (*H*, 125)

In a sense the sisters' shared memory of Itylus's death represents their mourning of an assertive (masculine) side of the female self, which they had to sacrifice in order to fit into the patriarchy.

Hermione's friendship with Fayne Rabb dominates the second half of the novel. Consolidated after she attends a production of *Pygmalion* in which Fayne plays the lead, the relationship offers the kind of mothering she craves, a temporary fusion of self and other that evokes the early ego state of "twin narcissism" common both to lovers and to creative artists.[15] Product of a fatherless childhood with a domineering mother, Fayne has psychic abilities that enable her to draw things out of Hermione, stimulating her first serious writing. Mutual acknowledgment of the worth of their creative work enhances feelings of self-regard and self-affirmation that are indispensable: "I am Her. She is Her. Knowing her, I know Her. She is some amplification of myself like amoeba giving birth, by breaking off, to amoeba. I am a sort of mother, a sort of sister to Her" (*H*, 158).

Unlike her romance with George, which threatens the fore-closure of subjectivity and original speech, intimacy with Fayne expands Hermione's spiritual horizon: "Words with Fayne in a room . . . became projections of things beyond one. Things beyond Her beat, beat to get through Her, to get through to Fayne" (*H*, 146). Free from the heterosexual script, the two nurture each other's poetic identities successfully, and Hermione feels empowered to supersede her father's "mathematical-biological definition" with one that reconciles writing with womanhood: "Words may be my heritage and with words I will prove conic sections a falsity and the very stars that wheel and frame concentric pattern as mere very-stars, gems put there, a gift, a diadem, a crown, a chair, a cart or a mere lady. A lady will be set back in the sky" (*H*, 76).

Recognizing a rival, George sides with Eugenia's disapproval of Fayne's influence, suggesting that Hermione's withdrawal from him is unwholesome, even sinister, and that she and Fayne "ought to be burnt for witchcraft" (*H*, 165). But though Hermione plans to break her engagement to George, a double betrayal temporarily sabotages both relationships. When Hermione discovers that Fayne and George have secretly seen each other, her confusion produces a complete physical and mental breakdown.

In an extended monologue during Hermione's delirium, H.D. conveys the troubled dialectic of her heroine's developing female self-definition in terms that reflect the inadequacy of "normal" sex roles as models for an ambitious young woman. Hermione describes herself as an "unborn butterfly" that tried to emerge too early from the cocoon of parental (particularly maternal) influence. Unable to trust her own impulses, no matter which way she turns, to Fayne or to George, she experiences loss:

> A white butterfly that hesitates a moment finds frost to break the wavering tenuous antennae. I put, so to speak, antennae out too early. I felt letting Her so delicately protrude prenatal antennae from the husk of the thing called Her, frost nip the delicate fibre of the starfish edges of the thing I clung to. I, Her clung to the most tenuous of antennae. Mama, Eugenia that is, Carl Gart and Lillian [George's mother] were so many leaves wrapped around the unborn butterfly. Outside a force wakened, drew Her out of Her. Call the thing Fayne Rabb. I clung to some sort of branch that wavered in the wind, something between Lillian and Eugenia, a sort of precise character George Lowndes. Wavering by instinct toward George I found George Lowndes inadequate. He would have pulled back quivering antennae. (*H*, 216)

Hermione's gestation of an autonomous self is successful in the end, however. In a finale that bridges the psychic chasm between procreativity and creativity, her breakdown becomes a breakthrough. Approximately nine months after the novel's beginning, she traces a fresh path across the virginal snow into the neighboring Farrand forest, "sure of finding something growing" (*H*, 225). Hermione's discovery of inner direction parallels the rainstorm that last summer had reminded Eugenia of the circumstances of her daughter's birth, but now there is an important difference in the location of creative agency: "Last summer the Creator had been white lightning brandished against blackness. Now the creator was Her's feet, narrow black crayon across the winter whiteness" (*H*, 223). Having disavowed her mother's role without losing fundamental affiliation with her strength, she discovers her own vocation.

Perhaps because it would have invited unbearable notoriety in her day or because it did not fully satisfy her, H.D. downplayed this emphasis on lesbian love in her published work, even though she recognized that it gave her access to the source of the power she was trying to unlock, a way of reexperiencing herself as a strong mother. In both *Palimpsest* and *Hedylus* she assigned a masculine gender to that in herself which did not fit in with the conventional ideology of womanliness, and she used historical masks to distance herself from the emotional issues associated with her trauma in childbirth.

In *Palimpsest* her first published attempt to connect the crucial personal "hieroglyph" with her poetic identity, H.D. takes an archaeological metaphor as the principle of coherence for her three related stories: a palimpsest is a "parchment from which one writing has been [imperfectly] erased to make room for another."[16] In order to represent the intersection of the historical, the personal, and the mythical, H.D. selects as related "scrapings" a story set in "War Rome" (the ancient city she associated with London), seventy-five years before Christ's birth; a second in "War and Post-war London," the place and period of her pregnancies; and a third in the timeless modernist locale of "Excavator's Egypt."

The central archaeological metaphor, "palimpsest," also allows H.D. to layer the psychological issues she was concerned with. Though she rearranges the crucial events of the war years in these stories, elaborating on some and downplaying others (particularly the fact of her second pregnancy and the importance of her lesbian attachments), all are easily identifiable after an acquaintance with the unpublished material. From this perspective, instead of providing concealment, her historical and mythical masks reveal the extent to which she internalized the conventions of an androcentric model for creativity, and they show her awareness of the need to modify this model in order to develop as an artist. Significantly, H.D. places heterosexual betrayal and a woman writer's troubled identification with her mother first in "Hipparchia," the inhibiting effect of a stillbirth upon artistic expression second in "Murex," and an enigmatic account of potential spiritual regeneration at a dead king's tomb last in "Secret Name."

In all three, the presence of another woman and the wish to ground creativity in female experience are central. By presenting the three stories as related "scrapings," H.D. interdigitates the heterosexual romance plot with an underlying story of mother-daughter attachment. In "Hipparchia" she demonstrates the uneasy conjoinment of the two plots; in "Murex" she shows how their intersection is destructive to the self-concept of a woman poet, especially if she becomes a mother; in "Secret Name" she implies that regeneration and artistic independence are contingent upon modifying androcentric myths that influence our fantasies.

The heroine of the first story, Hipparchia, Greek mistress of a Roman soldier, is enmeshed in a double bind that she must resolve before realizing her literary ambition, the restoration in her translations of the integrity of Greece: "Greece is now lost, the cities dissociated from any central ruling" (*P*, 71). Besides freeing herself from her lover's excessive sexual demands, she must work through a "family problem" in order to recover the Greek spirit and her flagging self-esteem. Named after her dead mother, an intellectual who is memorialized in an epigraph from Antipater of Sidon's tribute, Hipparchia must recover that primary identification but escape a similar fate of erotic self-denial in deference to a man: "that lovely wraith who followed blindly, cynic and philosopher, Hipparchia, who piled garment, purplefringed, golden-embroidered (ah, if I could forget her) and trailed in grey coarse linen, after my foolish father" (*P*, 8).

Cleverly showing how questions of relative power contaminate sexual play, H.D. tells the first part of this story from the Roman soldier's perspective. As Marius Decius waits in the coolness of her room, he attempts to analyze his attraction to Hipparchia. Remembering their arguments over religious values, in which he has insisted that her civilization is decadent and she, that "Romans are winepressers" who have cut her city and state to pieces, he realizes that guilt motivates him as well as fascination with her Greek intensity (*P*, 4). Yet he also fears that intensity, "the priestess in her" that dares to question Roman authority, and he is frustrated by her detachment from him, manifested in his inability to bring her to sexual climax. Fear and frustration turn to anger, as Decius' ambivalence about Hipparchia becomes infused with the rhetoric of Roman imperial conquest: "He had never brought to her thin lips, cut fine yet rather colourless, that cry that proved Rome conqueror. . . . Plunge dagger into a gold lilly. . . . You might as well plunge a dagger into the cold and unresponsive flesh of some tall flower" (*P*, 6).

Hipparchia, too, is concerned that she has not given her Roman lover the physical satisfaction that is "fair payment" for his protection (*P*, 12). Feeling constrained, she finds Decius "fat, like some overgrown tuberous vegetable" (*P*, 10) and is preoccupied with homesickness for her adventurous childhood when she hunted for insect specimens and flowers with her young uncle Philip, her first love. Decius seems like an "enormous child" whom she tries to satisfy with stories about her Macedonian past, to the point where he finds her indistinguishable from her mother, dour Crates' loyal wife who renounced her beauty and sexuality for wisdom and "the beggar's stick." Though Decius had always prided himself on choosing the most fragile and intellectually skilled women, Hipparchia's listlessness finally drives him into the arms of Lucullus' mistress Olivia, a lustier woman of the "general barrack preference" (*P*, 22).

Unfortunately, Hipparchia has internalized this stereotyping of women as either sensual and dumb or frigid and intellectual. When Decius' affection for her cools after he becomes engulfed by "the dark tide" of Olivia's sensuality, Hipparchia sees herself as "a field swept of its flowers, bare under arid sunlight" (*P*, 27) and consents to Decius' suggestion that she accompany their friend Quintus Verrus to Capua in order to lift her depression. Indeed, Hipparchia's affair with Quintus Verrus is partially caused by her wish to restore her fragmented integrity, a result of this separation of body from mind, to which she thinks her mother's fate bears witness. Relaxing in the comfort of Verrus' elegant chariot, she hopes to cure her nervous inhibition by "more than ever" repudiating "her mother and her mother's intellectual decision" to disavow erotic pleasure (*P*, 35). More suitably matched with Verrus, she feels restored to her body, recalled by Aphrodite to a more balanced realm of womankind:

> There had been no striving, no lacerating clutch and plunge such as soldiers parrying, counter-thrusting, practice at their sword-play. This was a different matter . . . belonging to realms of columned porches, of temples . . . and to the curious lap-lapping . . . that was the langorous yet distinctly measured, equalizing, balancing movement of the inner tideless ocean. (*P*, 39)

But though the "black torrent" of war Rome recedes temporarily in Capua's gardens, leaving her a "giant Thetis" among islands, Hipparchia cannot forget Decius, who besieges her still with love letters (*P*, 41). Like him, she finds absence an aphrodisiac, and when Verrus denies her request for a brazier in the bedroom, she uses the incident to idealize the earlier relationship: "She had found a Marius other than the Marius of Olivia. Other than the one she had, in the first ecstasy of her awakening, repudiated" (*P*, 47). During a severe thunderstorm, when Verrus remains impervious to the torrential rain that threatens to swamp her bedroom and to curtail her imaginative power (a thinly disguised allusion to H.D.'s fear of pregnancy), Hipparchia longs for her Roman maid Phaenna, who would answer should she shriek, and for Marius' alleviating humor. Though grateful to Verrus for sheltering her, Hipparchia finds fault with his petulance and sloth and decides to return to Rome.

Besides dissatisfaction with Verrus, Hipparchia's decision to return is also influenced by a changing perception of her relation to her dead mother. Now reconsidering "her mother's intellectual decision," she turns to her as to a reflection of herself for deepest validation (*P*, 53). As she gazes at her own image in a salt pool, as if at an oracle, the rich ornaments Verrus chose for her no longer seem appropriate. Realizing that she can interpret her mother's austerity in her own way and need not be defined by any man's love, she chooses herself alone, warmed only by the sun:

> She saw Hipparchia and she loved Hipparchia. Verrus could not love her as she loved herself, silver inviolable as she gazed back at herself standing with late autumn sun-light now a veritable lover, touching with electric warmth her smooth bared shoulders. Hipparchia loved the silver cold Hipparchia and with electric fervour of sun-light on bared shoulders she conceded further, Helios. Hipparchia an abstraction so loved beauty. (*P*, 55)

Once back in her old rooms in Rome, Hipparchia views the romantic triangle in a new light and attempts to give impetus to her aspirations by associating herself with her foster-uncle Philip. If she had once loved Decius because he helped her escape from the fate of an "assiduous and proper wife," now his touch repels her with "the very substance of Olivia" (*P*, 66). Away from Verrus, she realizes that she had been attracted by his similarity to dead young Philip (probably a composite of H.D.'s brothers Gilbert and Eric), her beloved childhood companion who had been struck down in his prime. Stripping her rooms of the costly gifts of both lovers, she determines to reinterpret her mother's renunciation by making a pilgrimage to Tusculum with only her manuscripts, thus choosing "intimacy without intercourse" in the communion of memory:

> Hipparchia, her mother's gesture, was a fit one. Wandering off with rough script, with nothing but the bare necessities. Hipparchia had wandered off with the dour old cynic on her pilgrimage. Hipparchia the second would do likewise. But her companion was not dour. He was young and frail with the frailty of some enduring cypress. (*P*, 68)

Remembering the details of Philip's death by a Roman arrow and her own capture, she resolves to avenge them both by completing the translations that are his bequest. She must finish her "fervid compilation of poetry, religion and ethics," for the very names of the Greek gods "still held virtue"; if written often enough "they would serve (as some Eastern charm) eventually to destroy Rome" (P, 72).

Though Hipparchia tries to use Philip's bequest, the "mind's eminence," to reestablish her integrity, substituting an inner marriage in which "body and brain merged like a sword and its very victim" for her mother's outward accommodation, she is inevitably paralyzed by such a self-defeating paradigm and falls ill (P, 73). In her delirium, memory of her mother issues a more positive directive: " 'You did not give back what you have never taken.' It was Hipparchia, a spark thrown off between the upper and nether stones of her betrayal who cried out to champion wan Hipparchia" (P, 78). As she focuses on what to keep instead of what to renounce, the "flame-tipped, insistent anguish" of a bird's song restores her vitality by validating her connection with the natural world: "It wasn't Philip who was writing. It was a bird outside singing . . . a bird scalded with spring this outer veil of winter" (P, 81). Realizing that all her past endeavor had been misdirected because she had "severed thought and creation" (P, 85), Hipparchia replaces the self-defeating phallocentric Roman model for creativity with the matrifocal Egyptian fertility legend, the mourning Isis' reconstitution of and impregnation by her dead brother-consort Osiris: "There is Isis in blue. I will claim her. I will be her" (P, 85). Though the intensity of her new vision threatens to engulf her temporarily, it ultimately leads to recovery, and to a visit by a young woman whose admiration for her poetry and offer of companionship recall her to herself.

If H.D. hides the woman artist's need to reclaim childbirth as a paradigm for successful self-expression behind Hipparchia's preoccupation with Isis, the Egyptian goddess whose protection Greco-Roman women sought for the whole span of events connected with the reproduction process, she makes that need the explicit theme of the central story in *Palimpsest*.[17] Titled after the spiny sea creature that the heroine associates with her verses, "Murex" explores the dynamics of her creative impulse from the perspective of guilt connected with a wartime stillbirth. In the spiritual twilight of a foggy autumn afternoon, Raymonde Ransome entertains a somewhat unwelcome visit from a younger counterpart, the Hampstead Jewess Ermentrude Solomon, whose story of blighted romance enables her to discover a truth about herself, which she then preserves in a new poem.

Raymonde listens to Ermy's tale of the loss of her lover to Mavis Landour (Brigit Patmore), the same older woman who ten years earlier had seduced Raymonde's husband, as if to something "from the other end of a psychic gramophone" (P, 107). Its familiar leitmotif of "How *could* she? *Why* did she?" forces her to confront her own moral confusion about events surrounding her wartime stillbirth and to recall repressed details of her emotional devastation and method of survival. As she recalls her suffering in a hostile wartime nursing home ten years earlier, Raymonde remembers feeling abandoned by her husband, being callously treated by nurses who thought she lacked courage since she was an American with a British husband not yet in uniform, and being consoled by a doctor who seemed to be the only other person who cared: "I'm sorry Mrs. Ransome, it was a beautiful little body—" (P, 111). She also remembers losing her husband to Mavis, whom she had asked to "look after Freddie" during that time, and Mavis's counterclaim that she had "prostituted herself" for Raymonde's sake (P, 113–114). Thus London had become the place of layer upon layer of pain and of "odd obliteration," a drift of the senses that produced an "over-consciousness that comes with pain annihilated" (P, 108). Superpain had led to a "nebulous Nirvana" that prevented her from apprehending her true feelings about the immediate past except through an intermediary, like Ermy, who could give her back herself.

Raymonde's personal agony in wartime has also affected her self-definition as an artist. Because she suffered a stillbirth while young men were marching to their deaths, her inner rhythm and creative essence have become inextricable from the wartime upheaval: "That pain and that sound and that rhythm of pain and that rhythm of departure were indissolubly wedded. Or was it her heart beating? Feet, feet, feet, feet" (P, 145). Fused with the sound of soldiers' feet tramping, Raymonde's heartbeat becomes transposed into metrical feet, "beat and throb of metre," almost against her will: "With the sound of feet in her head, something terrible had happened, was going to happen" (*P*, 142). A reactive fantasy only partially mediates these feelings of victimization and powerlessness, moreover, when Raymonde expresses her relation to her creative power in the "nom de guerre" Ray Bart. Imagined as a young spearman who "held a sword of pure steel," her poetic genius would clarify the moral blur of the situation, would fish up the truth and preserve it by means of the unrelenting laws of song: "The icy helmet of the thing she knew was Ray Bart's helmet closed above her . . . weighed heavy on her . . . where Raymonde would have worn small fragrant noncommittal and eternal field flowers" (*P*, 148).

Because it gives her a standard external to herself with which to measure her past suffering, Raymonde's poetic inspiration plagues her like a "festering splinter." Ermy's story makes Raymonde aware that her earlier ambivalence toward Mavis merely obstructed painful recollection of grief and guilt, which had been suppressed because of the war, at the stillbirth that had left her lifeless. Admitting that Mavis's assertion that she had encouraged her husband's infidelity is correct, Raymonde realizes that Ermy's story has given her back an "eternal Freddie," associated with a past layer of consciousness before her pregnancy and the war. This "ghost Freddie," fearing death in battle, had assured her that she would not become pregnant when they married and had admonished her to carry on their work: "I can't have you broken" (*P*, 140). As she reappraises her attitude toward Mavis in the poem she is writing, Raymonde recalls her ambivalence during the pregnancy, the hostile feelings she associates with the stillbirth, and her later numbness: She had never "wanted to set herself up for some plaster-of-paris model of virtue—of motherhood" (*P*, 150).

Yet Raymonde associates her verses, which "dyed all existence with their colour" (*P*, 160), with the sea creature from which purple dye is made, an image that has unmistakable fetal connotation in this context. Both the recurring question *"Who fished the murex up?"* and Raymonde's enlistment of Ray Bart to "ransom" the murex, her own "deep-sea jewel" and "irregular terse answer to everything" (*P*, 165), suggest her guilty dissociation and inhibition. Raymonde feels that because her baby died she must pay for her creativity with her womanhood. Further, since Raymonde's verses seek the "absolute form" that would enclose the "absolute vacuum behind it" (*P*, 165), that is, her experience of emptiness, it is not surprising that they become an instrument of twisted self-affirmation. A "reactionary Puritan," she had found laws of song "straighter than the laws of social Sinai" through which to discipline herself and assuage her guilt (*P*, 168). Ermy's story had shifted a bitter layer of volcanic ash: Raymonde would now worship the woman whose treachery had led her to recover a reflection of her sorrowing self:

> *See—I worship*
> *more, more, more—I*
> *love her*
> *who has sent you to my door.* (*P*, 172)

"Secret Name," the final story in *Palimpsest*, is probably based on a fusion of H.D.'s meeting with the mysterious "Man on the boat" aboard the *Borodino* en route to Greece with Bryher in 1920 and her later trip to Egypt in 1923 with her mother and Bryher. The most visionary of the three stories, it depicts research assistant Helen Fairwood's "super-normal" vision of the key to personal renewal in the recently uncovered temple at Karnak. Again H.D.'s epigraph is significant; this time it is a detail from a sacred Egyptian scroll referring to the magical power of Isis, to whom even the great god Ra is forced to reveal his secret name and thereby the means of divine authority and life-giving sustenance.[18] H.D. chooses the moment before the transfer of power, however. Drawing upon elements of Isis-Osiris myth and ritual, her story describes the psychological state that precedes her heroine's awakening to a buried creative dimension of herself.

War-weary and overwrought by her intensive research into Greco-Roman texts, Mrs. Fairwood feels strangely detached from everyday existence at the Luxor Hotel, like a tightrope walker who balances two "antagonistic worlds" of thought and emotion lest she topple over: "Yet she was well on guard, fearful from the start, lest for very rapture of this other world, this anodyne of Egypt, she might loose her slightly more familiar hard-won, specific Attic paradise" (*P*, 176). As she flirts casually with the English ex-captain seated beside her in the hotel garden, feigning ignorance about the statuary around her, she is conscious of interacting also at another level, of "making use of him," employing something "psychoemotional in her nature" to release "certain spiritual forces" (*P*, 177). Grateful for his assistance on that day's dizzying journey into King Amenophis' burial chamber, she associates Captain Rafton with the essence of that underground experience: her intuition that the "long graceful figure stretched in state in the centre of the minute and exquisite palace-tomb, was some potent opal," a "dark, substantial proof of her inheritance," a reward for the "sheer grit . . . the sheer physical nervous energy that had driven her to Egypt" (*P*, 182–83). Even though she is tired, she does not refuse when Rafton invites her to visit Karnak that evening, "the last night of the moon," but stands dead-silent, frozen with a sense of immanent revelation (*P*, 193).

H.D. describes Helen Fairwood's fateful visit to Karnak in the language of moonlit mystery and dream. Her intellect is "off guard," numbed by a "peculiar fatigue" (*P*, 203). Seated beside her in the "low-swung chariot," with his hat shading his face "helmet-wise," Captain Rafton seems to have come from London "by way . . . of Caesarian Rome," to be a traditional figure who would play "polite listener," confident guide, and potential protector (*P*, 203). As she follows his "outstanding dark form" through infinite corridors across starkly lit "Champs-de-Mar like" spaces into the hall of King Thothmes' banquet chamber, the very vastness of the setting suggests "magnificence of another order," freeing her from a mundane scale of values to measure herself by "new and yet unpremeditated standards" at once subhuman and transsexual (*P*, 209).

In this context of "curious shelter" that is both commonplace and yet infused with the aura of the Egyptian fertility myth, Isis' devotion to and self-induced insemination by her dead brother-consort Osiris, Helen Fairwood sees a "tiny temple or tomb or birth-house," emblem of rebirth and renewal:

It rose as if cut from one block of solid stone, at that distance she could not tell of quite what material, with the moon too working its common magic, making the little tomb or outer temple look square, geometric, set square with no imperfection or break in its excellent contour, like some exquisite square of yellow honeycomb. (*P*, 214)

In describing what this image means to her heroine, H.D. once again employs the imagery of virgin birth. As she follows Rafton down a related path, marveling at the precision of the giant hieroglyphs that even in the shadow shine clear, and he presses her gloved fingers into the "inset carved hieratic hawk" (*P*, 216), symbol of the Egyptian divine child, Helen Fairwood feels able to believe in him as an "uncommon Power" (*P*, 219). She is enabled to take the feminine position by means of this idealized substitute for the dead king.

Yet though she has been accompanied on her midnight journey by an idealized male figure, Helen Fairwood's fourth-dimensional encounter with Captain Rafton is framed by her relationship with Mary Thorpe-Wharton, which provides a sense of new direction. An adventurous, sensitive young American woman, Mary reminds her of an earlier self: "Maryland is exactly the sort of child . . . I was when I first crossed" (*P*, 204). Mary's mother, a "vain, overeducated" social climber (*P*, 194), has thrust Mrs. Fairwood into the position of chaperoning her daughter's courtship by a superficial young Englishman, about whom Mrs. Fairwood has serious reservations. But H.D. sets the tensions between mother and daughter off to the side here. From the perspective of her midnight intimation of psychic regeneration in the tomb of the dead king, the heroine of "Secret Name" comes to regard romance and marriage as merely temporary obstacles that would lead ultimately to inspiration: "The sun smote alike on her and on young Mary . . . alike, indifferently. Infatuated, both of them, come down to dots, with life, with some adventure, wherein Love might come, would come, temperamentally, destructively, but which in the end would free them" (*P*, 231).

In accord with the importance of this same-sex alliance, H.D. describes Helen Fairwood's response to Captain Rafton on the return ride in terms of the legendary prenatal mating of Isis and Osiris in the womb of their mother, the sky goddess Nut.[19] Her allusion to this tale, which symbolizes perfect union through the dissolution of ego boundaries and erasure of sexual polarity, may also screen the bonding with Bryher that took place after Perdita's birth:

> The town drew nearer, nearer, seeming to rush upon them, by some trick of consciousness, of itself, as if they stood static and the thud-thud of hoofs was only the heartbeat of some close, live body. As if they in some strange exact and precious period of pre-birth, twins, lovers, were held, sheltered beneath some throbbing heart. (*P*, 220)

Further, in her hotel room once more, when Mrs. Fairwood feels like one "who has been under ether," as if the whole exhausting day has been a "mist and lilly dream, an excursion into "some outre-mer where thought was transposed into form" (*P*, 224), H.D.'s description is like that of her second delivery, which she underwent with the aid of "twilight sleep" (arranged by Bryher), an anesthetic of scopolamine and morphine that produces ecstatic feelings and loss of memory. H.D. wrote to F. S. Flint, upon the death of his wife in childbirth, of her own brush with death during her delivery:

> Will you tell me (if it is not too distressing to you) about Violet and the baby? I feel so utterly understanding as I went through it all almost exactly as she did. And then I wanted to stop breathing—not from anguish of life, but, as it were, from perfection of being—as the tide pauses a moment when it turns. I could pray she went out like that into a full, rich life—flowers, some Italian landscape. It was coming back to life that was anguish to me. We must think that she is re-created and not alone in that happy flowering.[20]

Helen Fairwood feels wonderfully integrated and in possession of herself, as if "dykes and barriers had broken," when she returns to

the ruins with her young friend Mary in the brilliant morning sunlight
(*P*, 225). If last night she had been like a fish released very deep into
"layer on layer of sea" (or of the unconscious), now the sun at noon
"brought out a second layer of inter-related potentialities" a little
closer to the mind's surface: "For weren't she and Mary in their
outlook singularly, even as the captain had last night on the trip home
insinuated, alike?" (*P*, 230). As the two women turn together to
watch the vivid birds darting among the hieroglyphs, the brilliant
colors of morning further enliven the past night's vision of creative
possibility: "We didn't have this last night. We didn't, last night, have
these colours. Not even in that exquisite little Nike birth-house that
stood so clear" (*P*, 233). Though the "little . . . house of Power"
has vanished when Helen Fairwood turns to regard it a second time,
as if an earthquake had demolished it overnight, its image has left an
indelible psychological impression. As Mary returns to consider
marriage with her English suitor, Helen remains to wonder about the
outcome of union on a different plane. Would it result in a different
order of birth?

In her second published novel, *Hedylus*, which depicts the
psychological links between a mother and her poet-son, H.D. continues to explore the relation between gender identity, motherhood, and
creativity, focusing again upon the need to modify an androcentric
ideal. Like *Palimpsest*, this elegant parable of an artist's quest for
inspiration and self-transcendence is again set in a postapocalyptic
historical moment when the immediate past seems spiritually dead and
the future not yet recognizable. Hedyle, the aging Greek mistress of
the tyrant of Samos, stubbornly defines herself as "the Athenian" and
compels her illegitimate son, the poet Hedylus, in whom she sees
herself reflected, to do the same. Yet though Hedylus' need to leave his
mother in order to help found a new Alexandrian academy of poetry
gives the plot impetus, the two are linked even more intimately at the
novel's end. For, in an ironic double-play, H.D. makes Hedylus' quest
for autonomy and rebirth simultaneously a cautionary tale of dependency and inhibited creativity: Hedylus' leavetaking is counterbalanced by his mother's renewed decision to stay on the island.

The catalyst for this double transition is the traveler Demion (the name's demonic echoes are evident), who appears as an apparition upon the island at the same time as Hedyle's despised Athenian former lover stops on his way to Alexandria. An idealized father-figure conjured by Hedylus in his seaside hideaway, Demion helps the fatherless boy to integrate his imaginative life, which he has previously experienced as psychic blight, with his physical condition: "He realized . . . that his head was somehow adequately and suitably at one with the length of thin yet wiry, muscular young torso."[21] A "sort of courteous Helios" or "physical manifestation of omnipotence," the apparition also suggests another kind of poet Hedylus could become: "Your writing has only half expressed you. . . . One sees the struggle of some innate force. It breaks out at brief interval" (*Hed*, 76). Demion is also receptive to Hedylus' affection for Irene, an adventurous young woman who prefers the Artemisian pursuit of fishing to the stitching and weaving of more conventional women. Irene—iris— iridescent: Her name means "some sort of state, mystical almost, of innate quietude," and Demion advises Hedylus to take her with him on his journey (*Hed*, 81).

But if Hedylus' fall into consciousness and confrontation with his mother gives the story impetus, his departure invokes a deeper, parallel level of reflection that makes it double back. H.D. ends as she began, with Hedyle gazing narcissistically into her mirror, confirmed in her earlier premonition that something important is about to happen. Hedylus gone, she addresses Demion herself, admitting that her grief is mixed with relief, as if a heavy helmet has been lifted fron her head: "Her own son had been her standard, her threat, her constant heart-ache" (*Hed*, 121). Whereas earlier her mirror had caught reflections of her childhood, of her remote mathematician father and the mother she did not know, Hedylus' departure releases the memory of her own charged experience of motherhood:

> I mean the boy. I never meant to have him. Clarix, my first lover,
> had betrayed me. It was all due to papa. He was so remote.
> There was no competing with him. No one ever taught us. The

thing was a shock. Had nothing to do with formula, with numbers, with the why and the why . . . Papa was so fantastic. And Clio [her sister] wasn't well that year. Clarix shocked me, and with a turn, I ran straight into the arms of . . . I can't even name him. There was Clarix and this other. It seemed impossible. I lay on a rock outside Sunium, where we stayed with Lyda. Papa was so fantastic. There were, he had assured us no gods. There was a fiery pain at the back of my head and I had been taught that pure reason was the only goodness. Goodness, Goddess. There were others, I was certain. There was the Cytherean. (*Hed*, 124)

In direct contact with the demonic side of herself, Hedyle remembers that she chose to bear Hedylus in these difficult circumstances because her pregnancy was accompanied by a divine sign: the appearance of a tiny grass snake that she had not seen before. Her decision was not determined by "Aphrodite rising from the water," whom she associates with love's servitude, but rather by a small serpent, "signet of the god of Delphi," generator of vision and song (*Hed*, 126). In order to save her son from either of his repellant human fathers, and to attain a "glamorous victory of the mind over the mere physical defilement of childbearing," she regarded him as a divine child, the product of a "sacred marriage" or psychic parthenogenesis:[22] "This child, I said, won't be the child of Clarix or of the other lover. I would see to it. I said, 'I'll have the child because of that snake but it will be the sun's child' " (*Hed*, 126). In order to own up to her creativity, to connect it with the Eros principle within herself, Hedyle had to disown her son's (and her own) humanity. Hedyle also associates the conditions of Hedylus' conception with her Egyptian lapis bracelet, a serpent biting its tail, symbol of the uroboric beginning in which male and female elements of consciousness are undifferentiated. Her son's conception had been her test; he did not matter so much as a child, but rather as an "actual manifestation of an act of faith" in her creative power (*Hed*, 138). She had been a corpse wrapped in her own faith, like the dead original owner of the bracelet.

But though Hedyle's attraction to Demion is linked with an "absolute illiterate faith in the manifestation . . . of beauty" (*Hed*, 140), she also perceives that he spoils everything, and she is unwilling to accompany him to the East. Had she remained in Athens with Demetrius, she would have lost her identity; and she fears that her essence would likewise be absorbed were she to leave Samos with Demion: "Demion would have gathered me to him as the sun a raincloud" (*Hed*, 140). The hysteria of other women (Ariadne, Creusa, Cassandra), who had been "so importunate as to let God love them" (*Hed*, 133), serves as an inner warning of the need to modify this androcentric idea of creative inspiration. In a self-protective gesture, Hedyle chooses to remain behind.

H.D.'s clever eradication of the distinction between the "kept" mother and her poet son in the final lines of *Hedylus* serves to underline both her closeness to her own unconscious and her awareness of the special risks taken by the woman artist in a patriarchy. While she imagined her creative power as male in her two published pieces, her trauma in pregnancy deepened her discomfort at this falsification.[23] In *Palimpsest* Ray Bart and Captain Rafton effect only a twisted self-affirmation for Raymonde Ransome and Helen Fairwood, and in *Hedylus* Hedyle's exhausted confession underlies her poet-son's quest.

By giving both mother (Hedyle) and son (Hedylus) voice here, by showing their related responses to the enigmatic Demion, who is an idealized version of Hedylus' father, H.D. portrays the noxiousness of the traditional heterosexual romance plot for the psyche of the artist, even if he is male. She shows the damage done when a silenced mother (here a "kept" woman) is the object of the child's process of subject-formation, and not a subject in her own right. (Hedyle becomes the unconscious ground on which the confrontation between Hedylus and Demion is played out.) When Hedyle confronts Demion herself at the end, the pathology motivating the poet-son's quest for autonomy is revealed. H.D. will return to this motif, the connection between the silenced mother and her "wounded" son, more explicitly in *Helen in Egypt*.

H.D.'s attempts to resolve the conflict between motherhood and authorship by portraying access to the mother's potency in texts that celebrate lesbian love (a direction openly expressed in her unpublished fiction) did not satisfy her. Her published novels contain a broader deconstruction of gender identity. In them she shows the impact of motherhood as a heterosexist institution on the formation of both masculinity and femininity, which she portrays as an intertwined, conflictual whole. All of these early novels show H.D. trying to recover childbirth as a source of creative power for women, to integrate creativity and procreativity in a way that privileges neither. H.D.'s trauma in pregnancy sensitized her to the problem that feminine gender identity, in a patriarchy, means identifying with a devalued, passive mother.[24] Further, in her published novels she demonstrates implicitly that when women's natural power is debased by their role, the development of men is impaired, too.

3

~~~

H.D.'s Imagism

A Poetry of Loss and Rebellion

RAYMONDE RANSOME'S COMPLAINT in "Murex" that she is patronized and misunderstood by critics who find her poetry "cold" reflects H.D.'s own dissatisfaction with critical response to her early poetry (*P*, 166). In *Some Notes on Recent Writing*, written in the 1940s after her creative renewal, she deplored critical emphasis on the "crystalline" surfaces of her early poems, which implied a dismissal of their content, and she invited a more penetrating assessment. Noting the connection between the classical masks she used in her early fiction and the concentrated energy of her early poetry, she suggested that the poetry's highly wrought quality was the result of suppressing the personal narrative behind it:

> The Greek, or the Greek and Roman scenes and sequences of the prose studies are related to the early poems. I grew tired of hearing these poems referred to, as crystalline. Was there no other way of criticizing, of assessing them? But perhaps I did not see, did not dare see any further than my critics. Perhaps my annoyance with them was annoyance with myself. For what is crystal or any gem but the concentrated essence of the rough matrix, or the energy, either of over-intense heat or over-intense cold that projects it? The poems as a whole, and the "Greek" stories I have mentioned, contain that essence or that symbol,

69

symbol of concentration and of stubborn energy. The energy
itself and the matrix have not yet been assessed.[1]

H.D. suggested the reasons for that suppression in a later
memoir, in which she described her friendship with psychoanalyst
Erich Heydt. When Heydt asks her about the origin of a line in "Mid-
day," a poem from her first book, she recalls her sadness during its
composition in a way that also reveals an underlying mixture of denial,
survival guilt, and longing for spiritual absolution. She had left
America in order to be a poet, a goal that demanded self-assertion
and a degree of iconoclasm; then events that she considered unspeakable, which occurred during World War I, gripped her in a stran-
glehold of conflict and alienation. As she put it:

> I am surprised at the sadness in those poems—you see, I have
> never been able to discuss them. I don't think it was personal—
> that is—I had a—a—married life. There was something that I
> was looking for. I could not have reached artistic maturity in the
> America of that day. We had no signposts, at that time. I was
> married in England in 1913 and then the—the—I call it the Iron
> curtain, a term we all understand. That iron-curtain fell between
> me and my somewhat—well—not hot-house, but in a way, very
> comfortable surroundings—I mean, I had in a way, a very petted
> and spoiled American life—one girl with brothers—I don't
> know. It is hard to explain it. We say (old-fashioned people used
> to say) when someone dies, he or she has *gone home*. I was
> looking for home, I think. But a sort of heaven-is-my-home. I
> was looking for that—that super-ego—that father-lover—I don't
> know—How can I explain it? (*CF*, 12)

Though she did go on to specify the grief and guilt she felt after
her losses in childbirth, H.D. could not discuss these feelings when
they occurred. To have done so would have seemed selfish in view of
the larger national disaster. Nor was she able to express herself openly
in her published fiction or her verse. Instead, she encoded her story,

adopting strategies of concealment to depict the internal division that resulted from her trauma. As Jeanne Kammer has pointed out, her poems aim at evoking in us a response to what she has not said.[2] Inhibited by conventions of female self-sacrifice from more capacious uses of poetic voice, H.D. used a highly compressed visual mode of expression, which depended on juxtaposed metaphoric images, stripped of linguistic connectives, to convey complex emotional states that often included contradictions. Her irregular but distinctly musical cadences are built on patterns of internal rhyme and repetition that are deliberately inconspicuous. As Alicia Ostriker has written, "We are being invited to trust . . . our own interiority, not a transcendent still point outside of ourselves."[3]

In this chapter I consider the emotional matrix underlying the compressed surfaces of H.D.'s Imagist poetry. My view links questions of technique and sensibility, the laconic speech and "mythopoetic sense" noted by Ezra Pound, who invented the school of Imagism to describe H.D.'s poetry, with H.D.'s personal psychology.[4] From her first book *Sea Garden* (1916) to *Red Roses for Bronze* (1931), H.D. provides startling insights into a woman poet's relation to her own creative power from the perspective of one whose sense of mastery in the experience of childbirth was seriously shaken. Some poems enact the miscarriage of psychic qualities associated with childbirth and the archetype of the child, such as hope and a sense of fulfillment.[5] In others, she attempts to controvert these feelings of stricken imagination by divorcing female creative power from the ideologies of gender and the institutions of marriage and motherhood that circumscribe it. Some poems in this rebellious vein celebrate lesbian love as a refuge from the pain of heterosexual engagement. In many H.D. uses classical images of women to explore the discrepancy between her own experience and that already codified in culture. Because guilt partially blocked access to inner forms of her own, she projected her feelings, breathing new life into these figures of myth and classical poetry. Thus she conveyed the nonrational, overdetermined truths of dream in images from nature or Greek myth that were objective correlatives of her troubled emotional state.

71

Most of the poems of *Sea Garden* must have been written between 1913 and 1916, the years between H.D.'s marriage to Richard Aldington and the immediate aftermath of their stillborn child (spring, 1915). As the title suggests, the book's main theme is homage to a particular kind of rugged, natural beauty: a beauty of fierce struggle and endurance, which the speaker contrasts with the cloying "beauty without strength" of conventional, sheltered gardens, or to the urban blight of modern cities.[6] The sea rose is "harsh," "meagre," "stunted," but "more precious / than a wet rose / single on a stem" (*CP*, 5); the sea lily is "slashed and torn / but doubly rich" (*CP*, 14); the white violet, though "fragile as agate" (*CP*, 25), catches the light; and though sea poppies grow among "split conch shells" (*CP*, 21), they are more fragrant than the meadow variety.

Evidence of deep internal conflict undercuts this celebration of survival and kinship with nature, however. Conflict results in the debilitating erosion of erotic power that we find in such poems as "Storm," "Night," "Acon," and "Mid-day." In the first of these, the speaker accuses the storm of crushing the green out of the trees' live branches, burdening them with "black drops." A "weighted leaf," broken off in the wind, "whirls up and sinks, / a green stone" (*CP*, 36). "Night" curls petals and leaves back from the stalk till they break, leaving the "stark core / of the rose / to perish on the branch" (*CP*, 33). In "Acon" the speaker asks for "all-healing herbs" to cure the feverish "Hyella, / whom no god pities" (*CP*, 32). And the speaker of "Mid-day" is "defeated":

> My thoughts tear at me,
> I dread their fever.
> I am scattered in its whirl
> I am scattered like
> the hot shrivelled seeds. (*CP*, 10)

Unlike the poplar, which stands "deep-rooted among the hill-stones," she perishes "on the path / among the crevices of the rocks" (*CP*, 10).

Two short verses titled "Garden" suggest that the conflict is caused by the speaker's troubled relation to her sexuality, which she associates with spiritual inhibition and stasis. In the first she addresses a rose "cut in rock," asserting that its imprint is so clear that she "could scrape the colour / from the petals / like spilt dye" (*CP*, 24). But what begins as an assertion of female force quickly becomes an admission of paralysis as the text doubles back on itself:

> If I could break you
> I could break a tree.
>
> If I could stir
> I could break a tree—
> I could break you. (*CP*, 24)

In the second verse she implores the wind to "rend open the heat" (*CP*, 25); for in this state of aggravated suspension the process of her inner life is hindered, and its natural product is incompletely formed. Spiritual deadlock is conveyed by sound as well as sense in the cumulation of internal assonance that overlaps the field of the lines:

> Fruit cannot drop
> through this thick air—
> fruit cannot fall into heat
> that presses up and blunts
> the points of pears
> and rounds the grapes. (*CP*, 25)

In "The Gift," a poem that foreshadows an important later memoir, the problem becomes one of sexual role rather than one of sexual identity. A disillusioned speaker offers her consciousness of the pain of female experience to an uninitiated, conventionally feminine other woman: "Instead of pearls—a wrought clasp— / a bracelet— will you accept this?" (*CP*, 15). Distinguishing herself from this childlike other, whose world is yet "unspoiled" (her garden "over-sweet," her house "over-lovely"), she compares her own suffering with

73

traditional spiritual initiation. She has endured "the tense nerves / through the moment of ritual" (*CP*, 17). Forever marked by her experience, she no longer craves a lush garden, but rather a "still place" and "perhaps some outer horror / some hideousness to stamp beauty . . . in our hearts" (*CP*, 18). This mark of difference—"no changing it now" (*CP*, 18)—is her wry offering to the other.

That H.D. found it increasingly difficult to reconcile female sexual identity with creative power after her stillbirth becomes evident in "The God," the section in *Collected Poems* she devoted to the theme of inspiration. Some of the eleven lyrics there were first published in *Poetry* as early as 1913, before her stillbirth; others, namely, "Adonis," "The God," "Pygmalion," and "Eurydice," were written at Corfe Castle in 1917.[7] In the earlier poems—"Oread," "Moonrise," "Orion Dead," "Hermonax," and "The Pool"—H.D. writes about creativity either from a female perspective or from one that is sexually undifferentiated, but in the later ones she represents creative power as masculine in a way that reveals the pain of self-division.

As its title indicates, "Oread" dramatizes the perception of a mountain nymph as she regards the sea aroused in passion. The imagery of the reiterated commands, all projections of her own wooded environment, blurs the boundary between subject and object, suggesting that potency and receptivity are internally coexistent:

> Whirl up, sea—
> whirl your pointed pines,
> splash your great pines
> on our rocks,
> hurl your green over us,
> cover us with your pools of fir. (*CP*, 55)

In "Moonrise" a band of Amazons loose their arrows at the moon, hoping that her strength will empower their song: "She is great, / we measure her by the pine trees" (*CP*, 56). And even though she is desolate at having killed Orion, the huntress Artemis defiantly celebrates her destructive potential in "Orion Dead": "So arise and face me. / I am poisoned with rage of song" (*CP*, 56).

Both "Hermonax" and "The Pool" convey the primordial, undifferentiated quality of creativity. In the former a "caster of nets" makes a strange offering to the sea-gods Ino and her son Palemon. A gift of "sea-wrack," it is a "sea-gliding creature . . . like a weed, / covered with salt foam" (*CP*, 58). And in very few lines "The Pool" deftly calls on our sense of touch to convey the elemental quality of water (and the unconscious) together with its impenetrable mystery:

> Are you alive?
> I touch you.
> You quiver like a sea-fish.
> I cover you with my net.
> What are you—banded one? (*CP*, 56)

In the poems written at Corfe Castle after her stillbirth, H.D.'s masculinization of her creative power reveals increased anxiety and self-denigration. For example, "Adonis" emphasizes the negative dimension of the oriental god's regenerative power: "each of us like you / has died once" (*CP*, 47). And "Sitalkas" (Apollo's cult name) alludes to a ritual of purification by burning known as the "Delphic Stepteria": "thou art come at length / more beautiful / than any cool god" (*CP*, 58). In "The God" the speaker doubts whether the "mysterious" and "far distant" ebony face of ivy-garlanded Dionysus can turn toward her. She has felt cast out from the natural world, her creativity a destructive force, and she has turned inward, away from life:

> my very glance must shatter
> the purple fruit.
>
> I had drawn away into the salt,
> myself, a shell
> emptied of life. (*CP*, 46)

But she finds no escape from destruction. The fiery cyclamen that embodies Dionysus has ensnared even her consciousness: her creative power is turned inward to mortify a powerless self:

> I pluck the cyclamen,
> red by wine-red,
> and place the petals'
> stiff ivory and bright fire
> against my flesh,
>
> now I am powerless
> to draw back
> for the sea is cyclamen-purple,
> cyclamen-red, colour of the last grapes,
> colour of the purple of the flowers,
> cyclamen-coloured and dark. (*CP*, 47)

Such anxiety about creative power (when it is imagined as male) is also the subject of "Pygmalion." H.D.'s sculptor-king wonders whether he is the agent of his creative power or its object: "Which am I, / the stone or the power / that lifts the rock from the earth?" (*CP*, 49). He created innumerable gods out of the rocks, but once these images were finished, they mocked his inadequacy: "*you are useless, / no marble can bind me, / no stone suggests*" (*CP*, 50). Though he intended them to be subordinate, to represent his personal power, his statues have a perfection that reveals a fiery essence belonging to a suprapersonal, transcendent domain: "They have melted into the light / and I am desolate" (*CP*, 50). His desolation suggests the answer to his last rhetorical question: "am I the god? / or does this fire carve me? for its use?" (*CP*, 50).

In "Eurydice" the speaker gains a negative form of self-affirmation by rebelling against a culturally mandated pattern of male-female relationship that negates the possibility of independent female self-determination.[8] Addressing her musician husband Orpheus after he has glanced back on their journey out of Hades, sweeping her once more into the world of death, she angrily challenges his assumption that life with him is better. Accusing him of having been arrogant and self-aggrandizing in his attempt to recover her, she wishes he had let her be so that she could have forgotten him and the past without the pain of an anticipated return. She asks why he turned back, why he hesitated, why he bent his face to hers; and these repeated questions ring with suspicion and fury: "What was it you saw in my face? / the light of your own face, / the fire of your own presence?" (*CP*, 52).

Consigned now permanently to Hades, she determines to make this underworld a locus of growing autonomy and personal triumph. But her concluding image doubles back on itself, refusing even this limited inscription of female authority. Eurydice's comparison of "hell" with the opening of a "red rose" poignantly evokes the author's stillbirth:

> At least I have the flowers of myself,
> and my thoughts, no god
> can take that.
> I have the fervour of myself for a presence
> and my own spirit for light;
>
> and my spirit with its loss
> knows this;
> though small against the rocks,
> hell must break before I am lost;
>
> before I am lost,
> hell must open like a red rose
> for the dead to pass. (*CP*, 55)

Though the feeling in it is ambivalent, "Eurydice" introduces a technique H.D. will use repeatedly to controvert the pull toward self-renunciation we have seen in so many of these early poems. She identifies with heroines from classical literature, lending them interiority, either to validate her own experience or to critique the social organization of gender that has caused her emotional pain. As her *Notes on Euripides, Pausanias, and Greek Lyric Poets* (1920) indicates, she was attracted to the images of heroic women enshrined in the poetry of Sappho and those of a few, revolutionary male feminists.

77

Her notes on the "Fragments of Sappho" and the "Garland of Meleager" elaborate on this atypical womanly ideal.[9] We do not look for conventional warmth in Sappho's poems, H.D. writes, "not fire nor sunlight, not heat in the ordinary sense, diffused and comforting," but another element containing these, yet differing in essence, "as if the brittle crescent-moon gave heat to us, or some splendid, scintillating star turned warm suddenly in our head like a jewel" ("Notes on Greek Poets," 3). The wise Sappho represents a world of emotion entirely different from anything today. Spending her flawless talent to destroy "custom and mob-thought," she could construct from the single gesture of a half-grown girl, a "being, a companion, an equal" ("Notes on Greek Poets," 7). And though Aphrodite's beauty is the reiterated subject of her poetry, its distinctive quality is not a rosy eroticism, but rather a wry intellectual discernment: "The underlips curl out in the white face . . . the brows break the perfect line of the white forehead, her expression is not exactly sinister (sinister and dead), the spark of mockery between half-closed lids is rather living destructive irony" ("Notes on Greek Poets," 3).

Similarly, by her account, Meleager, the first great anthologizer of lyric poetry, particularized women in his *Garland* not as objects of sexual desire but as "co-workers with men"; he compared "the peculiarities of their creative spirit, with these most symbolic and sacred flowers" ("Notes on Greek Poets," 7). And in her essay on Euripides' "Helen," H.D. implies that Euripides eschews the sexual allure of this avatar of female beauty, preferring to idealize her demonic power:

It is good to meet Helen face to face, for [other] men and poets have visualized her so crudely. We had become tired of her sweetness, her contours painted for us, as soft and luxurious.

She is young but young like the statues dug from the dazzling sand in the desert behind the tomb of Proteus. Her face is not in any Praxitelian sense beautiful. It is white and beautiful as a skull or a bird's swift, destructive beak is beautiful. ("Notes on Greek Poets," 3)

78

In her earliest translation, choruses from Euripides' *Iphigeneia in Aulis*, H.D. attempts to rationalize the apparent inevitability of female pain and loss by showing how women internalize a value system that is inimical to them and then collude in their own victimization. In this play the young women of Chalkis witness the war-crazed sacrifice of a royal daughter who is on the edge of erotic power. Having journeyed to Aulis to see the battle line, "the thousand ships" gathered to retrieve Helen, they creep through the woods between the altars to Artemis. Disturbed by what they find, they try unsuccessfully to reconcile the dazzling imagery graven on their minds with the ignominious results of Paris's theft, which they see before them.

They predict the Greeks' vengeful destruction of Troy and the future slander of Helen:

> May no child of mine,
> Nor any child of my child
> Ever fashion such a tale
> As the Phrygians shall murmur. . . .
> "Helen has brought this." (*CP*, 78)

They also recall the wedding of Pelios and Thetis, where the frenzied centaur Chiron predicted that Thetis's son Achilles would "scatter fire" over the land; and they deplore the murder of innocent Iphigeneia, who is to be sacrificed like an animal, because of a civilization gone astray:

> They will leave you
> With stained throat—
> Though you never cropped hill-grass
> To the reed-cry
> And the shepherd's note.
>
> Some Greek hero is cheated
> And your mother's court
> Of its bride. (*CP*, 82)

"Of what use is valour," these women ask, in a world where "evil has conquered the race" (*CP*, 80, 81).

But then Iphegeneia herself accepts the social necessity of her death as a heroic tribute to Artemis that will serve to "break the curse" on her people, asserting that she goes "to a new place / Another life" (*CP*, 84). Though at first the chorus of "slight girls" laments their powerlessness to "cry out" in objection, overwhelming religious authority ultimately leads them to acquiesce in this sacrifice. Thus by their silence, they contribute to the Greek patriarchy's brutal ritual.

In *Hymen* (1921), the volume that became the fourth section of *Collected Poems*, H.D. connects women's self-sacrifice and silence with the institution of marriage for which they are socialized, suggesting that in marriage female procreative power is appropriated by men. The title poem, a verse-masque to be accompanied by music, draws upon the traditionally mournful bridal epithalamia of Sappho, which H.D. modulates to suit her own purposes.[10] In an early letter to Bryher she describes the subversive nature of her formal experimentation in this poem and two others in this volume:

> I am really very happy over your acceptance of *Hymen* as a form. I have already planned four or five others — would you call them masques? . . . One I want to be a Sicilian witch-piece — rocks, smoldering fires, anemones, twisted olives — very wild and savage. I have called it in my mind, *Simaetha*. (You remember the girl in Theocritus.) The *Leda*, I want quieter in tone — birds, flowering grass and hyacinths. I am planning several others, poems, with prose intervals and music.[11]

Though it ostensibly celebrates the consummation of a marriage, the stately masque "Hymen" is markedly funereal. Written after H.D. and Aldington separated, it depicts the psychosexual development of a silent bride by means of a sequence of gradually maturing choruses of young women. After sixteen matrons from the temple of Hera pray that the joy of sexual union will be long-lived, four "small maids" begin the developmental procession, offering a few, pale "first crocus buds." Four "rather fragile taller children" follow mournfully: "Like a bird out of our hand, like a light out of our heart, / You are gone" (*CP*, 104). Then four free, wild "wood-maidens of Artemis," who bring a basket of hyacinths and sing the "swallow-song of joy," lay their offering across the marble floor in a pattern that the bride's "bent eyes / May trace and follow / To the shut bridal door" (*CP*, 104). Next comes the bride-chorus, with the bride "a veiled symbolic figure" indistinguishable from the others, followed by two groups of young matrons. This last procession enters with coverlets and linen for the bridal bed, which they describe as if it were a coffin:

> Let the palings of her bed
> Be quince and box-wood overlaid
> With the scented bark of yew.
>
> That all the wood in blossoming,
> May calm her heart and cool her blood
> For losing of her maidenhood. (*CP*, 108)

The figure of Love, a tall youth with flaming hair and deep red wings, brings the masque to a climax when he pauses just outside the bride's door with his gift of black-purple cyclamen. The speaker likens these flowers to the crimson cover of the bridal bed, comparing phallic penetration in sexual intercourse, an act usually associated with insemination and fertility, with the plundering bee's part in pollination:

> There with his honey-seeking lips
> The bee clings close and warmly sips,
> And seeks with honey-thighs to sway
> And drink the very flower away.
>
> (Ah, stern the petals drawing back;
> Ah rare, ah virginal her breath!)
> Crimson, with honey-seeking lips,
> The sun lies hot across his back,
> The gold is flecked across his wings.
> Quivering he sways and quivering clings.
> (Ah, rare her shoulders drawing back!)

One moment, then the plunderer slips
Between the purple flower-lips. (*CP*, 109)

After Love passes offstage to a crash of cymbals, a band of boys
holding flickering torches sweep the fallen petals and conclude in half-
subdued voices: "Where love is king / Ah, there is little need / To
dance and sing" (*CP*, 110). The bitter irony of this conclusion serves
to underline the purposive choice of the form itself. For in its
Renaissance flowering, the court masque ended with the masquers
joining the audience in a dance that validated and celebrated the
reigning king's authority, a convention that H.D. calls into question.[12]

H.D.'s later addition of an opening epigraph to Pallas Athene
confirms her ironic intention in "Hymen." Added sometime after
1919, it defends the virgin goddess whom others have called remote
and blind, with the lines "now that my head is bowed / in sorrow, I find
/ she is most kind" (*CP*, 101). Carl Kerenyi's discussion of the tension
intrinsic in the Athene myth illuminates the defensive aspects of H.D.'s
poem. He points out that the worship of Athene in connection with
marriage and motherhood must be understood in terms of father-right.
Athenian maidens were led by their parents to the Acropolis on the
day before their wedding to secure the conception of a child, and the
priestess of Athene visited newly married women wearing Zeus' *aegis*.
The weapons of the goddess (helmet, lance, and shield) and the duality
inherent in her name exteriorize the inner contradiction associated with
her. Pallas, also a word for "robust young man," is linked with Athene,
from *atena*—a clay vessal used in sacrifice. Kerenyi writes that Pallas
protects Athene against the "loss of feminine choice and integrity,"
against "the attacking force of the archaic masculine."[13]

An alternative, "white" emotional state, linked with restored
integrity and lesbian love, informs a second important group of poems
in *Hymen*: "White World," "Prayer," "Song," "Evadne," "The Islands," "At Baia," "Fragment 113," and "Egypt." "The whole white
world is ours," H.D. writes in the first section of this group, and "delight
/ waits till our spirits tire / of forest, grove and bush / and purple flower
of the laurel tree" (*CP*, 134). "Prayer," "Song," and "Evadne" develop

nuances of this white world. As in her unpublished novel *Paint It Today*, H.D. associates whiteness with intactness, with the chaste terms of artistic inspiration, and with creation divorced from procreation. For example, the prayer to Athene asks that the goddess touch the speaker's forehead, thus restoring "glamour to our will, / the thought . . . the tool, the chisel" (*CP*, 142). "Song" personifies its subject as a rarefied fertility god or goddess, whose face is as "fair as rain, / yet as rain that lies clear / on white honey-comb" (*CP*, 133). And Evadne, united with Apollo, claims that "Between my chin and throat / his mouth slipped over and over" (*CP*, 132).

Similarly, "The Islands" and "At Baia" celebrate an inviolate artistic integrity. The former answers the question "What are the islands to me," with a luxurious catalogue of Greek place-names so euphonious and beautifully paced they should be set to music. The question is subtly complicated in the poem's seven sections to develop a finely honed contrast: "What can love of land give to me / that you have not?" (*CP*, 125). It finally comes to rest, unanswered, upon the "cold splendour of song / and its bleak sacrifice" (*CP*, 127). At Baia, the ancient port of Cumae, which is inseparably associated with the Sybil, the speaker meditates on the salutary gift of oracular expression. By elaborating on a comparison with "some lovely, perilous thing, / orchids piled in a great sheaf," she implies the ineffable, metaphysical fragrance she seeks: "Lover to lover, no kiss, / no touch, but forever and ever this" (*CP*, 128).

H.D. connects this alternative, "white," emotional state more explicitly with lesbian love in "Fragment 113" and "Egypt." In the former poem she dilates Sappho's "Neither honey nor bee for me" into an ingeniously wrought comparison between degrees and modes of passion. Throughout half of the poem the speaker's reiterated denials ring subtle changes upon the "old" sensual "plunder" she refuses because it has caused her to suffer:

> not honey, not the south;
> . . .
> not iris—old desire—old passion—

83

old forgetfulness — old pain —
not this, nor any flower. (*CP*, 131)

Finally, she admonishes the other to "touch as the god," to "seek strength of arm and throat," to prefer intellectual love, the lyre's "fiery-tempered" frame to the trembling lyre note.

Continuing the connection between whiteness and lesbian love, H.D.'s "Egypt" also countervails the nineteenth-century aesthetes' depiction of love between women as decadent and sinister. [14] At first the speaker thought Egypt had maimed her by offering "dream for life, / an opiate for a kiss, / and death for both" (*CP*, 140). But her experience has not been "days of trance, / shadow, foredoom of death," but rather "passionate grave thought, / belief enhanced, / ritual returned and magic" (*CP*, 141). Most important, she felt the beginning of personal regeneration, a return of female potency:

Even in the uttermost black pit
of the forbidden knowledge,
wisdom's glance,
the grey eyes following
in the mid-most desert —
great shaft of rose,
fire shed across our path,
upon the face grown grey, a light,
Hellas re-born from death. (*CP*, 141)

The institution of motherhood as a threat to female sexual and psychological potency is the theme of two other poems in *Hymen*: "Thetis" and "Demeter." That H.D. found the mother of Achilles an important subject is evident also in a second poem about her in *Heliodora* (1924) and in the prominent part she plays in *Helen in Egypt* (1961). That is, the speaker imagines Thetis' glamour before she gives birth, prophesying that she will step from a jeweled, solidly paved parapet into the amber-flecked sea at sunset. She will pass "beneath the island disk" to dare the glittering back of a swaying dolphin, that "uterine beast" which the Greeks revered. However, in the second poem Thetis's daring results in self-sabotage and a loss of identity because of the devaluation of motherhood in patriarchy. The Nereid grants her husband "love under the sea" in exchange for the coming of her mighty son Achilles. Unlike her sister sea nymphs who would have "a daughter for child," a "*stray self, furtive and wild,*" she dreams of a son who will "flatter" her wounded self-image (*CP*, 161). This wish propels her out of her natural home: she creeps over the sand to find Achilles' footprint and prostrates herself "along the burning sand" before it. Thus, "the mother, Thetis' self" melts into a blue rivulet (*CP*, 163).

Most compelling in its depiction of motherhood and loss of self is the complex "Demeter." In this early poem H.D. draws on her knowledge of Eleusinian ritual to reclaim for her subject a rightful place in our awareness and esteem. In the beginning the Greek goddess who was the mother of the grain and of a mysterious daughter complains of the way men imagine and worship her: "(men, fires, feasts, temple steps) — useless" (*CP*, 111). Compared with slender, more popular Aphrodite, she is wrought "heavy / and great of limb" (*CP*, 111), flattered but neglected. Not content with empty flattery, Demeter exhorts initiates to rank her highest, declaring that she offers a more profound truth: "never forget / in thought or mysterious trance— / I am greatest and least" (*CP*, 112). For though the hands of Love are soft, how many know that true beatitude demands sacrifice and loss, "black crocus against the black / locks of another" (*CP*, 113)? She supports her claim by referring to myths associated with the Eleusinian mysteries, in which initiates who imitated her mourning were promised fortitude in the face of death.

Demeter's own initiation was the finding of her daughter Persephone, who had been seduced while gathering narcissus flowers and taken by Hades to the underworld. But she enriches our understanding of the Eleusinian rite by first showing her relationship to the birth of Dionysus, lord of the soul's ecstasy. Calling him by his cult name Bromios, Demeter reshapes the most well-known version of the god's origins by stressing the long-term hardships of his nurturing rather

85

than the melodrama of his begetting. According to common legend, Dionysus was the child of Zeus and a mortal woman, Semele, who was destroyed by the lightning of the god's presence while the child lay in her womb. He was then saved from the flames and put in his father's thigh for the remainder of his gestation. H.D.'s Demeter angrily dismisses this version: "Enough of the lightning, / enough of the tales that speak of the death of the mother" (*CP*, 113). Emphasizing an adjacent fragment of myth, she claims Bromios as her adopted son. She found him asleep in the ivy brake; she scratched and foraged to keep him alive; she took him and his deserted mother to her heart.

H.D.'s linkage of Dionysus' origins with his mother's desertion and the seduction of Persephone alludes to lesser known dimensions of the Eleusinian ritual. Kerenyi writes that the core of these mysteries was the revelation that the queen of the dead herself had given birth in fire to a son. According to a variant of the myth, the mother of Dionysus was not Semele but Persephone, who gave birth to him under the earth.[15] H.D.'s reference to the ritual myrtle carried by the mystai, one of Dionysus' three sacred plants, suggests that she had this meaning in mind: In exchange for the myrtle, Hades was supposed to give Dionysus' mother back to him.

H.D.'s depiction of the meaning of Persephone's seduction is in keeping with its intrapsychic importance to her, with its suprapersonal dimension, and with its epiphanic essence. For Persephone and Demeter represent linked facets of a woman's life cycle, maidenhood and motherhood, which may be repeated throughout history. Motherhood, the more earthly and accessible facet, necessarily involves recognition of the loss of maidenhood, the rather ghostly, transcendent part of the duality. Therefore, in the last section, when a choric voice whispers "*What of her— / mistress of Death?*" (*CP*, 114), Demeter's response is particularly poignant. A miniature developmental history of herself in relation to her daughter, her answer stresses their joint role in cultural renewal while disclosing both a bond and a disjunction:

> Form of a golden wreath
> were my hands that girt her head,

fingers that strove to meet,
and met where the whisps escaped
from the fillet, of tenderest gold,
small circlet and slim
were my fingers then.

Now they are wrought of iron
to wrest from the earth
secrets; strong to protect,
strong to keep back the winter
when winter tracks too soon blanch the forest:
strong to break dead things. (*CP*, 114)

In the passage above Demeter implies that she is strong enough to protect her daughter, but the choric voice's renewed question insists on further insight: "*What of her— / mistress of Death— / what of his kiss?*" (*CP*, 114). As the distinction between "my" and "her" disappears in Demeter's second reply, so does the boundary between mother and daughter. In this early study of Demeter, H.D. experiences mourning as an inner descent to the moment of lost maidenhood. Capable only of a nascent recovery, she is unable to return fully. Demeter's "finding again" of her daughter and of her own essential quality as her daughter's mother remains overshadowed by the wrench of heterosexual initiation: "Ah, strong were the arms that took / (ah, evil the heart and graceless), / but the kiss was less passionate!" (*CP*, 115).

In "At Eleusis," published later in *Heliodora*, H.D. focuses again on the mother as lost maiden, this time depicting a preliminary stage of the ritual in which initiates imitate the purification of Persephone, Hades' bride. In this part the priestess of Demeter holds a *liknon*, or winnowing fan, over each initiate's head. This basket, in which grain was cleansed and in which accessories of the Dionysian rites were kept, also held infants who were regarded as seeds of the future.[16] Upon viewing the fan, initiates thought of their sins and of the state of infancy to which expiation would restore them. In keeping with the understanding that Demeter and Persephone, mother and maiden, are two parts of a woman's self (Persephone the hidden part), H.D.'s speaker in this poem seems to stand outside herself, to be both priestess and initiate:

> take the basket,
> think;
> think of the moment you count
> most foul in your life. (*CP*, 179)

And when her hidden self falters at the thought of the consequences of her rape, the priestess part enables her to proceed by evoking a suprapersonal, religious purpose: "What they did, / they did for Dionysus, / for ecstasy's sake" (*CP*, 179).

As "Thetis" and "At Eleusis" suggest, in *Heliodora* (1924), which became the fifth section of *Collected Poems*, H.D. continues her exposition of the damage done to the female psyche by restrictive gender roles. Not the least of this damage, emotional frigidity, is the subject of the book's poem-length epigraph "Wash of Cold River." By the chill Ionian water, rare wind-flowers grow that are "colder than a rose" (*CP*, 147). In their presence the speaker is inspired to mold "*a clear / and frigid statue*" for Artemis' inaccessible shrine (*CP*, 148). Similarly, H.D.'s title poem "Heliodora" celebrates the dead girl Meleager loved, who represented to him "the whole spirit of the Aegean and Ionian islands" ("Notes on Greek Poets," III, 2). In this witty tribute to Meleager's poetry (if not to his love), H.D. uses her rivalry with Aldington to dramatize the narcissism of the male artist.

The speaker, a rival poetess, describes an instance when she and the young Meleager stayed up all night "to quibble in flowers and verse / over a girl's name" (*CP*, 151). They vied with each other for perfect phrases and caught each other's inspiration: "So I saw the fire in his eyes, / it was almost my fire, (he was younger)" (*CP*, 154). In playful retribution for this theft, she raises the ante, challenging him to compose a verse so glorious it would awaken the muses: "What was one girl to the nine?" (*CP*, 153). But though his tribute is extraordinarily beautiful, the muses remain asleep. His ego wounded, he is thus provoked to reassert the purity of his love for Heliodora and to shout "that for the nine" as he rushes out the door. Therefore, having outwitted him, she has the last words—which were originally his:

> I thought:
> there will never be a poet
> in all the centuries after this,
> who will dare write,
> after my friend's verse
> "a girl's mouth
> is a lily kissed." (*CP*, 154)

Also in *Heliodora* H.D. reinterprets the existing images of Lais, Cassandra, Penelope, and Helen. In each case she shows how stories that have minimized female pain have also curtailed female potential. In "Lais" she establishes a wider context for Plato's epigram. When the speaker says, "Let her who walks in Paphos / take the glass" (*CP*, 149), she differentiates the goddess Aphrodite from this beautiful young woman who has given up her mirror after she is bereft of her lover. Lais has relinquished her mirror because she "sees no longer in its depth / the Lais' self / that laughed exultant / tyrannizing Greece," but rather a grieving face she does not recognize (*CP*, 150). Similarly, Cassandra, the prophetess cursed by Apollo always to be doubted, is pictured praying piteously to Hymen, god of marriage: "Hymen, O Hymen king / what bitter thing is this?" (*CP*, 171). She finds herself alone, shunned by humanity in the darkness of her second sight, so she pleads with Hymen for an unorthodox kind of union, and the fruit thereof. She wishes to wed Love and to create beautiful ritual, as Hymen has: "may it not break, beauty, / from out my hands, my head, my feet? / . . . O Hymen lord, be kind" (*CP*, 171).

In "At Ithaca" faithful Penelope is nameless. She is seated at her loom against a dark sea that "takes on that desperate tone / . . . that wives put on / when all their love is done" (*CP*, 163). In a traitorous moment she wishes "some fiery friend" would sweep her loom from her fingers and "tear the pattern there, / the flowers so deftly wrought"

(*CP*, 163). But the "web of pictures" that reflects her deprivation even more subtly contains her life. Contemplating the beauty of her artistry, she becomes further ensnared, this time in imaginative sympathy with her husband's will to conquer:

> Athene steels my soul,
> shooting across my brain,
> I see as shafts of rain
> his chariot and his shafts,
> I see the arrows fall,
> I see my lord who moves
> like Hector, lord of love,
> I see him matched with fair
> bright rivals and I see
> these rivals flee. (*CP*, 164)

In its striking depiction of patriarchy's devastating impact on woman's psyche, H.D.'s "Helen" foreshadows her epic poem *Helen in Egypt*. The symbol of irresistible beauty and illicit love, the cause and goal of a terrible war, Helen has become an object of denigration and hatred: "All Greece reviles / the wan face when she smiles . . . remembering past enchantments / and past ills" (*CP*, 155). Overlooking her divine origin, the prophecy (made in Egypt in the *Odyssey*) that she is "God's daughter, born of love," Homeric epic has degraded her to a wan shadow of herself, sacrificing her to its heroic theme.[17] The effect on *her* of this noxious cultural tradition, enacted in the poem, is increasing immobility and withdrawal. The once vital luster of her beauty turns to "white ash amid funereal cypresses" (*CP*, 155). As Susan Friedman has written, "Her smiles win her no mercy, and the only way she can become loved is through her death."[18]

I would single out H.D.'s haunting poem "Lethe" as that which best dramatizes her complex, troubled relation to her own feelings in this period, which best exemplifies the tension between silence and speech that characterizes her Imagist poems. Self-effacing in intent, it depicts psychic numbing, the condition Robert Jay Lifton describes as the "incapacity to feel or to confront certain kinds of experience, due to the blocking or absence of inner forms or imagery that can connect with such experience."[19] In a hypnotic, self-reflective reverie the speaker conveys both the unbearable loss that moves her to speak and the desperate effort to keep her feelings in control. She condemns an "other" to a death of sensation, to a loss of the sensible world, to the thanatotic state that is Lethe, the river of forgetfulness that separates the underworld from the world above. The subtly varied, rolling three-beat lines, eight of which begin with the word "nor," already contain the negation they solicit:

> Nor skin nor hide nor fleece
>   Shall cover you,
> Nor curtain of crimson nor fine
> Shelter of cedar-wood be over you,
>   Nor the fir-tree
>   Nor the pine.
>
> Nor sight of whin nor gorse
>   Nor river-yew,
> Nor fragrance of flowering bush,
> Nor wailing of reed-bird to waken you,
>   Nor of linnet,
>   Nor of thrush. (*CP*, 190)

In the third stanza, the powerful, rocking rhythm achieves a profound nullity, a travesty of sexual climax that replaces fulfillment and peace:

> Nor word nor touch nor sight
>   Of lover, you
> Shall long through the night but for this:
> The roll of the full tide to cover you
>   Without question,
>   Without kiss. (*CP*, 190)

Within a year after her mother's death in 1927, H.D. had an (illegal) abortion, an experience that exacerbated her guilt around the conflicting claims of womanhood and authorship.[20] More than ever it seemed that her creativity existed at the expense of her procreativity, that the creation of poems instead of children was transgressive, even criminal. Not surprisingly, her increasing psychic pain threatened the progress of her poetry. Though she had experimented with verse drama and fiction, the volume *Red Roses for Bronze* (1931) shows no formal development from her earlier *Collected Poems* (1925). As she indicates in her short poem "The Gift," her "ardent / yet chill and formal" poetics was becoming increasingly untenable (*CP*, 33).

Incipient emotional and artistic paralysis is the central theme of *Red Roses for Bronze*. In its title poem, in the translations, and in such poems as "Triplex," "When I Am a Cup," and "Epitaph," H.D. documents her pained recognition of her own aggression, an attribute that conflicted with socially accepted ideals of the "good woman" and exacerbated her guilt. Written while she was working on the film *Borderline*, in which she plays a self-destructive woman who is driven to violence by her lover's betrayal, the title poem reveals a more personal dimension of that film's demonic urgency. A woman sculptor who has been rejected by an attractive man, the speaker in the poem seeks to revenge herself by casting his figure in bronze as a form of tribute:

> if I might take dark bronze
> and hammer in
> the line beneath your underlip
> (the slightly mocking,
> slightly cynical smile
> you choose to wear)
> if I might ease my fingers and my brain
> with stroke,
> stroke,
> stroke,
> stroke,
> stroke at—something (stone, marble, intent, stable,
>   materialized)

peace,
even magic sleep
might come again. (*CP*, 211)

It is thought that H.D. had Paul Robeson in mind as the beautiful male figure from whom she wanted to force recognition, whose essential energy she wished to capture.[21] If this is so, then she is covertly using racial fantasies to exteriorize her guilt and vulnerability at having transgressed a gender role. In any case, her speaker cannot express her "fervour" directly.[22] Both her desire and her creative impulse become linked with a punitive sense of self. Couched in irony and self-deprecation, her tribute becomes inverted; jealousy and hatred effect both the severance of the head from the male body she admired and the sacrifice of her own female sexuality:

such is my jealousy
(that I discreetly veil
with just my smile)
that I would clear so fiery a space
that no mere woman's love could long endure;
and I would set your bronze head in its place. (*CP*, 215)

H.D. also chose to include in this volume two translations of choruses from Euripides' tragedies that not only reflect her growing obsession with the demonic side of inspiration but connect it with subverted motherhood. Both her selections from the Bacchantes' chorus in *The Bacchae* and her translation of the "Sea-Choros" from *Hecuba* focus on a mother's extreme suffering: her madness, isolation, and despair. From *The Bacchae*, Euripides' haunted dramatization of the terror of religious extremity, H.D. selected those passages that emphasize the ultimate victimization of Agave, Pentheus' mother, when she realizes she has killed her son: "O let me never see / haunted, mad Cithaeron / nor Cithaeron see me" (*CP*, 231). By making Agave's despair follow immediately upon the Asian women's frenzied

93

incitement to murder in the name of Dionysus, she underlines the grim irony of their attempt at justice. Similarly, in the sea chorus from *Hecuba* she depicts the bereaved matriarch's distraction in her last days after she learns that her son has been murdered, too. Grief has shrunk the horizons of her world so severely that no matter which goddess she serves, the sea wind can only confirm her worst fears:

> I am lost,
> I am dead
> . . . .
> the flower of my days is stricken,
> is broken,
> is gone
> with my fathers,
> my child
> and my home;
> wind,
> wind,
> we have found an end
> in the sword of the Greek
> and his fire-brand. (*CP*, 240–41)

In poems such as "Triplex," "When I Am a Cup," and "Epitaph" H.D. delineates the extreme self-division behind her incipient artistic paralysis. In "Triplex" a tormented speaker wishes that Athene, Aphrodite, and Artemis, each of whom represent valuable female qualities, would stop their internal warfare. In "When I Am a Cup" she alludes ironically to the female symbol of fertility associated with Persephone in order to depict sterility. When the speaker asks whether, when she is a cup, you can hear an "echo in a seashell," an answering voice only confirms her barrenness: *"there is no sound, / but of seaweed trailing / across sandy ground"* (*CP*, 294). Similarly, H.D.'s "Epitaph" offers three attitudes toward her death: first, a subjective view links death with the most intense moment of her life; second, she anticipates the judgmental mob who will accuse her of unlawful behavior; finally, she foresees the response of the sympathetic reader who acknowledges the "ai ai" written on the legendary hyacinth and understands the profound sorrow underlying "Greek ecstasy." These words are written on H.D.'s tombstone today:

> so you may say,
> "Greek flower; Greek ecstasy
> reclaims forever
>
> one who died
> following
> intricate song's last measure." (*CP*, 300)

Finally, one lyric sequence leavens the bleak emotional landscape of *Red Roses for Bronze* with a component of hope. In "The Mysteries, a Renaissance Choros" H.D. draws on her interest in occult practice as a means of integrating the demonic, foreshadowing *By Avon River*, her later tribute to Shakespeare and the poets of the Renaissance. Mindful of the Renaissance doctrine of correspondence among the natural, human, and divine spheres, a philosophy that supported such systems as astrology and alchemy, she compares the human with the natural order to show that renewal is inseparable from decay:

> one flower may kill the winter
> so this rare enchanter
> and magician
> and arch-mage;
> one flower may slay the winter
> and meet death,
> so this
> goes and returns
> and dies
> and comes to bless
> again. (*CP*, 301)

This knowledge of the role of death in the continuity of life is the most important gift of classical antiquity to Christian culture. It is particularly central to the Eleusinian myth, where Demeter's power derives not from her daughter's rape but from the ritual of descent and rising in which her grief becomes a force that compels change. The speaker's waning spirit derives strength from this paradigm:

> The mysteries remain,
> I keep the same
> cycle of seed-time
> and of sun and rain;
> Demeter in the grass
> I multiply. (CP, 305)

Despite the overlay of allusion, the line "one flower may kill the winter" (CP, 301) poignantly evokes the circumstances of H.D.'s daughter's birth and naming. It is as if Perdita's arrival, just in time to "take / The winds of March with beauty" at the end of a private winter's tale of profound loss, held the promise of H.D.'s artistic renewal.[23] To invoke the flower in the midst of loss, to invoke the Maiden, or the imaginal Child, is to invoke the power of the emergent self.

4

Creating the Imaginal Child
Freud and "The Flowering of the Rod"

AS THE DESPERATE PITCH of *Red Roses for Bronze*
indicates, the unresolved conflict between H.D.'s artistic identity and
her womanhood, newly exacerbated by an abortion, brought her to
the brink of emotional and artistic paralysis in the late 1920s. In 1930
she again sought psychiatric help, first from Mary Chadwick and
Elizabeth Ashby, then from Hans Sachs, and ultimately from Freud
himself in 1933 and 1934.[1] Though she continued to consult other
analysts throughout her life, this work with "Papa" (as she called
Freud) helped her to achieve the sought-after shift in perspective that
would bring about her greatest poetry.

Between 1931 and the publication of the first book of *Trilogy* in
1944, H.D. published no volumes of poetry except for her translation
of Euripides' *Ion* in 1937. But though relatively few poems were
published, she actually wrote a considerable amount of both prose and
poetry in this time, some of which was more overtly personal than her
earlier work. The private nature of much of H.D.'s literary work in the
1930s reveals that this crucial analysis with Freud served as an aid to
self-protection as well as self-reflection. That is, it permitted her to
express and clarify important emotional issues without the self-
censoring effect of intended publication. When pressed by her friend
Robert Herring, who wished to publish more of these poems in *Life
and Letters Today*, she refused, insisting that publication of "The

Master" (her poem about Freud), in particular, would spoil her analysis.[2]

Besides *Ion*, the chief works completed during this incubation period, between 1931 and the beginning of World War II, were a novel, *Pilate's Wife* (still unpublished), and the lyric sequence "A Dead Priestess Speaks" with the related poems "The Master," "The Dancer," and "The Poet," all written in the 1930s and recently published. Then came divorce from Aldington (1938) and the extremely productive war years. Between 1939 and 1944, having chosen to remain with Bryher in London during the Blitz, H.D. wrote *Within the Walls*, a collection of short stories based on her dreams; *The Gift*, a memoir of her childhood; *Writing on the Wall*, a memoir of her analysis; *Magic Ring*, an account of her séances with Arthur Bhaduri; "What Do I Love?" a lyric sequence based on encounters with victims of war; and the brilliant sequence *Trilogy*, which includes the poems "The Walls Do Not Fall," "Tribute to the Angels," and "The Flowering of the Rod."

This important artistic breakthrough is related to the "working through" of guilt associated with H.D.'s earlier trauma in pregnancy and to the adoption of a new sense of agency regarding the past. I analyze the underpinnings of it by comparing central emotional issues recorded in the journal she kept during her first psychoanalytic sessions in 1933, in her letters, and in relevant poems written in the 1930s with those recalled in the much later memoir *Writing on the Wall*, which she wrote in 1944 between the last two books of *Trilogy*. H.D.'s interpretative translation of *Ion*, completed shortly after her work with Freud, serves as an emotional bridge between the analysis and her later creative flowering. The psychological perspective she achieved in *The Gift*, that of the imaginal child, prepares the way for the emotional dynamics of *Trilogy*. In both the memoir and the poem H.D. integrates her experience as a woman and a poet by restructuring the conventional imagery of the family.

In *Writing on the Wall* (1944), her retrospective "translation" of her work with Freud, H.D. emphasizes the didactic dimension of her analysis more than the therapeutic one. Describing herself as an analysand rather than a patient, she recounts how she was drawn to Vienna a second time in 1934 by the plane crash of the Flying Dutchman, J. J. Van der Leeuw, the brilliant theosophist whose analytic hour preceded hers, and whose death reinvoked her brother's. She had come "to take his place," the Professor had said, to "carry on the torch" of Freud's teachings in an unstereotyped, visionary way (*TF*, 6). She felt, therefore, that her need to free herself from "repetitive thoughts and experiences" had broader social implications: She wished to find out "how best to steer [her] course" (*TF*, 13) in the event of oncoming war, partially in order to equip herself to help with "war-shocked and war-shattered people" (*TF*, 93). Psychoanalytical technique becomes aesthetic structure in the memoir's impressionistic, unchronological style, as H.D. demonstrates how Freud taught her to explore the truth of her own experience by free association upon memories, dreams, and visions. She explains how he validated her sense of the connection between her inner life and "the universal world of dream" embodied in the master plots of myth (*TF*, 71). And she shows how he helped her to reformulate her personal terrors and hopes by discovering the universal significance of her personal death encounter and its accompanying guilt: "The dead were living in so far as they lived in memory or were recalled in dream" (*TF*, 14).

The therapeutic reason that she had come to Vienna, "because [she] must not be broken," with that thought's accompanying association with feelings of painful alienation from her mother, the sense that "the child in me that called her mamma was dead," is played down in the memoir (*TF*, 17). Or, rather, the pain of this personal dimension is transformed. H.D. conveys this shift of emotional perspective most emphatically, first, in a self-possessed interpretation of the luminous "Princess dream," which both she and Freud considered central to her analysis, but which each viewed differently; and then in a bold narrative of her visions on Corfu, in which she emphasizes their value as inspired emblems of personal destiny, rather than their danger as psychological symptoms. In both accounts she presents her interaction with Freud as a creative collaboration in which she ultimately transforms his theories to serve the requirements of her individual vision.[3]

For example, in her account of the significance of her Princess dream, H.D. stresses that that figure became a link between herself and Freud — "our personal guardian or inspiration" — rather than the subject of contention that the entry in her journal implies. In this dream H.D. watches as an Egyptian princess descends a marble staircase to a river on which floats a basket containing a baby, which "the Princess must find" (*TF*, 32). Since the dream recalls the picture of Moses in the bulrushes, Freud interprets it to mean that H.D. wishes to be the male patriarch Moses in her fantasy, an interpretation in line with his theory of female penis envy. With a delicacy that merely hints at the more profound disagreement we find in her letters and poems written in the 1930s, H.D. both refuses this interpretation and transmutes it, attributing to Freud an alternative commensurate with her own woman-centered view: perhaps she is Miriam, Moses' sister, who is half-concealed in the rushes.

Similarly, in her account of the visions on Corfu, H.D. divests Freud's diagnosis of her mental state, megalomania, of its judgmental quality. Instead, she implies his complicity with her view, that the series of light-pictures she saw projected on her bedroom wall were like the visions of "psychics or clairvoyants," a testament to the strength of her prophetic power in poetry. H.D. describes the "writing on the wall" as taking place in two stages. In the first stage a series of three static light-pictures or stencils appear intact before her in the semidarkness: the undifferentiated silhouette of a helmeted head ("dead brother? lost friend?"); the equally large outline of a goblet or cup, "actually suggesting the mystic chalice"; and the "tripod of classic Delphi," traditionally a revered symbol of poetry and prophecy, associated here with an "ordinary," "friendly" domestic item, the three-legged lamp stand with which she and Bryher sometimes brewed tea (*TF*, 45, 46). She would reclaim or replace the helmeted head (symbol of the warrior ethos) with the mystic chalice, symbol of the womb, and thereby reappropriate the seat of prophetic power.

In the second stage, after Bryher's encouragement, the pictures take an upward course. A "ladder of light," timeless symbol of spiritual ascendancy, slowly draws itself out of the intensity of her concentration. It is followed by the figure of Niké (Victory) floating swiftly up the ladder, with a series of broken serpentine curves on its right, as if her mind were no longer caged, but "free and with wings" (*TF*, 55). Finally, after H.D. drops her head in mental exhaustion, her staunch friend sees the culminating picture: "a circle like the sun-disk and a figure within the disk; a man, she thought . . . reaching out to draw the image of a woman (my Niké) into the sun beside him" (*TF*, 56). A sign of her spiritual rebirth, this concluding symbol also signifies the reevaluation of woman's place in western culture that she is undertaking in her poetry.

Cognizant of the important differences between this selective later memoir and the actual content of her analysis, H.D. added the notes she had recorded during her first sessions in 1933, which she recovered from Vienna after the war, as a postlude titled "Advent," when *Writing on the Wall* was republished as *Tribute to Freud* in 1956. Together with her letters to Bryher during both periods of the analysis, "Advent" provides us with invaluable "raw" emotional data from her first sessions to set beside the more considered later memoir. For example, although all three sources describe the confrontational aspect of her first encounter with Freud—her stubborn refusal to be overwhelmed by his fame and authority in spite of her shyness and embarrassment—the contemporaneous accounts stress her tears at his recognition of her artistic achievement, an emotional response charged with guilt resulting from her losses in pregnancy.

Indeed, the most memorable part of H.D.'s letter to Bryher after her first session documents the disarming way in which Freud overcame her initial resistance by insisting upon her superior professional accomplishment. After she describes her discomfort at his request that she take off her coat and lie down on the couch, which she attempted to counter with accounts of how her earlier analysts had proceeded, she writes:

> he seemed vaguely shocked, then remarked, "I see you are going to be very difficult. Now although it is against the rules, I will tell you something: YOU *WERE* DISAPPOINTED IN ME, AND YOU *ARE* DISAPPOINTED IN ME." I then let out a howl,

and screamed, "but you do not realize you are everything, you are priest, you are magician." He said, "no. It is you who are poet and magician." I then cried so I could hardly utter and he said that I had looked at the pictures [in his office], preferring the mere dead shreds of antiquity to his living presence.[4]

The letter continues with mention of Freud's apology to her, a poet, for his "bad English," at which she "howled some more," and his declaration that she "had got to the same place as he," which induced even more tears, until "the hour was even more than half gone."[5]

The first entry in "Advent" (written the next day) confirms this emotional release and describes more fully its source in repressed conflict and guilt, particularly about her relationship with her mother after the traumatic war years, in which H.D. became both a recognized poet and eventually a mother herself. "I CRIED TOO HARD," H.D. writes and then recalls immediately thinking of her mother's paintings and a moment of closeness the two shared before her marriage. When her tears resumed, she remembered, almost in spite of herself, what she had been unable to express twenty years earlier: her sense of severance from her mother at the time of the stillbirth (which she associates with the *Lusitania*'s sinking) and her related fear of losing herself; the hostility of the nurses whom she felt disapproved of her; her reactive identification with male victims of war; and her costly method of psychic survival by identifying her creativity with the men in her family. Her omission from these associations of any mention of her second illegitimate pregnancy and successful delivery eloquently attests to her conflict about motherhood and her need to repress emotional access to the full complex of emotions associated with it:

I cried too hard . . . I do not know what I remembered: the hurt of the cold, nun-like nurses at the time of my first London confinement, spring 1915; the shock of the Lusitania going down just before the child was still-born; fear of drowning; young men on park benches in blue hospital uniform; my father's anti-war

102

sentiments and his violent *volte-face* in 1918; my broken marriage; a short period with friends in Cornwall in 1918; my father's
telescope, my grandfather's microscope. If I let go (I, this one
drop, this one ego under the microscope-telescope of Sigmund
Freud) I fear to be dissolved utterly. ("Advent," 115)

In this context of holding on at all costs, of fearing to be
"dissolved utterly," H.D. first recalls the " 'jelly-fish' experience of
double ego," which she had on the Scilly Isles after her second delivery
in 1919. She describes having felt insulated from "the war disaster" by
two separate bell jars, one over her head, the other over her body.
Discounting earlier attempts to understand this experience in terms of
the need to integrate her mind and body (cf. *Notes on Thought and
Vision*), she associates her enhanced vision here with the double lenses
of her father's telescope, rather than with the more immediate experience of birthing a child with whom she would be permanently
emotionally linked.

The defensive aspect of this account was not lost on Freud.
Unlike Havelock Ellis whose earlier lack of interest had disappointed
H.D., Freud sensed that the two bell jars could aptly symbolize the
self-division H.D. felt because of her problematic connection with her
mother, and he understood Bryher's importance as a sympathetic
artist-mother substitute. Indeed, in all reports of her analysis H.D.
stresses her gratitude to Freud for recognizing her need to recover
inner access to her mother in order to integrate her poetic identity with
her womanhood.[6] Through the transference, Freud encouraged H.D. to
associate attributes of her mother with him.

In "Advent" H.D. also reports having told Freud about her
irredeemable situation in 1918, when, pregnant and critically ill with
pneumonia, she believed that either she or her child would die. Freud,
in turn, assured her that he remembered the wartime epidemic well
because in it he lost his favorite daughter Sophie in childbirth, a loss
unmitigated even though her baby survived. His tender remembrance
of his dead daughter, the picture of her he carried in a locket attached
to his watch chain, deeply moved H.D.; it must have helped her to feel

absolved from guilt attached to earlier fears for her own safety during her second pregnancy—particularly after the concurrent losses of her brother and father and the preceding stillbirth. And it may also have helped her to accept her decision to have an abortion.

Though it is unmentioned in *Writing on the Wall*, the relation between H.D.'s need for absolution from guilt and the writing block she hoped to undo through analysis is an important motif in "Advent." H.D. notes that she deliberately began her analysis on March 1, Ash Wednesday, traditionally a day of penitence, because March was the month when she heard from America of her father's death and, later, the month when her mother died. She describes Havelock Ellis and Freud as latter-day prophets who could provide absolution by tempering Victorian law, which she felt was as severe as the old law of Leviticus: "death by stoning for the vagrant, and unimaginable punishment for the lawless" ("Advent," 117). And she derives hope of personal regeneration from the thought that though March is "traditionally the House of the Crucifixion," the astrological calendar also shows that the last week of March, when her daughter was born, "sometimes coincides with the spiritual vernal equinox, the resurrection" ("Advent," 142).

Guilt may also explain the content of the second supernormal experience H.D. describes in "Advent" (also omitted in *Writing on the Wall*), her shipboard encounter with the mysterious "Man on the boat" aboard the *Borodino* en route to Greece in 1920. H.D.'s account of this dream (which seemed real to her) follows the admission in her journal that she felt "unnerved" when Freud denied that her girlhood infatuation with Frances Gregg could have made her happy, thus appearing to prefer those of her relationships that served the functional goal of biological reproduction. Perhaps his diminishment of the worth of her first lesbian attachment (which H.D. associated with writing) reminded her of the dissatisfaction with conventional sex roles that had been revived after her trauma in childbirth. In any case, after Freud suggested that she was dodging "unwonted memories" and leaving "the solution up to psychoanalysis," H.D. tried to convey to him the significance of this enigmatic encounter ("Advent," 152).

H.D. describes a brief encounter with an attractive architect, Peter Van Eck (Peter Rodeck), who sat beside her at dinner, replacing a deaf old lady whose questions about her plans were embarrassing. The flirtation became unsettling when it led to a vivid dream meeting with a sympathetic, perfected double of Van Eck on the ship's upper deck at twilight. The whole experience occurred after a stormy day at sea during which she had felt adolescent and renewed, after having behaved in an unladylike manner: "I am indeed in a new element. I am in an old element too; I am adolescent and a fresh strength has come to me even in these few days at sea, out from London" ("Advent," 155). In her dream state she saw not the real Van Eck, who had a deep scar over his left eyebrow and wore thick-rimmed glasses, but a mythic "Man on the boat" whose eyes were uncovered and whose forehead was unblemished. Most important, she shared with him a vision of dolphins leaping rhythmically "like crescent moons" from an unnaturally serene and artfully mannered sea, in a dance that seemed "curiously unconvincing" ("Advent," 158, 160). Disconcertingly, the real Van Eck seemed to confirm the sight of these dolphins later at dinner.

In two later sources H.D. elaborates on the emotional significance of this dream meeting. In a letter to George Plank she suggests unabashedly that her wish for a sympathetic companion after the abandonment and loss accompanying Perdita's birth generated this vision of a perfected man. (She had been abandoned by her husband during her second pregnancy.) Her infatuation with Van Eck was related to her intimacy with Bryher, who took that supportive role:

> He had a very dynamic manner and rather got what Br. felt for me—it was with him, a sort of "marriage by prozy" [sic] that I had a very lovely relationship with Br in Greece. . . . He became a symbol of everything that I had not had, the perfect balance in my life, and the support and the father for Perdita.[7]

And in *Magic Ring* she emphasizes the fantasied power of the "Man on the boat" to bridge the rift in her integrity caused by guilt following her losses in childbirth. She writes that the mysterious meeting represented the way in which her "shivering" ego met the accumulated shocks of the World War I years by momentarily transporting her into another dimension, where she and this emanation were counterparts. In this account she writes that she felt singularly blessed by the appearance of dolphins. Sacred to Apollo as symbols of regeneration, these "uterine" beasts often rescued their mortal favorites in Greek legend or carried the dead to safety.[8] Therefore, when her mysterious companion held his palm above the water, drew one dolphin up, and assured her that he loved her despite her earlier losses, his approval absolved her of the survivor guilt that had become connected with artistic achievement: "all at once the burden of mortality—the albatross—fell off into the sea."[9]

Such emotional poise is not evident in H.D.'s account of her meeting with Van Eck in "Advent," however. H.D. describes having felt confused by her inability to relinquish either the real man or the idealized one without loss. Moreover, she is irritated that Freud seems more interested in his pregnant chow Yofi, who wanders about the office, than in these "faded" memories. H.D.'s letters to Bryher indicate that Freud attributed her vision of Van Eck's idealized double to revived oedipal issues, particularly guilt toward the devalued oedipal mother. And they show how he used H.D.'s awareness of Yofi's pregnancy to help her confront her ambivalence about maternity, particularly her concerns about the incompatibility between motherhood and achievement.

H.D.'s letters show that Freud acknowledged her artistic accomplishment while prompting her to reexperience and examine these earlier fears. For example, over the course of a few days, H.D. writes first that Freud remarked that she was excessively modest about her writing and then that he embarrassed her by praising her "rare type of mind." Next she reports a dream that he interpreted as indicating her fear of pregnancy: "Evidently I was afraid of becoming pregnant by papa Freud, funny??? But no Freud-cat, or esoteric Yofi, I can assure you, will be stranded on your front door step like the last one, vintage 1919."[10] Then, almost with comic inevitability, she writes that

Freud has offered them one of Yofi's pups, implying, self-mockingly, that refusal to accept it would constitute a sacred offense:

> I feel like the Virgin Mary at the entrance of the dove. Papa has offered us one of Yofi's pups. What will we do about it??? . . . Fido [Bryher], why have you gone and got me in this awful mess??? I feel pregnant. I feel Fido is cruelly and sadistically laughing, howling.[11]

Several of H.D.'s letters in 1933, which are less jocular in tone, also report false labor pains ("tummy cramp") accompanied by nightmares that suggest to her that the "puppy equates death, impregnation."[12] But the most important result of this "pregnancy phase" was the resolution of conflict over "rival loyalties" between mother and father, which H.D. felt to be the therapeutic goal of her analysis ("Advent," 146). The dynamic of this reintegration is evident in a dream that both H.D. and Freud thought was particularly significant. In it her fear of loss of self in pregnancy is modified after the threatening father-imago is de-idealized.

In a letter several pages long H.D. conceptualizes this dream as having three stages. First, she mentions an "emotional crise" the previous night in which a frightening caterpillar-beetle (associated with her father, whose birthday is in November, the house of Scorpio) miraculously grows wings. She says that this "gave the clue to the whole interpretation" of the main dream sequence because it meant that "the fear and dread of the Scorpio, my father, a cold, distant, upright, devoted father and husband but for whose profession [astronomy] I had only terror . . . is removed."[13] Second, she describes a "prologue" to the main dream sequence in which she is "trying to play a piano on the open deck" of a boat (trying to perform), when a storm at sea interferes. Fortunately, Bryher and Perdita are on board, and Perdita tells her not to be afraid. This reassurance of her personal spiritual survival makes her feel detached from the storm, as if viewing it on a movie screen, but she still feels pity and sadness for the other women, whose smaller boat overturns. She writes, "Freud said it was obviously a mixed death and birth dream, fear of death in birth, hence you and P., and a pity for the other women doomed to drown, or to die in agony of childbirth."[14] The third part, the dream sequence itself, modifies this fear of losing herself in pregnancy by means of contact with an exiled young prince whom Bryher takes her to visit. This prince (Freud) comes up out of a riverbed to greet her accompanied by beautiful white bulls, which are not "phallic" but associated with her mother—"mother-bulls." In the prince's house she sits by him while "he makes charming sketches, drawings" reminiscent of her mother.[15]

The main dream sequence continues with a series of incidents that seem a reprise on a deeper emotional level of H.D.'s fear of losing her integrity in childbirth. First, she finds herself alone in the prince's bedroom, except for a clothed figure asleep on the bed. When she looks at herself naked in a series of mirrors, she is surprised that her front is like her back—"entirely smooth, like a child." She feels ecstatic at this discovery of herself "a Virgin in the magic-mirrors" and leaves secretly before the sleeping figure wakes.[16] Then her departure brings her to another room in the house, heavily Victorian in furnishing, in which a church bazaar is about to take place. Here she finds two Siamese cats at large, one of which is a great favorite of hers. Remembering that she once had two kittens who tore her life to shreds, however, she worries that Bryher will buy her one of these cats. Her wish to escape this possibility leaves her outside the house on a road at which a gang of workmen are busy. Their leader tells her that in order to get through a dangerous tunnel she must board a passing train.

The next dream incidents have an eerie historical precision. H.D. associates the three men she encounters aboard the train with her three "husbands" during the first war years and with her fears of being perceived as an inadequate woman. The first man (Aldington) is dissatisfied with the half-shilling tip she gives him. Then she gives the second man (Gray) a whole shilling but worries that he will misunderstand her intentions and hand her change. Feeling "self-distrustful," she leaves the train and finds her daughter waiting near the station in the charge of her disapproving mother and aunt. After quarreling with them over her daughter, she boards another train carrying a third man (Rodeck), who approves of her. He gives her the "right" or "white" journal, which brings her to her desired destination. The dream ends with Bryher arranging a seventy-seventh birthday party in Vienna for Freud, who attends with his wife wearing "a new hat." Now H.D.'s "one concern" is to speak German well enough to "talk with Mrs. Freud."[17]

The structure of this dream anticipates the psychic process that H.D. will recapitulate in both *The Gift* and *Trilogy*. We see how deidealization of the father-imago (inner representative of the patriarchy) enables her to reassess her relationship to her mother in analysis. Her sense of joyous integration at the end of the dream, her "one concern" to speak the mother-tongue at Freud's birthday party, suggests the successful incorporation of the positive aspects of her mother's power into her poetic identity. H.D.'s letters to Bryher also reveal that following this dream she and Freud debated theoretical questions that helped H.D. to clarify her emotional position further. Specifically, she describes Freud's theory of penis envy to Bryher, implying that he interpreted her conflict around artistic achievement (as well as her bisexuality) in this context.

H.D.'s letters refer to the following theory of female psychosexual development: Seeing the world androcentrically, Freud accounted for the oedipal girl's shift of affection from mother to father by attributing to her a sense of genital deficiency for which she blames her mother. The "normal" woman assuages this recognition of her "lack" by converting her desire for a penis into a wish for a child.[18] H.D.'s letters indicate that Freud viewed her as an "advanced or intellectual woman" who did not repress the "masculine" elements of her libido in order to become properly feminine and heterosexual, but who remained arrested at the preoedipal stage.[19]

At first H.D. seems interested in this theory. Penis envy, as the desire for phallic privilege, appeared to explain to her why certain of her women friends stayed in bad marriages.[20] But later letters show a fundamental disagreement stemming from discomfort with Freud's treatment of her creative impulse as compensation for a genital deficiency. For example, H.D. finds "most odd" Freud's idea that her dreams about literary men (Shaw, Coward, Lawrence) are evidence of penis envy because, in his view, "book means *penis*" and as "a 'writer' only" was she "equal in uc-n [sic], in the right way, with men."[21] Bothered by the implication that women are inherently inferior as prototypes for creativity, she insists that she and Freud must "work it out." And in a description of a particularly prophetic dream, she suggests that her creative life is shaped by an identification with the mother's childbearing capacity as potentially powerful, rather than by a sense of blocked masculinity.

In this dream, which H.D. associates with "having a pup" and in which she has "none of the usual p-envy reactions," H.D., Bryher, and another woman leave a play about male infidelity in their own car.[22] They drive to open country where H.D. has a vision of female divinity that foreshadows the goddess-muse of *Tribute to the Angels*:

> We got to the country. I looked up. There was a giant moon, bigger than the sun. It was rainbow coloured and like a pool of rainbow in the sky. Enormous. As I looked, there was a dim figure of a woman in the moon. She was clothed with "samite, mystic, wonderful," if you know what I mean, draped in flowing rainbow coloured robes, seated like a madonna in a curved frame. But she was not Madonna in that sense, she was Greek, she was Artemis, yet she was pregnant. A perfect renaissance idea . . . VIRGIN but pregnant. "O moon of my delight that knows no wane." I shouted to you and Joan to look. A bird crossed the surface, a dark pigeon, a dove. Freud tells me it is an almost perfect mythological state I was in. The moon, of course, equated mother, but it was "mother-in-heaven." You and Joan and I were a sort of band of sisters, the Graces or Fates.[23]

Here H.D. contrasts the patriarchal Christian ideal of motherhood symbolized by the Madonna, who piously yields her body to the Lord in passive submission, with an ancient idea of a virgin moon-goddess, whose power to foster life does not depend on her relation to a husband-god. This goddess bears divinity and its prerogatives in her own right.[24]

H.D.'s poem "The Master" recapitulates her dispute with Freud over the ramifications of his assumption of male primacy. More explicitly than in *Writing on the Wall*, in which her questions about Freud's view of psychosexual development are subsumed to a generalized and muted dissatisfaction with his rationalist perspective, H.D. dramatizes both her disagreement with him and the creative release engendered by his validation of her independent vision. Like *Writing on the Wall*, "The Master" is primarily a tribute; but like her other contemporaneous accounts of the analysis, it reveals more directly the intimacy and anguish of their analytic confrontation.[25]

H.D. begins with love of the master and fear of his death—fear that resonates with the pain of earlier losses. Freud's spiritual beauty, enhanced in old age, makes him seem "nearer to God" than other men. This mixture of love and fear deepens the significance of their disagreement over woman's nature as the poem evolves. For, as Rachel Blau DuPlessis and Susan Friedman point out, the poem's syntax sometimes fuses Freud and God so that they seem like "two aspects of one being," and though this fusion graphically expresses H.D.'s awe, it also "makes her challenge to his interpretations a form of blasphemy."[26]

H.D.'s fusion of Freud with God initially inhibits self-expression. When she prays that God reward Freud for his receptivity to her with "some surprise in heaven," contemplation of His supernatural powers renders her temporarily speechless: she cannot suggest anything suitable (*CP*, 452). Slyly critical of the crippling effect on women of Judeo-Christian misogyny (inherited by Freud), she attributes her speechlessness to internalization of woman's subordinated role: In the creation story God's Word supplants female fecundity and only man is granted the power of naming:

> I do not know what to say to God,
> for the hills
> answer his nod,
> and the sea
> when he tells his daughter,

111

white Mother
of green
leaves
and green rills
and silver,
to still
tempest
or send peace
and surcease of peril
when a mountain has spit fire. (*CP*, 453)

This image of the obedient daughter as compliant Mother, sanctified in western religious tradition, underwrites woman's cultural subjugation in patriarchy. It justifies the suppression of her aggression, without which she is deprived of the subjective strength necessary for expression.

In the next lines of the poem H.D. calls attention to the confusion that such a monolithic ideal of womanhood causes in the woman poet. She credits Freud with helping her to understand and integrate the dissociated parts of her self, with enabling her to accept the ambivalent responses of her nature, and with permitting her to see herself as sexually multivoiced:

I did not know how to differentiate
between volcanic desire,
anemones like embers
and purple fire of violets
like red heat,
and the cold
silver
of her feet:

I had two loves separate;
God who loves all mountains,
alone knew why
and understood
and told the old man
to explain

112

the impossible

which he did. (*CP*, 453)

H.D. suggests that she achieved this psychic reintegration, not by compliance with Freud's theories, but after a dispute in which she opposed his phallocentrism with her own woman-centered vision. Four times in section IV she mentions her "anger" at "the old man" for his "talk of the man-strength" and his related theory of male moral and spiritual superiority: "I was angry with his mystery, his mysteries. / I argued till day-break" (*CP*, 455). Then she shows how she countered his unexamined assumptions about female inferiority with an affirmation of woman's perfection based on her own experience: "I could not accept from wisdom / what love taught, / *woman is perfect*" (*CP*, 455). Rachel Blau DuPlessis and Susan Friedman describe how H.D.'s vision of perfection, based on the female body, eloquently opposes Freud's phallocentrism: At the center of "The Master" is "a lyrical and erotic celebration of woman's physical being, where the woman's ecstatic dance fuses the human form to earth, tree and flower; where the woman's erotic mysteries connect sexuality, fertility, and spiritual renewal."[27] H.D.'s woman is not passive nor incomplete, as Freud had defined her, but "full of the mysterious power emanating from her orgasmic presence."[28]

> O God, what is it,
> this flower
> that in itself had power over the whole earth?
> for she needs no man,
> herself
> is that dart and pulse of the male,
> hands, feet, thighs,
> herself perfect. (*CP*, 456)

H.D. also makes Freud's validation of her independent vision instrumental to her creative release. Carefully distinguishing herself from his more doctrinaire followers who would derive their status from reflected glory, she insists that his respect for the prescience of the artist set her free to prophecy. In Section VIII her moving tribute to Freud's magnanimity reminds us of his famous admission that his theories about women were incomplete and his suggestion that those who wished to know more should "Enquire from [their] experience of life, or turn to the poets, or wait until science can give [them] deeper and more coherent information."[29] He did not demand that she be a "disciple," that she "seal / documents in [his] name," or that she think his every word was "sacred":

> no,
> he was rather casual,
> "we won't argue about that"
> (he said)
> "you are a poet." (*CP*, 458)

In the last sections of the poem Freud's validation of H.D. as a woman poet and "seer" enables her to imagine a future in which the moral significance of woman's experience will be recognized by a society in which men will "turn from easy pleasure / to hardship / of the spirit" (*CP*, 461). She prophesies that "men will see how long they have been blind": They will see how "this thought of the man-pulse has tricked them" into an ethos of domination and destruction (*CP*, 460). Anticipating the insight and flowering of *Trilogy*, she invokes a universally acclaimed vision of godhead that incorporates the female: "you are near beauty the sun, / you are that Lord become woman" (*CP*, 461).

Other poems written in the 1930s also reflect central motifs of H.D.'s analysis: both her desire for absolution from guilt associated with her losses and her need to integrate her artistic achievement with her womanhood. In "The Dead Priestess Speaks," the title poem of an experimental volume that includes several older "Greek" pieces written before her work with Freud, an impure female speaker is "nominated for the Herald's place" instead of being stoned "from the altar" after she comes home to Miletus [Vienna] (*CP*, 372, 374). As

Louis Martz points out, this tone of personal confession establishes both the direction of this volume and of H.D.'s work in the 1930s. She conveys a sense of resurrection by "moving from Greek masks toward a more personal voice."[30] Martz also speculates that H.D. saw "The Master" as the central link between "The Dancer" and "The Poet." In the former, H.D. bases her celebration of the female artist's achievement on a sense of restored sexual and psychic integrity that implies the new self-knowledge brought about in her analysis.[31] I would add that in the latter, a poignant elegy to D. H. Lawrence (whose criticism hurt her deeply), her metaphoric representation of the male artist's defensiveness seems informed by the Freudian theory that man is developmentally mandated to distance himself from his primary female affectional tie. She is a butterfly whose moral authority depends on emergence from her husk; he is a "singing snail" who is "true / to the irony / of [his] shell" (*CP*, 464).

The resurrection of a dead woman is also the theme of H.D.'s translation of Euripides' *Ion*, which she began in 1917 but did not complete until after her analysis. H.D.'s letters to Bryher indicate that she saw mirrored in this play her own desire for the powerful preoedipal mother, that is, the mother who could serve as a role model for her artistic ambitions. The poignant reunion of Kreousa and Ion represented "a sort of fancy-dress edition of [her] phallic fantasy."[32] As she progressed with the translation, she linked the success of her creative work with the memory of her successful second pregnancy, even postponing gynecological surgery until after the play was completed. In the following letter, her awareness of the female body as an ideological construct anticipates her use of the childbirth metaphor in the late lyric sequences:

> This was work I was doing after the first confinement and during my pregnancy with old Pups [Perdita]. Probably I have it linked up with my physical creative force. As that is going, I translate it into this out-put of plays. The attitude one takes at this time is all-important for the rest of one's life—therefore, as a trailer, I will not go to Dr. H. for the moment. The swimming has

tightened me up. To cut the thing now, might be to break across this urge.[33]

In keeping with the more personal mode of her work in the 1930s, H.D. directly inserts her own voice into the play in an ongoing interpretative prose commentary. At the outset, she finds the tragedy's central problem to be the meaning of the "betrayal and desertion, by one of its most luminous figures, of a woman and her first child."[34] And at the conclusion, the mutual recognition of mother and son is more crucial to the future glory of Ionian culture, in her view, than the confirmation of Ion's divine paternity.

H.D.'s commentary especially stresses the modernity of Euripides' characterization of Kreousa. Forcibly married to Xouthos, the childless Athenian queen once bore Apollo's child in secret and, in accordance with his plan, left it exposed to die. Having endured her loss in stoic silence, she "has the inhumanity of a meteor, sunk under the sea" (*I*, 28). As she begins to question the god's honor and to deplore the fate of woman in patriarchy, she seems "to step out of stone, in the manner of a late Rodin":

> O, poor
> lost woman
> and race of woman,
> alike;
> O, chaste,
> O, lawless;
> man made your law;
> for you all,
> there is one
> judgment. (*I*, 39)

The intensity of Kreousa's suffering goads her to attempt a fearful crime. When Apollo's oracle overlooks her plea for a child and awards the boy-priest Ion to her husband as his child alone, she becomes inflamed by the injustice of this apparent double desertion.

The chorus of women, who express the play's inner mood, wish death to the child "as if to prophecy the unconscious reaction" of the bitter queen (*I*, 59). When Kreousa returns, accompanied by an Old Man who is "Fate's prompter," she is ready to consider this "melodramatic solution . . . with suspicious alacrity" (*I*, 76, 77).

Here H.D.'s interpretation of Kreousa's motivation reflects the self-acceptance she gained in analysis. Differing with critics who describe the Athenian queen as " 'savage' at heart," she finds nobility in Euripides' portrayal of her aggression. According to H.D., Kreousa "predicts the figure of the new world-woman" in whom "tenderness and gallantry merge" (*I*, 64). She "yearns in neurotic abandon for a child she has lost, yet at the same time retains a perfectly abstract sense of justice, of judgment toward the highest religious symbol of the then known world" (*I*, 64). Earlier she had felt violated by Apollo, "by inspiration," but she had clung to her integrity even in defeat. In the same spirit she plots to kill this boy, even though she feels a psychic affinity with him, in order to prevent a second betrayal. "This is not the gesture of a frenzied, over-balanced woman," H.D. argues, but a tragic sacrifice, an action of "unquestionable authority" befitting the descendant of Pallas Athene:

> Kreousa, the queen, stands shoulder to shoulder with the sword-bearer of the Acropolis. She, too, holds a weapon; she, too, strikes infallibly at the enemy of her city. Kreousa, the queen, standing shoulder to shoulder with Pallas Athene, becomes Kreousa the goddess. The price? Kreousa the woman. (*I*, 77)

Fortunately for the history of civilization, Kreousa's plot fails. And in the ensuing crisis H.D. attributes to her a new dimension of self-knowledge. In the moment before Ion is prevented from hurling her from Apollo's altar where she has taken refuge, Kreousa recognizes in his hesitancy a mirroring of her own inner conflict. Like the boy's overblown invective against her, her vilification of Apollo represents projected self-hate. She has "arguing down something in her own spirit, rather than inveighing against mere outside circumstance" (*I*, 99). Kreousa is reconciled with her lost child following this insight into her ambivalence, and the two proceed to Athens where Ion will be crowned king. Having joyfully recognized herself as Ion's mother, Kreousa will also be the mother "of a new culture, of an aesthetic drive and concentrated spiritual force, not to be reckoned with, in terms of any then known values" (*I*, 123).

H.D.'s final glowing tribute to Athene (upon which Freud congratulated her) alludes to the radical change in her own mental structure achieved in analysis: the achievement of a less punitive sense of self. The appearance of the goddess represents the mind's capacity to "achieve kinship with unconscious forces of most subtle definition" and thereby to bring about the welding of "strength and delicacy" that marks the high water of human achievement (*I*, 123).

The years immediately following the publication of *Ion* brought both divorce from Richard Aldington (1938) and the onset of World War II. Though H.D.'s divorce revived the recrimination that caused the marriage's failure during World War I and her anxiety over Perdita's parentage, it also gave her a chance to clear the record. In this period she roughed out the first two-thirds of *Bid Me to Live [A Madrigal]*, which is her final version of people, events, and feelings in 1917–18. She had participated in the romanticization of violence during the Great War. And she had felt prematurely crushed just as she was beginning to blossom, as if the war had been an act of wrath directed at her personally for her sins.[35] As she wrote later, "I had accepted the Establishment. That is, I had accepted the whole cosmic, bloody show. *The war was my husband.*"[36] Now she was prepared by Freud to face disaster a second time. Here was another generation poised on the edge of destruction upon whom the same punishment was being visited. What was the meaning of her survival and that of her friends, she asks in the first book of *Trilogy*: "We passed the flame: we wonder / what saved us? what for?"[37] How could she make spiritual reparation, "scratch out // indelible ink of the palimpsest / of past misadventure?" (*T*, 6).

As she endured the bombing of London, H.D.'s horror at the "orgy of destruction" was mixed with an extraordinary euphoria.[38]

She wrote during the 1940 Battle of Britain that she felt "exaltation" rising "like sap in a tree," because she had been able "night after night, to pass out of the unrealities and the chaos of night-battle and see clear."[39] Unafraid, she regretted only that she might not be able to "bear witness" to the truth that "when things become unbearable, a door swings open or a window."[40] The very proximity of death reawakened in H.D. a promise of resurrection that was rooted in her earlier survival of death in childbirth. Supported now by Freud's theories of the importance of the "family complex" in both personal and cultural development and by her own recovery of her mother in analysis, she felt that the war had uncovered the matriarchal foundation of civilization: "the shrine lies open to the sky" (*T*, 3). Spiritually reunited with her mother in dream and vision, she would reassess maternity and ascribe new cultural meaning to the womb.

Like T. S. Eliot in *The Four Quartets* and Edith Sitwell in "Still Falls the Rain," H.D. was driven inward by the outward threat of war. But the uniqueness of her findings resulted from their being rooted in the primal physical experience of childbearing. As she wrote in her introduction to *Within the Walls*, the collection of short stories based on her dreams in 1940–41, those who miraculously endured within the walls of the city under siege must "re-value" the "whole conception of time."[41] For them, every day was literally a "birth-day," because for the time being they were "within the walls of [their] own bodies" (*WW*, 2). In one of these remarkable stories she depicts the emotional deliverance that this return to the female body signified. Her imagery here graphically reflects the integration of her artistic achievement with her womanhood, foreshadowing the central vision of *Trilogy*.

In "Before the Battle" (1940), H.D.'s heroine finds that her personal war is over, the conflict between creativity and procreativity resolved, once she is able to restore the connection between mother and daughter that she felt was broken during her trauma in childbirth. She compares the "waves of terror" that sweep over the citizenry with the "rhythm of birth pangs" necessary to beget a new age (*WW*, 1). In her reverie, fear of bombardment becomes fused with concern that the publication of her daughter's autobiography will provoke misunderstanding and criticism. The "child's book" becomes "the child her-self," and she is plunged back into the terror of death she felt before her daughter's birth. Just then the doorbell rings and a grown-up Perdita returns from a party "attired like a very Primavera"; her face "round and rose-coloured" (like that of the goddess-muse in "Tribute to the Angels") is the answer to her prayer (*WW*, 4).

In the story H.D. implies that her heroine's emotional balance and self-confidence have been restored by a new insight into the psychology of male domination. When Perdita complains that one of her male friends has disparaged her book, her sympathetic mother offers an explanation of womb envy that indicates a new attitude toward the criticism directed at her by her own youthful literary companions. She implies that patriarchy's confinement of women to the domestic sphere (the reason for her own earlier conflict) results from male sexual jealousy and fear of woman's biological potency:

> I say, it's this way. Men, the nice sensitive men . . . are creative and really they would like a child, not a child as a man has a child but a child actually. So they get jealous when something like a child, a book, comes to a woman who can have a child any-way. . . . That's why so many of them hate things women do. . . . They think why should a girl have everything? (*WW*, 8)

This shared moment between the heroine and her writer-daughter is followed by a dream in which the generational cycle is completed. She and her own mother visit the frozen graveyard in her hometown where they find a "white blossom on a flowering branch" amid the graves, proof that "there is summer in mother and daughter" (*WW*, 12). Though nothing can completely erase the pain of her earlier marriage to death, she feels protected and restored by this Eleusinian fantasy: "We built a great fire, brought back a dead log to life . . . she and I together brought back the spring. The war is over, I tell you" (*WW*, 12).

Like *Within the Walls*, H.D.'s wartime memoir *The Gift* also focuses on her matrilineal inheritance and relates her artistic inspira-tion to imagery of the female body. Dedicated to her mother "Helen /

who has / *brought me home*" with the notation "for Bethlehem Pennsylvania 1741 / from Chelsea London 1941," it affirms a revolutionary psychic power, a "Gift of Vision" handed down to her from her Moravian grandmother.[42] The childhood recipient of Mamalie's stories about destroyed church documents and extravagant devotees of the "Ritual of the Wound," H.D. felt connected with these ancestral "initiates" through her own suffering and spiritual redemption (*G*, 86). And her extensive reading in Moravian church history in the 1940s gave her an evocative religious context for her personal psychological findings.[43]

H.D.'s allusion to Count Zinzendorf in *The Gift's* dedication (1741 is the year he founded the Moravian settlement at Bethlehem) is particularly significant in view of the memoir's emotional content. Zinzendorf's Pietist emphasis on the heart as the seat of religious worship and his preoccupation with the imagery of Christ's atonement implied a feminization of the deity. Under his leadership, Christ's wounds came to be revered as mystical entities deserving adoration in their own right; the wound in His side was spoken of frequently as the birthplace from which all souls are born. Believers were advised to be like little children "who feel at home in the Sidehole and crawl in deep."[44] Such devotional practice, which linked the wound (suffering and death) with the womb (birth and life), particularly suited H.D.'s spiritual needs. Her Moravian ancestors had imagined the miracle of pain and blood becoming joy and health in terms of a female mystery, childbirth.[45] They had given her an image of the divine, of salvation, that was located in the procreative matrix of her own body.

In *The Gift* H.D. does not refer directly to the suffering she underwent during her second pregnancy. She focuses instead on a childhood shock she received while witnessing her father's near-fatal head wound, an earlier memory that is charged with feeling and that she repressed during the pregnancy. In that state of extreme vulnerability she must have felt her father's death as an abandonment (especially since her husband had also left her). But she must also have felt too guilty to acknowledge her anger at her father's loss and so have idealized him instead. H.D. encodes these ambivalent feelings in the memoir by exaggerating her childhood shock at the sight "of blood running down from the side of his face" and linking it with her grand-mother's "secret" that God had been literally present when the Moravian pact with the Indians had been violently broken at *Wunden Eiland* (*G*, 84). As she notes in *Magic Ring*, "I worked the story of myself and Gareth [Bryher] into my own family and made my grandmother reconstruct a strange psychic experience to me, a child" (*MR*, II, 119). Magnifying the importance of having witnessed her father's head wound (and glorifying her own part as his nurse) was a way of de-idealizing him, of feminizing him, and of establishing a new bond.

Now H.D. was undergoing another massacre perpetrated by modern-day savages on another island "pock-marked with formidable craters, with Death stalking . . . at every corner" (*G*, 140). Connect-ing her father's wound with Zinzendorf's feminization of the deity gave new meaning to the Moravian motto *"L'amitié passe même le tom-beau."* In the context of this ancestral sanction, she was free to view paternal authority as a social and political construct. Having realized that legitimate power is rooted in maternal love as well as in paternal authority, she was free to resurrect an archaic female divine pantheon. Thus, immersion in the imagery of death facilitated a personal and cultural all-clear:

> Under every shrine to Zeus, to Jupiter, to Zeus-pater or Theus-pater or God-the-father . . . there is an earlier altar. There is, beneath the carved superstructure of every temple to God-the father, the dark cave or grotto or inner hall or cellar to Mary, Mere, Mut, mutter, pray for us.[46]

As Deborah Kloepfer points out, in this passage from *The Gift* H.D. invokes a universal mother "who will manifest herself not only within an arcanum but within *language*: a maternal voice and rhythm, a mutter-ing, a grotto in language that is the mother's space."[47] I would add that this maternal voice and rhythm is already implicit in the memoir's narrative method. Writing in the voice of the imaginal child, that is, of the child reconceived by the adult in memory, H.D. reclaims her mother as an inspirational muse by giving her childhood impressions a compassionate new context derived from the insight she gained in her analysis.

In a letter to Norman Holmes Pearson, H.D. stresses the importance of this double perspective, in which the newly perceived interconnection of past and present reveals a pattern conducive to artistic growth. In order for *The Gift* to be completed, "it had to be worked through the minds of the children or the child."[48] Earlier attempts to describe her history had put her in the position of the passive sufferer of events. Her analysis put her in touch with herself as a child in a way that enabled her to see herself as the agent of her experience, as having unconsciously arranged her life so that she repeated certain prototypical scenes and crises. It permitted her to transform the story of her past into a form more adaptively useful.[49] For example, she describes her childhood hurt at her mother's failure to realize that any of her children were "gifted" but then subsumes it to an adult recognition that her mother's denial of her daughter's talent was a projection of her own self-hatred.[50]

H.D. attributes her mother's self-limitation (and her own earlier silence) to woman's historical oppression in patriarchy and its perpetuation in the family. They had both been preconditioned to accept a family myth of "the girl who had died," starting with Fanny who had been burnt to death at Christmas in the seminary — imprisoned in her hoop skirt — and continuing with other girl-children who had died in infancy, whom no one seemed to care about. H.D. subtly relates this unwritten history of female sacrifice in the family to the glorification of conquest condoned by society in wartime. Paradoxically, in the midst of a second world war, in which many men were to be wounded, killed, and memorialized, she opens her memoir by mourning previously unattended female losses[51]:

> Why was it always a girl who had died? Why did Alice die and not Alfred? Why did Edith die and not Gilbert? I did not cry because Fanny died, but I had inherited Fanny. Mama cried

(although I had seldom seen her cry) because Fanny died, so Mama had cried. I did not cry. The crying was frozen in me, but it was my own, it was my own crying. . . . The gift was there, but the expression of the gift was somewhere else. (G, 4)

Further, H.D. relates the thwarting of her mother's self-expression to the fear and mystery surrounding female sexuality in restrictive Victorian society. In its uncut form, the memoir's second chapter consists of a fantasy of her mother as a romantic young girl who secretly visits a gypsy fortune-teller and is told she will have a gifted child. Here H.D. imagines the constraints of her mother's life as "Miss Helen," the dutiful daughter of the principal of the Moravian seminary. Though as a child her mother had been singled out as talented by her exotic music teacher, her father had discouraged her singing and she did not believe in her own gift: "*Gift?* That was the German for poison."[52] Though as a young girl she had been infatuated with a handsome Spanish student who had kissed her and sent her red carnations, she had experienced her own sexual feelings as mysterious and dangerous, as somehow "not right." She had been proverbially afraid of snakes. No wonder that her daughter, having dreamt that a monstrous snake had bitten her on the mouth, later thinks: "We must go further than Helen, then Helle, than Helios, than light, we must go to the darkness, out of which the monster has been born" (G, 58).

H.D.'s grandmother provides the numinous force with which the child will penetrate the darkness and transform this noxious pattern of female self-sacrifice. As she listens to her stories of promises broken and documents destroyed, she wonders for the first time in her life "who we all are," and why Mamalie always asks Uncle Fred [Wolle] to sing *The Four Marys* "the last thing after Thanksgiving or Christmas parties" (G, 80). This poignant Celtic ballad, "Mary Hamilton," is about a Scottish queen's handmaiden who prepares for execution after giving birth to and abandoning the child of the king. H.D. related the story to the painful dispossession that later became her own subject. Seeing this dispossession in historical perspective allowed her to align self-creation and procreation with less ambivalence than before. In notes to *The Gift* she wrote:

> But this Mary and this song did make a furrow or runnel in my emotional or spiritual being that later let through a stream-of-consciousness that, in retrospect, is more precious to me than the St. Matthew Passion and the Mass in B Minor. For it was my own interpretation of the Gift, as mamalie later in this story reveals it to me.[53]

The figure of Mary, the sinner or "neurotic woman," reappears as a combination of Mary Magdalen and Mary of Bethany to the reviving speaker in "The Flowering of the Rod," the final poem of H.D.'s *Trilogy*. She is transformed in this poem, "healed of soul," by her own persistent mourning and by the Mage Kaspar's validating memory of a prelapsarian paradise in which the feminine and the masculine were equally venerated: *"I am Mary, the incense-flower of the incense-tree, / myself worshipping, weeping, shall be changed to myrrh"* (*T*, 138). Crucial to this healing has been the speaker's earlier revision of masculine culture's definition of her femininity, particularly in the institution of motherhood. She rejects the prevailing stereotypes that would split the image of woman into chaste madonna or devil-ridden whore, thus denying her the strong sense of identity necessary for self-representation, and she reinstates an integrated female perspective into the moral, religious, and linguistic status quo.

Prepared by Freud to experience mother and father in a new way, H.D. becomes her own child in *Trilogy*: She gives birth to an imaginal self, a revitalized woman who appears finally "shy and simple and young" (*T*, 172). Drawing upon her own unconscious as the source of her inspiration, she reenacts the dynamics of her analysis. In the first book of *Trilogy* the de-idealization of the father and recovery of the mother's power that H.D. achieved in analysis prompts a critique of Judeo-Christian misogyny and a prophetic call for the reestablishment of older matriarchal values. Dedicated to Bryher "for

Karnak 1923 / from London 1942," "The Walls Do Not Fall" begins ironically by comparing the bombing of London in 1942 with the opening in 1923 of King Tutenkhamen's tomb, where ancient buried treasure was uncovered along with the king's remains: "still the Luxor bee, chick and hare / pursue unalterable purpose" (*T*, 3). As "thoughts stir" in her desolation, H.D.'s speaker invokes the prophet Samuel, probably referring to his alleged denunciation of the institution of kingship:[54] "unaware, Spirit announces the Presence; / shivering overtakes us, / as of old, Samuel" (*T*, 3). Then she specifically links the biblical identification of woman with sin—augmented by the church fathers—with the ethos of domination and coercion that resulted in "ruin everywhere": "Devill was after us, / tricked up like Jehovah" (*T*, 5). Psychologically adept, however, she is cognizant that "gods always face two ways" (*T*, 5), that the very severity of this denigration implies a different primary reality. Therefore she would "search the old highways / for the true-rune," risking castigation as a "harlot" in order to "recover old values" and restore the beauty of "Isis, Aset or Astarte" (*T*, 5).

As Susan Friedman has written, H.D. draws on dream and ecstatic vision to accomplish her task of spiritual recovery.[55] The dream, acting as interpreter between the collective unconscious and the individual psyche, "explains symbols of the past / in today's imagery" (*T*, 29). By means of the dream work, the dreamer's unconscious impulses, perhaps repugnant to his superego (the psychic embodiment of cultural values), are transformed into visual images and the doors of repression are partially opened. In the successive poems of *Trilogy* three revelatory dreams represent divine agency, mediating between stultifying, outmoded tradition and redemptive vision. Through them H.D. reconstitutes Father, Mother, and herself as Child, constructing a female "family romance" that departs from Freud's male prototype.

In the first of these dreams the speaker envisions a form of male divinity who is "not at all like Jehovah" (*T*, 25). Appearing to her in the "spacious, bare meeting-house" of her paternal colonial ancestors, he is "Ra, Osiris, *Amen* . . . the world-father" (*T*, 25). Slender and beardless, he has shining amber eyes that are "coals for the world's burning"; they emit a regenerative fire that also suggests the healing fragrance of "sea-incense" (*T*, 26). Similar in feature to the idealized double of Peter van Eck described in *Magic Ring*, Amen represents the "Christos-image," the symbol of redemption disentangled "from its art-craft junk-shop / paint-and-plaster medieval jumble / of pain-worship and death-symbol" (*T*, 27). Through his manifestation as the astral Ram who (like Freud) is both father and mother, she will "be Lamb, mothered again," the "splintered . . . crystal of [her] identity" recomposed (*T*, 30). Indeed, after her invocation to this feminized "All-father," the poet proclaims ecstatically "my heart-shell / breaks open" (*T*, 35). Her longing to return "home" to a revised child world, the world of *The Gift*, where the blazing stars can be called on to heal and even grasshoppers witness divinity, fosters a "grain" of faith lodged long ago between "a heart-beat of pleasure // and a heart-beat of pain" (*T*, 38). Nourished thus in the "heart-core," this kernel of grain will grow into the paradisiacal Tree of eternal life.

As Susan Gubar has written, the "grain" that will break open "the heart's alabaster" also signifies the poet's desired escape from the "entrapment" suggested by male culture's imagery of female sexuality and creativity, indicating H.D.'s growing identification with more overtly female symbolic forms.[56] At the beginning of "The Walls Do Not Fall" the poet identified herself and her work with the "craftsman" shellfish, hidden and therefore protected, whose "shell-jaws snap shut / at invasion of the limitless" (*T*, 9). "An emblem of defensive survival in a hostile world," the shellfish has been traditionally associated with the artist, Gubar writes, because it "transforms living substance into formal object and thereby mysteriously creates the beautiful circularity of its house and . . . the perfectly spherical pearl."[57] H.D. must initially have been drawn to the imagery of shell and pearl also because it links the creation of art with female procreative process. Because the pearl can be seen as a seed in the womb of the shellfish, the shell enclosing the pearl is a common image of pregnancy in literary history. As Gubar notes, the "self-enclosed, non-referential completeness of shell and pearl recalls

H.D.'s own earlier imagistic poems."[58] Like the product of the shellfish, who will not be "cracked open or digested," they are shaped by a poet "rigidly and self-consciously in control of her material."[59] But this "locked-in" imagery of female creativity—particularly its association with impenetrability and purity—is deemed inadequate as the poem develops. I would add that shells become identified with "old thoughts, old conventions" because H.D. wished to incorporate hitherto unacceptable feelings of aggression into the female sphere. In order to "recover the rod of power," to reexperience vitality, mastery, and control, the speaker must admit inundation and allow primitive terrors to resurface. She must "surrender / sterile logic, trivial reason" and dare to flounder in the "sub-conscious ocean where Fish / move two ways, devour" (*T*, 40). Though not forgetting the beneficent image of woman, "Love, the Creator, / her chariot and white doves," she must rededicate her gifts to "spiritual realism" and entreat also "the original great-mother, / who drove // harnessed scorpions / before her" (*T*, 47). Only when she dares a "personal approach / to the eternal realities," substituting the defeat and impotency she has herself experienced for what has been consecrated or deemed heretical by culture, will words reveal their hidden meanings and become "little boxes, conditioned to / hatch butterflies," the emblems of renewal (*T*, 53).

After she has discovered "a new Master" over Love by touching her own depths, the speaker identifies her creativity with the despised but tenacious worm instead of the defensive, self-righteous shellfish: "In me (the worm) clearly / is no righteousness, but this— // persistence" (*T*, 11). Attracted by the apparently miraculous changes of the worm-cycle (which in its dramatic shifts resembles female biological growth), she will spin a cocoon that is both "shroud" and a new womb, the locus of rebirth.[60] Also, the worm (like the snake) is a bisexual symbol: most important, it "profit[s] from every calamity," better encompassing her capacity for aggression and for growth (*T*, 12). Along with such male poets who are also "nameless initiates / born of one mother," she will bridge the "schism in consciousness" created by rigidly assigned sex roles (*T*, 21). Drawing upon Egyptian resurrection myth, which recognizes that the sibling lovers Isis and Osiris were

once united in their mother's womb, she will reassign to the feminine
the creative agency that androcentric Judeo-Christian religious tradition had appropriated. She will recover the "secret of Isis":

> which is: there was One
> in the beginning, Creator,
> Fosterer, Begetter, the Same-forever
>
> in the papyrus-swamp
> in the Judean meadow. (*T*, 55)

"*Still the walls do not fall*"; instead they preserve liberating messages
that will permit her to "reach haven / heaven" (*T*, 58). Like the bone-
frame of her body, they withstand the shock of new life.

In "Tribute to the Angels" H.D.'s speaker continues the process
of psychic modification begun in the first volume of *Trilogy*, this time
gaining assistance from Hermes Trismegistus, patron of alchemists.
Mentor of "orators, thieves and poets," Hermes offers a precedent
method for spiritual transformation (as well as a metaphor), the
double alchemical process of destruction and creation. As Adalaide
Morris has written, alchemy involved a process of purification
through which destruction was to prefigure and permit new life.[61] A
modernist alchemist, H.D. will melt down the broken, scattered
fragments of her psyche in the "fire and breath" of her poem-crucible
to re-create new jewels of spiritual health. She will purge androcentric
language of its destructive connotations and restore to the feminine its
original potency.

Hermes Trismegistus also provides H.D.'s speaker with a syn-
cretic, heretical religious philosophy that enables her to reintegrate
pagan myth with Christian, to incorporate "what the old church found
in Mithra's tomb" with "what the new church spat upon" (*T*, 63).
Continuing with her critique of Judeo-Christian tradition, she deliberately sets the narrative of "Tribute to the Angels" in the context of the
Book of Revelation, using its legacy as a blueprint of social renewal to
question John's version of redemption while offering her own revision.

As Gubar points out, H.D. quotes from Revelation directly in order to alter John's severely vengeful version of apocalypse. She replaces his seven angels who pour out God's wrath upon the earth from their golden bowls with seven angels whose presence in embattled London testifies to the "promise of rebirth that her bowl holds."[62] Whereas "*I John saw*" a series of abominations and disasters upon the earth, she sees a sign of "beauty incarnate" (*T*, 67).

Specifically, H.D. places Uriel, angel of the thunder and terror of war, into a system that he cannot dominate, balancing him with Azrael, "the last and greatest, Death," with Raphael, "the first who giveth life" (*T*, 67), and with Gabriel, the angel of annunciation and mercy.[63] She performs this shift in perspective by reevaluating the meaning of Uriel, whose symbol is an open hand holding a flame.[64] "God's very breath," Uriel is that in us which watches and worships "with unbroken will, / with unbowed head"; he represents the fire of "strength, endurance, anger" in our hearts (*T*, 68). Uriel provides the "jet of flame" with which we light the poem-bowl to begin the process of transformation. In his name we pause "to give / thanks that we rise again from the dead and live" (*T*, 70).

Compelled by the "unsatisfied duality" of "mother-father" within herself, H.D.'s speaker deplores how Judeo-Christian culture has divided woman from her own psychic strength by sacralizing motherhood, on one hand, and denouncing independent female erotic power, on the other. Calling upon earlier traditions in which the goddess of beauty, love, and fertility were one, she restores the desecrated name of Venus, which has become connected with "venery . . . venereous, lascivious," to its earlier religious associations with "venerate, / venerator" (*T*, 75). Thus the companion of Uriel, the fire-to-endure, is "*Annael*, peace of God" (*T*, 79).

Like her substitution of the grain in the heart's core for inadequate shell and pearl imagery, H.D.'s use of the alchemist's bowl to symbolize the womb's transformative power represents a revision of traditional vessel imagery that implies woman's passivity in the creative act. (Consider the Christian idea that Christ was conceived by the Holy Spirit as He overshadowed the virgin.)[65] No mere passive receptacle, H.D.'s poem-crucible comprises psychic and linguistic exertion that resembles physical labor. The poet distills, fuses, melts, changes, alters, conjoining the feminine and masculine forms of the Hebrew word for bitter (*marah*) — the root of the word Mary — to create a new concept of the maternal matrix:

> now polish the crucible
> and set the jet of flame
>
> under, till *marah-mar*
> are melted, fuse and join
>
> and change and alter,
> mer, mere, mère, mater, Maia, Mary,
>
> Star of the Sea,
> Mother. (*T*, 71)

Further demonstrating the effect of female experience on her expression of the sacred, the poet refuses to label the "jewel colour" in the heart of her bowl in any limiting way. She prefers instead to "minimize thought," to feel the "faint / heart-beat, pulse-beat" of new life and be "drawn into it" (*T*, 77). An act of apperception, performed with full awareness of the past, her linguistic creation is a feat of memory that approximates a return to life's source. Here H.D. transfers to the creation of poetry qualities of empathy and receptivity that she derived from her experience in childbirth.

After she reconstitutes the matrix, H.D.'s speaker is rewarded with a vision and a second revelatory dream. Her vision of a "half-burnt-out apple-tree / blossoming" represents the triumph of her own "invisible, indivisible Spirit" (*T*, 87, 83). This is the "flowering of the rood" (*T*, 87), the transformation of the cross on which Christ was crucified. By etymology also a rod, the flowering branch signifies the conversion of Aaron's rod from its original designation as an emblem of Moses' spiritual authority in a contest with Pharoah's priests, to the symbol of a new relation with the mysteries of nature presaging a female presence.[66] Fittingly, a dream follows bringing an image of a

Lady. A representative of lunar time whom the dream work liberates from her traditional role as chaste mother of a male god, she is clothed in snow-white garments of transfiguration without the "golden girdle" associated with the sanctification of her reproductive capacity. Different from conventional representations of the madonna-muse found in "cathedral, museum, cloister," she bears "none of her usual attributes; / the Child [is] not with her" (*T*, 97). In its place, suggesting her satisfaction with the speaker's purpose of writing a tribute, she carries a book containing "the blank pages / of the unwritten volume of the new" (*T*, 103).

This Lady, who carries an unwritten book instead of "the Child," mediates between the speaker's deepest psychic needs and the war-torn, misogynist world in which she finds herself. In its first appearance in H.D.'s poetry, the symbol of the child functions in two ways: it underlines woman's historical entrapment in a biological function and it signals the cultural benefit to be gained by her potential freedom. An emblem of yet unnamed imaginative power, the Lady who carries a book instead of a child is "the counter-coin-side / of primitive terror; she is not-fear, she is not-war" (*T*, 104). No mere "symbolic figure" of traditional female values such as "peace, charity, chastity" that have been privatized and devalued or channeled to serve male interests (and ultimately to service a war machine), the Lady does not allow her attention to be diverted to a divine husband or a male-god-child. It is devoted to the daughter-writer, who numbers herself among those "who did not deny their birthright" at the grave's edge: "we are her bridegroom and lamb; / her book is our book" (*T*, 100, 104). An avatar of the Goddess, who represents female power, she represents the speaker's ability to integrate her poetic identity with her procreative experience. "Different yet the same as before," she is her own unfettered soul freed from guilt caused by the mystification of woman's nature in patriarchy, freed from the "darkness of ignorance" that had imprisoned her: "she is Psyche, the butterfly, / out of the cocoon" (*T*, 103).

At the conclusion of her tribute to the angels, H.D.'s speaker testifies to a point of perfect psychic integration in which "all lights become one" and she may begin again. When the jewel melts in her crucible, she sees not John's holy city, "prepared as a bride adorned for her husband" (Rev. 21: 2), an image that represents to her "ashes . . . ash-of-rose" (*T*, 109). She sees "not a tall vase and a staff of lillies," traditional symbols of the Blessed Virgin's purity, but a visage full of color—"a cluster of garden-pinks / or a face like a Christmas-rose,"—which suggests vitality, sexuality, and the rediscovery of god-in-herself: *"this is the flowering of the burnt-out wood, / where, Zadkiel, we pause to give / thanks that we rise again from death and live"* (*T*, 110).

In "The Walls Do Not Fall" and "Tribute to the Angels" the reviving speaker recapitulates the psychological process of de-idealizing the father and recovering the mother's power that was evident in more literal accounts of her analysis and in the emotional pattern of *The Gift*. In the third long poem, "The Flowering of the Rod," she places the completion of her psychic renewal once more in that context by imagining her vision validated by another. Again H.D. breaks down a conventional reading of scripture, retelling the story of the birth and death of Christ from the perspective of two peripheral characters in the gospel—Kaspar, the wise heathen, and Mary Magdalen, the inspired whore. Imagining an extension of Kaspar's consciousness, she dramatizes her psychic reanimation as the product of a moment of recognition between these two. For, like *Writing on the Wall* (immediately precedent), which memorializes the poet's Freud, "the tale of a jar or jars" that embodies the speaker's flowering is as much the story of Kaspar's transformation as Mary's own (*T*, 105). In the final volume of *Trilogy* H.D.'s story of their encounter completes the "translation" of her own meeting with Freud begun earlier.

Having shown that she has withstood "anger, frustration, / bitter destruction," in "The Flowering of the Rod," H.D.'s speaker prepares us to "leave the smoldering cities below" (*T*, 114). She will satisfy her longing to "equilibrate," to resolve the "double nostalgia" produced by the polarities that seem inherent in existence, by rising beyond anger or pity to a harmony based on "love—resurrection" (*T*, 114). Like those mythical geese, whose ecstatic hunger for a lost paradise resembles the quest of Christ who was "the first to wing / from that sad Tree," she finds resurrection in a renewed "sense of direction" (*T*, 128, 123).

Like other lines, images, and scenes in "The Flowering" that recall her memoir, H.D.'s poetic statement that "in resurrection there is simple affirmation" strikes the same poignant note of mutual understanding with which she begins and ends *Writing on the Wall* (*T*, 115). Remembering that she could not find the gardenias that represented her special knowledge of Freud in time for his seventy-seventh birthday in Vienna but sent them later in 1938 when he was exiled in London, she recalls that even though she did not sign the card, he guessed correctly that they were from her and acknowledged them affectionately. Like her memoir, "The Flowering" moves beyond the "argument implicit in our very bones" that is more central in her contemporary accounts of their meeting to the "gardenias . . . of utmost veneration" (*TF*, 13, 111). Both testify to the experience of being known and its liberating effect on knowing.

When I assert that the tone of "The Flowering" is comparable to the *Tribute*, I differ with Susan Friedman and Rachel Blau DuPlessis, who read the *Tribute* as tacit evidence of H.D.'s debate with Freud. Though I agree with their general thesis, I would distinguish between the tone of that debate in "The Master" or in "Advent" and that in the *Tribute*. For example, consider the passage when H.D. describes Freud showing her the statue of Pallas Athene from his collection:

> "This is my favorite," he said. He held the object toward me. I took it in my hand. It was a little bronze statue, helmeted, clothed to the foot in carved robe with the upper incised chiton or peplum. One hand was extended as if holding a staff or rod. "She is perfect," he said, *"only she has lost her spear."* I did not say anything. He knew that I loved Greece. He knew that I loved Hellas. . . . He might have been talking Greek. (*TF*, 69)

Arguing that this story of the statue "represents a retreat from open conflict into the relative safety of nuanced code," Friedman and

134

DuPlessis interpret H.D.'s silence here as "speechless" rebellion.[67] I think not. H.D. was well past the need to establish her autonomy by insisting on difference here. Rather, she goes on to translate Freud's "Greek" words into her own language, citing the "singing quality" of his voice that made the "spoken word live in another dimension" (reminiscent of her mother's family) (*TF*, 69).

Similarly, in "The Flowering of the Rod" H.D. transforms Freud from a master into a muse. In a series of dramatic episodes that alludes to central issues of her analysis as well as to the gospels, H.D. reminds us that the first to witness Christ's "life-after-death" was "an unbalanced, neurotic woman" who was "out of step with world so-called progress" (*T*, 129). A fusion of Mary of Bethany (who disavowed housework) and the "reviled" Mary Magdalen, she also becomes associated with the Madonna in the revised nativity scene with which H.D. concludes the *Trilogy*. Leading up to this epiphany is an imaginative re-creation of how Mary Magdalen acquires the precious jar of myrrh with which she anoints the feet of Christ.

In H.D.'s version Mary receives the contents of the alabaster jar as a gift from the merchant Kaspar after an amusing scene in the Arab bazaar that is a comic transposition of her own encounter with Freud. Like the old professor (who had felt "the fangs of the pack" as a Jew in Vienna), Kaspar is no ordinary entrepreneur but a "stranger in the marketplace"; his "priceless" burial spice is "not for sale" (*T*, 130). A philosopher-alchemist who knows the "secret of the sacred processes of distillation," he is taking it to a "coronation and a funeral — a double affair" (*T*, 133, 130). Also something of a male chauvinist, Kaspar snubs Mary at first, fixing his eyes on the half-open door "in a gesture of implied dismissal" after she ignores his insulting sexual overtures (*T*, 131). Here H.D. burlesques Freud's phallocentrism. When Kaspar draws aside his robe "in a noble manner," the "unmaidenly" Mary does not "take the hint" (*T*, 130). Having seen "nobility herself at first hand," she is not impressed (*T*, 130). Simply detaching herself, she firmly holds her ground and finally leaves on her own terms: "I am Mary, a great tower; / through my will and my power, / Mary shall be myrrh" (*T*, 135).

Yet, though he has been conditioned to think that it is "unseemly" for a woman to "appear disordered, dishevelled," Kaspar is struck by Mary's unpredictability. And when he momentarily abandons his patriarchal stiffness, bending down in a posture of reverence to pick up the scarf that has slipped from her hair, he is granted a vision that complements the poet's own. For unlike the Christian Simon the leper, who later derides Mary as "devil-ridden" because he fears her lack of inhibition, the heathen Kaspar recognizes that she embodies the once-revered female deities of a prebiblical period. Realizing that they are "unalterably part of the picture," he "might call // the devils *daemons*," invoking them tenderly "under his breath . . . without fear of eternal damnation":

> Isis, Astarte, Cyprus
> and the other four;
>
> he might re-name them,
> Ge-meter, De-meter, earth-mother
>
> or Venus
> in a star. (*T*, 145)

When Mary's scarf slips to the floor, Kaspar recognizes that she represents "Venus in the ascendant // or Venus in conjunction with Jupiter" (*T*, 148). Here is the poetic counterpart to H.D.'s culminating vision at Corfu, in which an ascendant Niké is drawn into the sun-disk by a welcoming male figure.

In that half-second, when his intuition is in "direct contradiction" with the "hedges and fences and fortresses" of his thought (*T*, 159, 158), Kaspar has an experience that echoes the speaker's earlier vision of the Lady and recalls the luminous Princess dream of the Freud memoir. He sees that the light from Mary's hair is "as of moonlight on a lost river" and he remembers (*T*, 148). Through a fleck of light in the jeweled crown of the tripartite goddess who appears to his inner eye, Kaspar sees backward to the "islands of the Blest" and "the lost centre-island, Atlantis," and he sees forward to "the whole scope and plan // of our and his civilization on this, / his and our earth, before Adam" (*T*, 153, 154). This vision leads him, along with the poet, to hear an extremely important message.

Like "the echo of an echo in a shell," which does not conform to any known words but conveys itself rhythmically, the spell Kaspar hears reminds him of "the drowned cities of pre-history" as it translates itself (*T*, 156). Implying that a matriarchal genealogy has been erased from record, it recalls an ancient female trinity that suggests a condition of female potential quite different from that of Genesis:

> *Lilith born before Eve*
> *and one born before Lilith*
> *and Eve; we three are forgiven,*
> *we are three of the seven*
> *daemons cast out of her. (T, 157)*

Created not from Adam's rib but from the dust, Lilith was a woman who refused sexual subordination and dared to pronounce the Ineffable Name. As Susan Gubar has written, she and the unnamed daemon actually predate the Bible, establishing a link back to Kaspar's pagan deities: "together they promise a submerged but now recoverable time of female strength, female speech and female sexuality, all of which have mysteriously managed to survive, although in radically subdued ways, incarnate in the body of Mary Magdala."[68] Like Freud, who compared his new understanding of the preoedipal phase of female development to the discovery of Mycenean civilization behind Greece, Kaspar is a healer, a shaman of sorts. By recapturing Mary's "stolen soul, her lost ancestors," he reestablishes "the matriarchal genealogy that confers divinity upon her."[69]

After the Arab merchant Kaspar has apprehended the full nature of Mary Magdalen, he is transformed into the Mage worthy of the epiphany in the final sections. Dramatically reversing the chronology of his life, H.D. turns backward from his confrontation with this Mary to reinterpret his delivery of the gift of myrrh to Mary in the manger. When Kaspar places his jar on the stable floor, he has a premonition that "there were always two jars, / the two were always together," and he vows *someday I will bring the other*" (*T*, 168). When Kaspar remembers that there were two jars originally together, H.D. alludes to the legendary jar of spikenard that was believed to have magical properties because it contained Christ's circumcised foreskin. The "other jar" that Kaspar will bring someday contains a substance that is the male counterpart of female reproductive power: in the lore of magic, myrrh was credited with the power to cause menstruation.[70] But we already know that his wish has been or will be fulfilled. For when Kaspar gives the myrrh to Mary mother, the poet has already informed us that he is destined to give the other jar to Mary Magdalen.[71]

Finally both Marys recede from the foreground of the poem. For in the closing epiphany of this revised nativity scene, Kaspar's celebration of "the Holy-Presence-Manifest" refers not simply to the child in Mary's lap but to the speaker's recentering, to the appearance "in-herself" that her speech and virginal demeanor imply: "But she spoke so he looked at her, / she was shy and simple and young" (*T*, 168). Realizing that she herself contains the mystery of her trans-formed sorrow, he wonders if she knows that the "beautiful fragrance" she acknowledges comes not from his sealed jar but from "the bundle of myrrh" she holds in her arms (*T*, 170). In this final vision, which alludes to the Song of Songs, Kaspar finds manifest the triumph of eros over death.

This fragrant bundle of myrrh in the arms of the revived speaker at the end of *Trilogy* recalls the sprig of orange blossom H.D. received from Freud one winter day during her analysis, one of the concluding memories recorded in *Writing on the Wall*. Both represent the poet's conversion of Aaron's rod to a female symbol: to a goldenrod, to a golden bough "with its cluster of golden fruit" (*TF*, 90). Both signify her recovery and ownership of the indwelling spirit of fertility. For H.D.'s changed attitude toward authoritative men, facilitated in analysis, culminated in reconnection with her mother, with herself as imaginal child, and with her dream of prophecy in poetry. Reinventing Freud in her memoir, she made him a muse instead of a master. As a poetic complement to that tribute, she appears in "The Flowering" restored to herself.

5

"*Child-Consciousness,*" *a Vision of Eros*

From By Avon River *to* Bid Me to Live

LIKE MANY LONDONERS at the end of World War II, H.D. and Bryher celebrated their personal survival and Hitler's defeat by visiting Shakespeare's grave on Shakespeare Day. In her account of this occasion Bryher describes the air of reverence and gratitude with which the crowd proceeded to the church, an attitude at once chastened and childlike that also appears, more fully elaborated, in the poems and prose of H.D.'s tribute to Shakespeare, *By Avon River*:

> If it were the wish of any artist to paint the spirit of a country emerging from almost six years of war, he had a blueprint in the procession to the church on Shakespeare's birthday. Almost everyone was carrying a tribute, mostly from their own gardens. . . . We had stuck it somehow as England had stuck it at the time of the Armada. The flowers were masking the smell of the polluted London dust and we felt in a way that we could not explain that Shakespeare had helped to pull us through so that we were alive this April morning and we were taking him primroses in remembrance, the flowers that are the first a lot of children recognize by name, from his Warwickshire lanes. [1]

A more literary memoir than Bryher's, H.D.'s *By Avon River* is a meditation on those qualities traditionally associated with the child in literature: simplicity and vulnerability and growth, wonder, an intuition of and capacity for the miraculous. Like the great Romantic poets before her, Blake and Wordsworth, she considered such qualities essential in the artist and mystic alike. Like the Romantics, in her mature work H.D. used the symbol of the child not only to signify the artist's newly conceived subjective inquiry into the self but also to represent her deepest moral concern — dissatisfaction with the values and priorities of modern society.[2]

Though she first uses the symbol of the child in *Trilogy*, H.D. defines and clarifies her usage in *By Avon River* when she extends the conception to include an "unconscious longing for ultimate union" (*BAR*, 89) that imitates the reversible empathy of the parent-child bond. In *Bid Me to Live*, in which she lays to rest her personal trauma during World War I by means of a debate with D. H. Lawrence, H.D. terms the source of her creative vision "child-consciousness" or "the *gloire*."[3] By this she means a mystical psychic state inspired by love yet suprasexual, in which she feels herself part of the uncreated reservoir of all beauty, part of nature before it has been distorted by culture. Soon after, this newly crystallized perspective would prompt a critique of the noxious psychological effects of sexual romanticism in her epic poem *Helen in Egypt*.

In this chapter I discuss H.D.'s meditation on Shakespeare and her dialogue with Lawrence, her imaginative responses to two of several writers whose views of love and of the emotional source of creativity she found seminal. In her original reading of Shakespeare, which resulted from the need to connect her own experience with that of the literary tradition he represents, H.D. reconceptualized the erotic basis of creativity in a patriarchy. She claimed the source of inspiration to be the affiliative bond between parent and child instead of the oppositionally charged connection between man and woman. She then made this more primary emotional connection the basis of a theory of creativity that would counter the phallocentrism of her male contemporaries.

In "Good Frend," the three poems that constitute the first part of *By Avon River*, H.D. establishes the volume's tone and literary mode. As the first poem, "The Tempest," indicates, we are in the world of Shakespearean romance, a world of merited reconciliation. Here circumstances, though they may be antagonistic for a long time, eventually yield to meritorious humanity; and desires, though perhaps once perceived as too ambitious, tend to fall within a realm of moral possibility. H.D. chooses as her persona *"the king's fair daughter / Claribel,"* a speechless character in *The Tempest*, to whom she gives a voice that is gradually amplified in the three poems in the section.[4] In the third poem, "Claribel's Way to God," we are also in the tradition of Romance as that term refers to courtly love, a tradition of heretical religious mysticism veiled in the language of sexual passion, which was transmitted by the troubadours to European poets from the mystery religions of the Near East.[5] Ultimately, we are in a realm of profound inner quest, where the personal impulse does not dominate reality, because beyond the individual, beyond even death, there lies an independent force that offers alternative possibilities. We are in the world of the redemptive sea journey; in *By Avon River*, at the end of *Bid Me to Live*, and especially in *Helen in Egypt*, the sea represents that ultimately beneficent, numinous force. A comment on *The Tempest* applies equally well to *Helen in Egypt*, "the sea . . . washes through every nook and cranny of the play, moving the characters to their destiny both by carrying them there and by washing right up into their consciousness."[6]

"Come as you will, but I came home // Driven by *The Tempest*," H.D. begins her poem by that name (*BAR*, 5). She means not only that she came home, after World War II, to her domicile and to her family, but also that she "came home" in the old-fashioned Christian sense, in which death is viewed as the ultimate return home to a better life. As she wrote in a later memoir, thinking of her losses during World War I, of her psychic death, and of the sadness in her early poems, "We say (old-fashioned people used to say) when someone dies, he or she has *gone home*, I was looking for home, I think. But a sort of heaven-is-my-home, I was looking for that—that super-ego—that father-lover—I don't know—How can I explain it?" (*CF*, 12). After World War II, H.D. felt she had achieved the sense of reconciliation, of reintegration, that she had searched for earlier. Now she came home to her literary heritage, represented by Shakespeare, with renewed poise and artistic purpose. Her decision to incarnate the invisible character Claribel in her tribute to Shakespeare demonstrates this renewed purpose. She is unseen in the play and heard of only indirectly, but Claribel's name nevertheless "echoes from this rainbow-shell," confirming her artistic calling (*BAR*, 6).

H.D. chooses the persona of Claribel, Ferdinand's sister who was married off to the King of Tunis, because her story develops outside of the play's main action but yet is subtly instrumental: "*The Tempest* came after they left her" (*BAR*, 6). Claribel's marriage took place before the storm at sea (which occurs on the wedding party's return), yet we continue to hear about her after it, in allusions that culminate in Gonzalo's reference to her marriage, along with Ferdinand's, in his summation of the series of paradoxes that have led to the final restoration. H.D. quotes from these passages, ringing changes on them that give them new life:

> I came home driven by *The Tempest*;
> That was after the wedding-feast;
> *'Twas a sweet marriage*, we are told;
> And she *a paragon* . . . *who is now queen*,
> *And the rarest that e'er came there*;
>
> We know little of *the king's fair daughter*
> *Claribel*; her father was Alonso. (*BAR*, 5)

Where did Shakespeare find such a character, H.D. wonders. Did he read about her in pamphlets that reported the journeys of the *Sea-Adventure*, the ship that bore colonists to the new world? Did he have in mind the state occasion — the wedding of Princess Elizabeth to "a foreign fellow," the Elector Palatine? Or could he have found her likeness in the poet herself, standing shyly with the crowd before the church door in the "soft mist" on Shakespeare Day, April 23, 1945?

In describing the crowd passing through the church door, H.D. clarifies her interpretation of the ultimate meaning of Sebastian's

144

comment, " *'Twas a sweet marriage,* " by inserting a line from the Song of Songs to complement it. Besides depicting the love triangle between King Solomon, the Shulamite, and the Shulamite's lover, this psalm has also been read as an allegory of God's love. Similarly, H.D. attributes to Claribel's marriage a resonance far beyond Sebastian's particular vision in Shakespeare's play. She implies a bond between Shakespeare and the English spirit that sustains all who partake of it:

> Ring, ring and ring again,
> *'Twas a sweet marriage,*
> So they say, *my beloved is mine*
> *And I am his;* Claribel
> The chimes peel;
> . . . .
>
> Tenderly, tenderly,
> We stand with our flowers,
> Our beloved is ours,
> Our beloved is ours,
> Today? Yesterday? (*BAR*, 9)

H.D. continues her meditation on the power of love in the second poem in this section, "Rosemary." Here the epitaph on Shakespeare's tombstone provides the poem's subject: transformation or the possibility of life in death. H.D. begins by describing herself as she approached the tombstone, eagerly hoping to touch the letters inscribed on it, certain that "a rhythm would pass on, / And out of it, if I could stoop / And run my bare palm over it" (*BAR*, 10). But when she actually reaches the grave, she finds that the "stone had vanished as if under / Azure and green of deep-sea water" (*BAR*, 10). In its place grows a resplendent array of flowers: "laurel, iris, rosemary, / Heartsease and every sort of lily" (*BAR*, 11). As once Apollo's discus, "idly thrown," had accidentally "slain the Spring and yet forever, / That death had blossomed" (*BAR*, 11), so these flowers represent the power of Love to transform Death. Though there were "no letters anywhere," words of blessing are written in them that

"Speak through all flowers eternally, / *Blest be ye man*—that one who knows / His heart glows in the growing rose" (*BAR*, 11). In "Rosemary" H.D. focuses on the transformative power of love as it expresses itself in memory, a central motif in *The Tempest*, which H.D. will also stress in *Helen in Egypt*. Viewed as tokens of memory, neither Claribel nor asphodel is a "flower of death" but rather a bright "flower-de-luce" that signifies an end to strife not "after death / But now and here" (*BAR*, 11–12). In her poem, therefore, those who hold Shakespeare dear bring rosemary, the aromatic herb of remembrance, that outlasts time and tyranny: "What rose of memory, / *Ros maris*, / From what sea of bliss!" (*BAR*, 13).

Consequently, H.D. chooses as her persona Claribel, "a mere marriage token," particularly because (she imagines) Shakespeare remembered her last when he had not long to live (*BAR*, 14). Though Claribel "only threw a shadow / On his page," yet she "was his"—his brain-child—because he named her (*BAR*, 15). Neither witty nor forceful nor pathetic, like his more famous women characters, she stood "invisible on the water-stair" (*BAR*, 16) (like "our Princess" of the Freud memoir). Yet her very invisibility gave her versatility and a patient persistence less evident in his more developed characters: "Call me most proud who wait" (*BAR*, 15). But most importantly, her invisibility gave Claribel spiritual freedom, prompting H.D. to wonder who best attends Shakespeare, those who speak from his past, "shapes seen and sensed clearly," or "dim shapes" who unroll "mysteriously / Into the future" (*BAR*, 17). Finally (like T. S. Eliot in "Marina," which was also inspired by Shakespearean romance), H.D. claims for Claribel an affinity with the very essence of spirituality:

> And then I wondered . . .
> What voice it was from Avallon,
> Calling that last April,
> *Farewell, farewell,*
> *But only to pain, regret, disaster,*
> *O friend, farewell*
> *Is only to fear, despair, torture*

Say not farewell,
But hail, Master.
Was it Ariel?
Was it Claribel? (*BAR*, 17)

In the third poem in this section, "Claribel's Way to God," H.D. attributes Claribel's lack of entitlement to the patriarchal religious tradition that has denied women a voice. In an elaborate dream the speaker undertakes a spiritual journey in search of authentic selfhood. First, she compares herself with a "Poor Clare," a nun in the order of Saint Francis of Assisi, whose rosary and vows of self-abnegation are familiar. The sister's "Rose of Mary" reminds her of "the *ros maris*," so she asks a wood-carver to make her some comparable beads (*BAR*, 18). But the wooden beads hewn for her turn out to be "made of rosemary, / and fashioned and strung differently" (*BAR*, 18). Still seeking the way to God, she asks a wandering friar "who Saint Francis was" and finds that he achieved sainthood by devoting himself to his Lady "Poverty" and her Lord: "God and God's son, / The spoken and the written Word; / These three . . . but One" (*BAR*, 19).

Since she is not a "Poor Clare," but "Clare-the-fair" — too "well-endowed" to accept this ascetic alternative, she turns then to a richly ornamented prelate for enlightenment. But the prelate swiftly ushers her through the crowd to "His Holiness" himself, who apprises her of the latest trends in theological disputation instead. Finding nothing helpful there, Claribel wanders in Italy, joins the Clares, and for a long time brews "rue and thyme" and stuffs "rose petals in tall jars" in silent resignation (*BAR*, 21).

Finally, when she continues her journey, she meets a dying Knight Templar, who understands her need for validation. A kindred spirit who has been persecuted for his heretical matriarchal religious beliefs, he responds to the significance of her speechlessness:

The others thought that I had lived,
The others thought that I had died,
They never seemed to sense or know
That I was a mere marriage token,

147

> Who never had a word to say;
> But he, it seemed, regarded me,
> As if myself, I were the play,
> Players and a great company. (*BAR*, 22)

When she responds to this crusader's request that she confirm his beliefs, he describes to her the worship of "Supernal light" that the trouvères hid in the aubade. The Arabs, he says, told a "tale of passion and beauty, / Disguised as Lover and Lady, / To hide the ineffable mystery" (*BAR*, 23). His words provide her with a practical means of consolation and empowerment. For, unlike the Clares, who sought "*consolomentum*" in heaven (or H.D.'s contemporary Rupert Brooke, to whose despairing poem she alludes), Claribel finds the answer to her prayers "*this side of paradise*" — in the shared interpretation of her name:

> To him alone, I told my secret,
> Sir, I am nothing but a name,
>
> Claribel. Brightly fair, he said,
> O clearly beautiful, thou Spirit. (*BAR*, 24)

As the mage Kaspar's validation of her vision enabled the speaker of "The Flowering of the Rod" to appear restored to herself, so the Knight Templar's recognition of Claribel's spiritual essence breaks the spell and enables this middle-aged sleeping beauty to awaken from her dream and greet the dawn. For when the knight bids "farewell, farewell," the churchbells ring so clearly that "the pavement seemed to melt away," and the speaker finds herself, not in Venice but "in Avon meadow," standing "by Avon river" (*BAR*, 24). This time, when her chaplet tells its "*ora, ave*," it is to the music of "Ariel's song," whereupon one chime peals "so sweetly" that Claribel replaces the conventional Christian Trinity with "Avon's Trinity" (*BAR*, 25).

In the poem's final lines H.D. spells out the specific meaning of "Avon's Trinity." She offers an artist's version of the nature of the divine, which is based, not on self-denying obeisance to a patriarchal hierarchy ("These Three . . . but One"), but on a more egalitarian and celebratory conception of piety and love that includes women. In Avon's trinity "Love is God . . . Love is Strong," when a new Three are in perfect accord: the Dream, that personal and collective unconscious that is a "well of living water"; the Dreamer or artist, who may be either man or woman; and felicitous expression, the Song:

> And suddenly, I saw it fair,
> How Love is God, how Love is strong,
> When One is Three and Three are One,
> The Dream, the Dreamer and the Song. (*BAR*, 25)

Because she and Bryher had survived World War II together as well as World War I, H.D. dedicated her essay "The Guest," which constitutes the second section of *By Avon River*, to Bryher. Dated September 19 to November 1, 1946, this essay was completed at the clinic where H.D. was sent to recuperate from the terrible strain of living through that war. Very thin and frail, H.D. had been taxing her physical and emotional resources too severely during the war years. Despite warnings from her friends, she had spent an increasing amount of time engaged in spiritualist séances, first with Arthur Bhaduri and then on her own, until she was on the edge of mental breakdown. Finally Bryher, fearing the worst, chartered a plane and flew her to Zurich. Barbara Guest provides a startling account of H.D.'s behavior and possible state of mind in these months. Her words cast another, more somber light on H.D.'s preference for Shakespeare's invisible Claribel:

> The séances are evidence of a more and more frantic search into the unknown, the invisible—flights from a visible reality whose strain must have pressed upon her consciousness. It is at this time that she began tearing the bookplates out of her books, destroying those plates, so much a part of her identity, that had been designed for her by George Plank. She began moving furniture into the hall. Was she preparing for invisibility?[7]

All the more significant, then, is H.D.'s accomplishment in "The Guest." Here she offers the unique, intuitive kind of literary criticism that only a great poet could write. As she stated in her note of thanks to Norman Pearson, in this essay on Shakespeare and his contemporaries she has "endeavoured to preserve the living tradition, though sometimes at variance with the discoveries of modern scholarship" (*BAR*, 30). Indeed, the relation between literary tradition and the individual talent becomes more poignant after one reads her opening statement. For in her effort to remember Shakespeare "differently," H.D. describes a state of disorientation and isolation—of "dark night . . . dream or delirium"—the psychic state she may have experienced when she arrived at Kusnacht. We are to "murmer a number, 1-5-6-4 and follow it with another, 1-6-1-6. But that is no telephone number" (*BAR*, 31). Anchoring her essay about Shakespeare and his contemporaries on the merest shreds of biographical data, H.D. invites us to suspend mundane reason for awhile, to wander with her through the labyrinth of the mind. She considers aspects of Shakespeare's life and work that serve her need to connect her own experience with the predominantly male literary tradition he represents. She asks us to imagine why Shakespeare left court society in London and "came home" to New Place before he died.

In the course of her sixty-five-page essay, H.D. compares Shakespeare with fifty-nine of the one hundred Elizabethan poets and dramatists who are represented in the more complete anthologies of *Songs and Lyrics* (*BAR*, 32). She takes her title from Sir Walter Raleigh's poem "Go, Soul, the Body's guest / Upon a thankless arrant," a passionate attack on social corruption that also serves as her epigraph (*BAR*, 34). An accomplished courtier who spent his last years "eating his heart out in the Tower," Raleigh was also, "of necessity," a poet (*BAR*, 34). Like Philip Sidney, Christopher Marlowe, and Fulke Greville, Raleigh met a violent end—typical in that era of rampant intrigue. With the exception of Shakespeare, H.D. writes, we cannot picture any of these legendary figures in peaceful retirement. Locating Shakespeare's difference from his contemporaries in the ultimate priority he gave his domestic life, she continues, "Of William Shakespeare, alone, can we visualize a chair drawn up before an open window, an apple-tree in blossom, a friend or two and children. There was Elizabeth and, with her, Judith. Hamnet, Judith's twin, is not forgotten" (*BAR*, 34).

Considering the influence of Shakespeare's experience as a parent on his work, H.D. imagines what he was thinking in his last days. She pictures him planning Knotte Garden at New Place, and she suggests that specific kinds of flowers evoked lines from his poems and plays and were associated, in turn, with thoughts about his children. He thinks particularly of Judith, whose recent marriage worried him, and about her twin Hamnet, who died in childhood. For example, H.D. implies that the question of how to design Knotte Garden reminds Shakespeare that Judith "has gone away," which prompts him to wonder about his son Hamnet, "Now where is Hamnet?" Macbeth's despairing utterance follows. "Out, out brief candle" reminds Shakespeare that his life did not feel very brief at times, that there were "long waits between," long absences. These associations culminate in recalled lines from that most poignant sonnet, "From you have I been absent in the spring," the melancholy tone of which H.D. connects with Shakespeare's longing for his children. After quoting Shakespeare's beautiful lines, "They were but sweet, but figures of delight, / Drawn after you, you pattern of all those," she asks:

> But who was the pattern of all those? A child tugged at the knotted edge of his grey shawl. Another child was laughing, but it wasn't Hamnet. He looked at her-his face. They were both his children, but Judith with her hair tucked over her ears, was no Juliet. Judith was Hamnet. Hamnet was Judith. And he had left them at the bridge and spurred his horse through Oxford for an idle fantasy. Perfection dwelt in two separate. There was no *master-mistress of my passion*. It was late now. But Judith understood what he wanted with the garden. (*BAR*, 36)

In this passage not only does H.D. imply that longing for his children inspired this sonnet, she finds in Shakespeare a view of creativity, of creative inspiration and the relation of art to life that she will elaborate further in *Bid Me to Live* and *Helen in Egypt.* H.D. attributes to Shakespeare's parentage of the twins, Hamnet and Judith, several related insights. First, when he remembers Hamnet (and simultaneously hears Judith's laughter), Shakespeare envisions no tragic romantic heroine or hero (no Juliet or Romeo), but rather his own little girl, her dead brother's twin, who is still very much alive: "Judith was Hamnet. Hamnet was Judith." Second, he realizes that his journey through Oxford, away from home and children, had been in pursuit of an "idle fantasy" of spiritual fulfillment. For though the emotional source of creativity lies in an inward experience of love—an experience of creative bisexuality or self-love—Shakespeare realizes now that love's external objects, which exist differentiated in the world, are perhaps more important: "Perfection dwelt in two separate. There was no *master-mistress of my passion*" (*BAR*, 36). These thoughts, which come from his experience as a parent (here he remembers a song from *Cymbeline*), prompt him to hope that Judith will plant marigolds ("Mary-buds") in the garden, the flowers he associates with his mother (*BAR*, 36).

In an extended passage in which she compares Shakespeare with his contemporaries, H.D. continues her meditation on the parent-child relationship as the source of Shakespeare's vision, focusing particularly on the empathy between son and mother. For example, she compares Shakespeare with Ben Jonson, "a Scotsman, traditionally of poor parents," who "wrote plays solely, he said, to gain a livelihood": "His was an old head upon young shoulders, but he never, in any sense of the word, lost that head. We feel in some way, that there was no Mary Arden in his background" (*BAR*, 39). We cannot imagine Jonson "other than preoccupied with the classics." A "bookish child . . . with few books," he "would have given literally, his soul for more Latin and Greek." Not so "the child at Avon," H.D. continues, who "boasted in later life of other exploits. With moon-light on the snow, he sought the forest of Sir Thomas Lucy" (*BAR*, 40).

Further, in this period of religious conflict, court intrigue, and deadly plague, when such writers as Nash, Marlowe, Donne, and Webster were overwhelmed by the terror of death, Shakespeare was sustained by his earliest memories of Stratford's natural beauty, an alternative to the infected world of the court. Lines like Nash's "Come, come the bells do cry; / I am sick, I must die" express his profound despondency (*BAR*, 48). But the "inspirational tenderness" of Shakespeare's "Come away, come away death," or Herrick's "Fair daffodils, we weep to see" transcends the death that they invoke (*BAR*, 66). Shakespeare, Campion, and Herrick did not need "Dante's geometric circle within circle, to show the way from Hell to Paradise" (*BAR*, 67). Unlike Marlowe and Raleigh, Shakespeare left the court and returned home when "infection had completed the devastation," when his "royal throne of kings" was no longer royal: "If Hell was implicit in court and city, there were flowers to sweeten the stench of death. There were flowers to heal and flowers to be *strewn . . . on my black coffin*" (*BAR*, 67).

Similarly, H.D. attributes to Shakespeare's memory of a loving, nurturant childhood a quality of consciousness that liberated him from potentially debilitating ideas about religious hierarchy and sin prevalent in his time. In this era of revolution, of conflict between Catholic and Protestant, between church and state, the "church was plundered by the palace," and the "palace became the background for new ritual," she continues. Yet Shakespeare seldom mentions the Deity, and "sin is a word that is almost absent from [his] vast wealth of word and phrase" (*BAR*, 76). Instead of sin and dread, she bids us think of all the references to love in his work, as in these lines from the beautiful dirge in *Cymbeline*, "All lovers young, all lovers must / Consign to thee and come to dust" (*BAR*, 74). There is no sadness in this song, she asserts, because "we know from the beginning, that the child Fidele is not dead, but will re-emerge as the woman Imogen" (*BAR*, 77).

Such thoughts lead H.D. to the intellectual core of this essay, her discussion of how the tenets of the *School of Love* reached and influenced the poets of the English Renaissance — Shakespeare among them:

> The Inquisition had destroyed the cult of Our Lady, as an embodiment of or rather personification of the Church Spiritual, but the Lady banished from the churches of Provence, found

refuge elsewhere. The Troubadours, wandering along the flowering highways, carried with them the lute that Thomas Wyatt, some three hundred years later, touched for the last time, at the Court of Henry VIII. (*BAR*, 80)

A secularized version of the cult of Our Lady became a courtly convention, she asserts, implicit in Shakespeare's *John* and *Richard II*. In the latter "the golden flower is trodden underfoot, in the hundred years' frightful conflict over roses, white and red" (*BAR*, 81). She argues that England's greatest resource lies not in its official royal panoply but in Shakespeare's version of British history, which he veils in the foreign settings of his later comedies and tragedies. Without the plays of Shakespeare and the poems of his contemporaries, many of whom died violently or in poverty and disgrace, England "in the light of the world's culture, would rank at best as a bulwark of material strength": "It is the weakness, not the strength of England that defies time" (*BAR*, 81).

The troubadours, those poet-heretics in whom love was stronger than reason, had spread "the germs of deadly heresy" to the poets of the Renaissance: they worshiped beauty in the form of a blessed woman who mediated between God and themselves. Forced to renounce the official language of the church, their worship disguised itself in terms of earthly passion. The seeds of this spiritual inheritance, "blown by the tempest" throughout Europe, took root and continued to send out thorny branches: "In France, the popularity of the *Roman de la Rose* was at its height when Richmond proclaims, at the end of *Richard III*, 'We will unite the white rose and the red'" (*BAR*, 84). Suspect always, as they were in Shakespeare's time, when the boundaries of the known world were being extended, descendants of these poet-heretics extended the boundaries of the unknown world out of spiritual necessity. Lesser and greater among them agreed "in the unanimous acceptance of one article of faith," that "the dream was greater than reality" (*BAR*, 84). Out of this single tenet they built a body of literary work as formidable as any religious edifice.

Besides the ubiquity of violent death, this spiritual inheritance from the troubadours was the chief cultural factor that led our "cautious citizen of Stratford to be careful of his last belongings," H.D. speculates (*BAR*, 86). To find the more specific personal factors, she reinterprets the rather spiteful legend that Shakespeare died of a fever contracted after a "merry meeting" with his drinking buddies Michael Drayton and Ben Jonson. According to H.D.'s version of this legend, which lies at the heart of her meditation, Shakespeare's death followed an attempt to recall forgotten images from his childhood, images that led him to reconsider the emotional origin of his tragedies from a perspective that is at once that of a child and that of a parent. While discussing the effect of tragedy with Drayton and Jonson one beautiful spring evening, Shakespeare remembers the "long-purples" that grow beside the Avon and then those other flowers that some called "deadmen's fingers." But his mother never called them that, he knew. What did she call them?

> He couldn't remember what she had called them. He saw the fire reflected in the row of pewter plates. Then he was back in the kitchen and smelt wood-smoke and spice, and the delicate fragrance of the flowers with the too-long green-white stems that he held toward Mary Arden. (*BAR*, 87)

Frustrated by his imperfect memory of his mother's language, and therefore by his lack of access to the hidden world of childhood, Shakespeare turned his thoughts to the alleged "mistakes" in his plays, to other problems of language or structure. Perhaps he should have cut the last act of *Macbeth* after "to-morrow and to-morrow and to-morrow," as his friends implied. Should he have paid more attention to "the unities"? The *Merchant* lacked unity, certainly, and *Juliet* was still worse—two plays, really: "It had started as a romance, but as the Jew spoiled the unity of the *Merchant*, so some alien voice had shouted down the lovers' triumph" (*BAR*, 88). He had tried to "intimidate" that voice by having Mercutio delay the action, and by inserting a long poem that he should have omitted. There was *courtezia* in the play and

155

the *aubade* that Juliet "tried in vain to nullify"; but she could not succeed because fulfilled love was "powerless against the old forces of unconscious longing for ultimate union" (*BAR*, 89).

When she describes the overpowering impulse behind Shakespeare's first tragedy as an "unconscious longing for ultimate union" (*BAR*, 89), H.D. attributes to him an experience of love that is essentially mystical. That is, she refers to an experience in which, as W. H. Auden writes, "the love inspired by a created human being [is] intended to lead the lover towards the love of the uncreated source of all beauty."[8] She describes a variation of what Auden calls the "Vision of Eros," of which classic versions are found in Plato's *Symposium*, Dante's *La Vita Nuova*, and some of Shakespeare's sonnets. H.D. will elaborate further on her own version of this experience in her discussion of "the *gloire*" in *Bid Me to Live*, where she will connect it with the blissful state of being unborn. Here these associations lead her to consider the spiritual qualities of innocence and simplicity that such a vision entails: "All worldly gifts must be offered" (*BAR*, 89). Such qualities are what wandering mendicants like Saint Francis of Assisi, also a descendant of the troubadours, really contributed to western spiritual history. The *Fioretti* of Saint Francis, that ingenuous testament to the saint's sweetness of character that inspired so many Renaissance painters, had "vied with the prophyry and marble of Diocletian" (*BAR*, 89). And the "myths of Capitoline Jupiter," which posited the eternal indestructibility of the Roman Empire, had ceded to the spiritual priorities represented by this vision of ideal love: "The Child was the symbol of ultimate union" (*BAR*, 89).

When Shakespeare's thoughts returned to *Romeo and Juliet*, H.D. imagines, he realized that the tragedy of love he had depicted there was inspired by the thwarting of this unconscious impulse. For despite controversy as to the marriage-age of girls in Renaissance Italy, Juliet had been little more than a child: "In fact, Juliet was two children, though one of them was doomed. Both of them were doomed, finally, for how could one of them live without the other?" (*BAR*, 89). Friar Lawrence, "gathering his herbs," was Saint Francis come to life; but he could only "delay the dissolution by a few days, no longer" (*BAR*, 90). For though Friar Lawrence, Francis, and "the gentle Shakespeare" waited patiently, hoping there would be "new life" when the bridegroom returned from Mantua, events beyond their control took over the play, and "the lovers [were] united, as only they could be, beyond the grave" (*BAR*, 90).

This play became a tragedy instead of a romance, H.D. suggests, because unlike Fidele and Imogen who were not two children, but one, Juliet was herself only: she sought "ultimate fulfillment in another" (*BAR*, 91). But according to the "old creed and canon of the Kathars," the mystical sect that viewed the soul as entrapped by the body, such earthly fulfillment was impossible (*BAR*, 91). When he conceived of a romantic tragedy in which true union could occur only after death, H.D. argues, Shakespeare returned, perhaps unconsciously, to Eleanor of Aquitaine and the *School of Love*.

Then, in a particularly imaginative interpretation of the personal source of Shakespeare's first tragedy (like the library scene in Joyce's *Ulysses*), H.D. pictures Shakespeare ignoring Drayton's concern about "the unities." Instead, he remembers his daughter Judith on the night her twin brother Hamnet died, lying asleep: "They were children, huddled together in Judith's bed. Capulet found only one of them" (*BAR*, 91). Here personal and fictive fuse in the crucible of Shakespeare's memory, as do child and parent:

> Would she ever wake up and if she did, who would tell her about Hamnet? *But that the dread of something after death* — that was later, but it was Juliet's fear. The lines were overlaid with the horror of the old plague. But she would wake up. Or perhaps she would not wake up. Or she would wake up and find Hamnet dead, and refuse to live without him. Michael said it was Queen Eleanor who brought the song to England. . . . Richard's mother. Which Richard? . . . But that was Mary's brother. Mary? He smelt the saffron cakes, as she drew them from the oven. He held the flowers toward her. He had forgotten what she called them — not deadmen's fingers, anyway. (*BAR*, 92)

157

In this train of associations H.D. pictures Shakespeare's empathy with his daughter leading him back to his own primary connection with his mother. Then he realizes that the healing implicit in tragedy does not come only from the unities and the katharsis of Aristotle, as his friends implied. Queen Eleanor and Provence and a ritual that evoked the Church Spiritual also have something to do with it: "It was the bride of God these Kathars . . . worshipped" (*BAR*, 92). But finally, no such intellectually abstract questions ever really roused Shakespeare's deepest response, H.D. suggests, returning to her essay's starting point.

At last, H.D. pictures Shakespeare remembering why he did not take up Francis Bacon's flattering offer of foreign travel, why he preferred instead to return home to New Place for his retirement. Here he recalls Antony's line, "Let Rome in Tiber melt" (*BAR*, 94). As he sits savoring a glass of wine with Jonson and Drayton, he remembers another elegant Venetian goblet filled with wine, on that earlier occasion when the courtier had tried unsuccessfully to press him into the queen's service. When his friends stop talking and prepare to leave, the break of day brings Shakespeare the "darkness of knowledge" (*BAR*, 96). His final thoughts are of his earlier loss, of his guilt, and of the self-serving yet potentially redemptive power of the imagination:

> They were huddled together in Judith's bed, as he remembered them last together, though that was after he left London. That is, he remembered, as he drove his tired horse through Oxford, on the way back. He remembered them huddled together. They were cold. Did he speak harshly to Hamnet? He could not remember. He remembered words out of his own play,
>
> > Or bid me go into a new-made grave
> > And hide me with a dead man in his shroud.
>
> That was the child, Juliet, Judith. He himself had prophesied the whole thing. If he had not written the play, it never would have happened. (*BAR*, 96)

Shakespeare did not go with Bacon on the queen's business, H.D. asserts, because he sensed that "the Queen's business was waiting beyond Oxford" (*BAR*, 96). Conversation with his friends had revived an image of the desire for ultimate union that had motivated his first tragedy: "It was Judith, it was Juliet, it was Queen Eleanor" (*BAR*, 96). Hardly understanding the "impact of what he felt," he had refused Bacon and returned home because of his concern for Judith, whom he felt was as fragile as the glass stem he held between his fingers. Because he wanted to imagine a further work that would memorialize the life of the other of his children, he had held back:

> It was keeping back something. They had all, always kept back something. The metres ran on, recklessly or bound or ruled rather, like Campion's music. But something snapped. It was not the Venetian glass stem. He had come home because he loved Judith. (*BAR*, 96)

Thus H.D. suggests that parental empathy governed the last moments of Shakespeare's life. Just as she had earlier feminized Freud in her tribute to him, she imagines that Shakespeare's vision was shaped by the mysteries of the parent-child relationship.

H.D. had planned to deliver "The Guest" as a seminar at Bryn Mawr, but she was too frail after the war to travel. Recuperating at Kusnacht, she wrote "the *Sword* cycle" of prose fiction, experimental novels that were inspired by messages she believed she had received from the spirits of dead RAF pilots while she was engaged in séances with Arthur Bhaduri. H.D.'s "*Sword* cycle" consists of *The Sword Went Out to Sea* (1947), a detailed account of the occurrence and meaning of these messages; *The White Rose and the Red* (1947–48), which reconstructs the life of Elizabeth Siddall, Dante Gabriel Rossetti's wife, who committed suicide after a stillbirth; *Madrigal* (1949), a *roman à clef* about the World War I years, published as *Bid Me to Live* in 1960; and *The Mystery* (1949–51), which explores intersecting family and Moravian church history. Like H.D.'s tribute to Shakespeare, these novels offer an idiosyncratic, self-referential version of portions of cultural history.

The cycle is a tribute to William Morris, whose tripod-table H.D. inherited from Violet Hunt and used to invoke the messages from the lost airmen. Like Yeats, who called Morris the most lovable of English poets, H.D. considered herself, and the friends she depicts in *Madrigal*, to be the "inheritors" of Morris and the group of writers and painters around him. "That inheritance was of necessity, imperfect," she wrote. "But the perfect inheritance came to me actually and symbolically, with the tripod-table and the messages from the 'warriors of the Viking ship,' as described in the *Sword*" (*Some Notes*, 13).

These messages, H.D. writes, manifested her personal vindication, her conviction that she was "not a God-less child," but rather was "possessed in a serene, protected way, by his idea"—an understanding of the source of creative inspiration that had vital social implications (*Some Notes*, 11). She believed that the dead pilots' instruction to "stop the atom bomb" was directed through her to Lord Howell (Lord Dowding), the British air marshall whose lecture about the possibility of communication "at this time of conflict . . . with Beings of a higher order" she found deeply moving.[9] H.D. invited Howell (Dowding), who had lost a son in the Battle of Britain, to join her spiritualist circle, but when he learned what she was doing, he refused to participate. Warning her that she was going too far, he repudiated the pleas for peace from the lost pilots as "utterly impossible" (*Sword*, I, 21).

H.D. felt that this repudiation and Dowding's remarriage, which evoked her earlier rejection by Aldington, precipitated her emotional breakdown after the war. She regarded her vision of the Viking ship, which carried the airmen lost in World War II, as a counterpart to the tragic sinking of the *Lusitania* in World War I, which she associated with the death of her unborn child. In a later novel, *Magic Mirror* (1956), her heroine Rica (from America) elucidates the dynamics of her distress:

> Yes, I am Julia Ashton, she thought, and I am other names in other stories. There was Rafe Ashton and a child. Actually, the

star went on. Delia Alton wrote this in *Madrigal*. She went through the series, the second War, but actually, they were superimposed on one another, so that the child, the 1000 (and more), those lost in the air, and the Ship that brought them back, as final summons to the Air Marshall, became, in some way, that *Totenschiff* of the *Lusitania* going down, and one child (one still-born child) merged with them or became them and the Air Marshal became their father, finally repudiating them or seeming to repudiate them, as Rafe Ashton (though not so stated in *Madrigal*) destroyed the unborn, the child Amor, when a few days before it was due, he burst in upon Julia of that story, with "don't you realize what this means? Don't you feel anything? *The Lusitania has gone down*. (*MM*, 7)

In the quotation above, Rica's comment "the Star went on" reflects H.D.'s wish to redress that loss in her writing. Thus, though it is about her life in World War I, she considered *Madrigal* part of her World War II cycle—a "romance" that could not have been completed without the first two novels. Though a novel in "historical time," she writes, *Madrigal* contains the "eternal story of the search. The mythical or religious love-story continues through all the writing" (*Some Notes*, 1). Upon her return, February 1923, from the drowned Isis-temple at Philae, Julia (H.D.) knew that "women are individually seeking, as one woman, fragments of the Eternal Lover":

As the Eternal Lover has been scattered or disassociated, so she, in her search for him. In *Madrigal*, she seeks for him in contemporary time, among her associates of England and America, in the years immediately preceding and in the actual years of War I. (*Some Notes*, 3)

In *The Sword Went Out to Sea* H.D. formulated an idiosyncratic myth of romantic quest for this Eternal Lover, whom she conceived of as a "lost companion, [or] twin" (*Sword*, I, 118). From her new perspective, Lord Howell (Dowding) was the most recent in a series of men (beginning with Pound and including Lawrence) who repudi-

161

ated her in life, yet with whom she is reunited in fantasy: "The formula is established. She knows that to keep him, she must loose [*sic*] him" (*Some Notes*, 3). In *The White Rose and the Red* H.D. explored this pattern in an earlier period. She reconstructed the life of Elizabeth Siddall, emphasizing the unusual mental capacities that (finding no better outlet) caused her unhappiness and illness. H.D. implies that Siddall's wish to be an artist in her own right, and her friendship with Morris who was a kindred spirit, ultimately enabled her to transform the horror of her stillbirth into a redemptive dream that she began to record before her death. Unwilling to let her die, H.D. continued the story of Elizabeth Siddall in *The Mystery*. At Norman Pearson's suggestion, she moved her backward into Zinzendorf's eighteenth century (through a historical namesake, Elizabeth de Watteville) and forward to her own time, through her grandmother's maiden name, Elizabeth Seidel. Written just after the *Sword*, *The White Rose and the Red* and *The Mystery* stands on the "right side" of that work, H.D. writes, while *Madrigal* "stands on the left" (*Some Notes*, 15).

Though H.D. wrote most of what is now *Bid Me to Live [A Madrigal]* in 1938, during her divorce from Aldington, she was unable to complete it, to write Julia's concluding letter to Rico (D. H. Lawrence), until after she had received "the answer, the certainty of the War II experience" (*Some Notes*, 19). Based on events of 1917–18, particularly the three months in which H.D. gave refuge to D. H. Lawrence and his wife when they were forced to leave Cornwall, *Bid Me to Live* depicts the impact of war and of prescribed sociosexual roles on the psyche of a woman poet. With a detachment and acuteness different from the occasionally raw, sometimes "hallucinated" style of the early autobiographical fiction, H.D. explores Julia's precarious emotional state in the years after a stillbirth during the war. She documents Julia's relationships both with Rafe (Aldington), her estranged soldier-husband, whose accusations and infidelities make her feel guilty and inadequate, and with Rico (Lawrence), the artist with whom she feels spiritually mated, from whose rejection she unexpectedly benefits. Ultimately, Julia reinvents this rejection, transforming it into acceptance on a mythic plane. It leads her to a new view of creative inspiration, based on insight gained from her trauma in pregnancy, which obviates culturally determined sex roles.

Referring to the "cosmic, crucifying times of history," the novel's hyperbolic opening suggests that the ultramodern marriage of Julia and Rafe does not really have a chance. Though they "might have made a signal success" of it, these "liberated" times "set whirling outmoded romanticism" (*BML*, 7, 8). Robert Herrick's gallant, uncomplicated devotion to his mistress in the novel's epigraph, the madrigal "To Anthea," is bitterly ironic. For the young men of this war generation, "flagrant pawns in a flagrant game," are not *rosenkavaliere* but victims, "victimised and victimising" (*BML*, 7). When Julia falls and cuts her leg in an air raid, she fleetingly remembers the specific occasion of her particular victimization. She had lost a child a short time before, but because of the national mood of wartime stoicism, she had been unable to mourn adequately. Thus, she had turned her grief inward, becoming emotionally numb and sexually frigid in an unconscious attempt to remain connected with the infant: "A door had shuttered it in, shuttering her in, something had died that was going to die. Or because something had died, something would die. But she did not think that" (*BML*, 12).

Though they try to maintain the surface of their marriage, the festering wound caused by this inadequately acknowledged loss alters Julia's relationship with Rafe irrevocably: "They were just where they had been except for a gap in her consciousness, a sort of black hollow, a cave, a pit of blackness; black nebula was not yet concentrated out into clear thought" (*BML*, 12). Furthermore, she had been warned in the nursing home not to have any more babies until after the war; while Rafe, afraid that he would rot to death in a battle-trench, had become "another person"—a hearty "oversexed . . . young officer on leave" (*BML*, 47). With her complicity, he was having an affair with the promiscuous Bella (Dorothy Yorke): "I love you," he tells Julia, "I desire *l'autre*" (*BML*, 56).

Because Rico had been the only one who understood how she felt after the loss of her child, Julia turns to him again for comfort and validation. In "flaming" letters to Corfe Castle, where she had lived while Rafe was in army training, he had encouraged her poems. Now he appears in their embattled London flat, "with his fire-blue eyes in the burnt-out face," like some archaic Greek god of "pure being," in welcome opposition to Rafe's new coarse animality (*BML*, 51). Rico's was an "Orpheus-head," a live head, as opposed to Rafe's "late-Roman head": his letters seemed to hold "the flame and the fire, the burning, the believing" (*BML*, 52). Sensing the destructiveness of her relationship with Rafe, Rico had written "Kick over your tiresome house of life." Yet, what "did he really know about her house of life?" (*BML*, 61).

This explosive connection between Julia and Rico begins to sizzle when Cyril Vane (Cecil Gray) enters the picture. After supper on the first night in Julia's flat, in the presence of his wife Elsa, Rico had paid Julia an enigmatic romantic compliment. With a detached eye for the theatrical quality of this charged situation, H.D. underscores Rico's egocentricity and Julia's ambiguous role in what she sees as a parodic "family romance":

> Last night he had sat there and Elsa had sat in the chair where Julia was now sitting and Julia had sat like a good child between them. "Elsa is there," said Rico, "you are here. Elsa is there at my right hand," he said. "You are here," he said, while Elsa went on placidly hemming the torn edge of an old jumper. Her work-bag spilled homely contents on the floor. . . . Rico said, "You are there for all eternity; our love is written in blood," he said, "for all eternity." But whose love? (*BML*, 78)

Since Rico's love for Elsa is taken for granted, Julia is puzzled by her acquiescent reply, which appears to indicate her interest in a love affair with Vane. Elsa had muttered in her "guttural German," "This will leave me free . . . for Vanio."

A somewhat confused Julia decides to explore the implications of Rico's statement the next day, when Elsa goes shopping and leaves them alone together. When she finds Rico watching her as she stares out the window in the "dim grey afternoon light," Julia feels a "trail, a communication between them" that causes her to cross the room and sit beside him (*BML*, 80). More than an account of a conventional sexual overture, H.D.'s description of the following scene evokes both her imaginative earlier picture of Shakespeare's child Judith tugging at his sleeve and her poignant portrait of her childhood wish, in *The Gift*, to aid her wounded father:

> She sat at his elbow, a child waiting for instruction. Now was the moment to answer his amazing proposal of last night, his "for all eternity." She put out her hand. Her hand touched his sleeve. He shivered, he seemed to move back, move away, like a hurt animal, there was something untamed, even the slight touch of her hand on his sleeve seemed to have annoyed him. Yet, last night sitting there, with Elsa sitting opposite, he had blazed at her; those words had cut blood and lava-trail on this air. . . . Yet only a touch on his arm made him shiver away, hurt, like a hurt jaguar. (*BML*, 81)

In the lines that follow H.D. simultaneously emphasizes Julia's intense childlike empathy and her adult understanding of Rico's vulnerability, her intuition of the tenuous hold he has on his masculinity. Realizing the connection between the preceding night's brazen "open request for this relationship" and his withdrawal from any physical contact with her, Julia withdraws her hand (*BML*, 81).

When he rejects her, Rico unwittingly provides Julia with the "last drop of acid" in this "seething test-tube" (*BML*, 86). The very presence in the room of his "poignant personality," with its clear contradictions, allows her to "take command of a situation that was beyond any definition" (*BML*, 86). Now she interprets Rico's "for all eternity" to refer to their shared destiny as artists. As such they exist not only here in the historical moment but also in "another dimension . . . so starkly separate from this room, this city, this war, that it actually seemed to be taking place somewhere else, so that there was no confusion" (*BML*, 87). Rico's calculated detachment in the face of illness and public ignominy allows Julia to see herself, too, as a "most experimental" element in a wartime crucible. Like his, her sensibility is a product of life "lived to the very extreme edge of possibility" (*BML*, 88). Like him, she is obsessed with the desire to create a "great-mother" and would illumine in her poetry such casual details as Elsa's work-bag spilling its homely contents on the floor. To her now they all seemed like "trained actors" in an updated renaissance tragicomedy: "These exits, these entrances were taken out of her hands" (*BML*, 90).

Yet Julia's relationship with Rico is not without conflict. As Peter Firchow has noted, there is "a textual dialogue" going on in *Bid Me to Live*, with H.D. implicitly addressing herself to both Lawrence and Aldington.[10] H.D.'s choice of Julia as the name for her protagonist almost certainly derives from Lawrence's portrait of her in *Aaron's Rod*, Julia Cunningham. But, as Firchow writes, instead of Lawrence's "vicious, taunting, heavily ironic, half-hysterical Julia," we have here a suffering, bewildered woman, Julia Ashton.[11] Specifically, Julia is dissatisfied with Rico's fierce insistence on maintaining rigidly defined sex roles, a defensive dogmatism that she feels taints his worldview as well as his criticism of her work: "Frederico, for all his acceptance of her verses, had shouted his man-is-man, his woman-is-woman at her; his shrill peacock cry sounded a love cry, death-cry for their generation" (*BML*, 136). Employing an artistic double standard, he had tried to set sexually defined limits to her imaginative range, while he himself was free. He had written:

"Your frozen altars mean something, but I don't like the second half of the Orpheus sequence as well as the first. Stick to the woman speaking. How can you know what Orpheus feels? It's your part to be woman, the woman vibration. Eurydice should be enough. You can't deal with both." (*BML*, 51)

Ironically, when Julia heeds Rico's advice and "sticks to the woman speaking" in other areas of her life, she arrives at an understanding of creative inspiration different from his. As she begins to perceive her connection with Bella, to penetrate her rival's trendy, carefully lacquered exterior, she realizes that though they may appear opposite to the casual observer ("rose-red, rose-white"), Bella's tearful story about an "unauthorized" abortion provides a fundamental experiential link. Julia's new self-awareness permits her to apprehend the source of what Rico termed the "repressed hysteria" beneath Bella's "oriental" quietness, her "toneless" voice, her mindless promiscuity. "Slashed by unauthorized abortionists," Bella, too, had lost a child, that in spite of her poorly expressed reservations, she had "really wanted to have" (*BML*, 100). Confronted by Bella's pathetic plea that Julia stop tyrannizing Rafe's soul, Julia feels "that she was looking at herself in a mirror, another self, another dimension but nevertheless herself" (*BML*, 103).

Similar to the scene between Raymonde Ransome and Ermentrude Solomon in the "Murex" segment of *Palimpsest*, this confrontation between the two women provides one measure of the emotional distance H.D. traveled in the twenty-five years between these novels. As I have written earlier, Raymonde/H.D. felt disassociated from her grief and from ownership of her creativity ("Who fished the murex up?"); therefore, she encoded her feelings in "Greek" poems — composed by a masculinized alter ego. Unlike Raymonde, Julia feels her loss and her connection with Bella directly (and thus with all women). They have been brought together by the war, by men's need to deny their vulnerability in order to face it, and by a pervasive institutionalized ignorance and fear of woman's essential humanity; in other words, by "Rafe's problem": "She and Bella were simply abstractions, were women of the period, were WOMAN of the period, the same one" (*BML*, 103).

Julia's realization that Rico's response to her was like that of a "hurt animal" enables her to understand that his rigidity about sex roles also resulted, in part, from the untenable position of creative men in a society that fashions its ideal of masculinity from an ethos of heroism in war. Acknowledging that Rico's interest in "sex emotion and understanding" had given him extraordinary insight into human relations and institutions, Julia also sees that he is sometimes led to self-falsification by what she terms "man's problem" in such a society. Here H.D. recognizes what David Cavitch has called "the conscious shame of effeminacy" that often led Lawrence to voice "the authoritarian ideals of a fierce masculinity that did not accurately reflect his own deeper nature."[12]

As an alternative to Rico's shrill dogmatism and also to Rafe's desperate sexual exploits, Julia offers a view of creative inspiration that obviates culturally determined sex roles. She argues that though "this vaunted business of experience, of sex emotion and understanding" might (doubtfully) be all right for men, it was clearly dangerous for women because "there was a biological catch" (*BML*, 136). The only real "loophole" for man or woman was to be spiritually bisexual or androgynous, a view of creative inspiration that Lawrence could not accept:

> There was one loophole, one might be an artist. Then the danger met the danger, the woman was man-woman, the man was woman-man. But Frederico, for all his acceptance of her verses, had shouted his man-is-man, his woman-is-woman at her; his shrill peacock-cry sounded a love-cry, death-cry for their generation.
>
> He was willing to die for what he believed, would die probably. But that was his problem. It was a man's problem, the man-artist. There was also the woman, not only the great mother-goddess that he worshipped, but the woman gifted as the man, with the same, with other problems. Each two people, making four people. As she and Rafe had been in the beginning. (*BML*, 136)

In the second half of this passage Julia not only refers to "man's problem" in our society, she also suggests how that problem devolves on woman. Her observation that the pairing of artists results in "four people" alludes to Freud's statement that he was coming to regard every sexual act as "a process in which four persons are involved: the other as a mirror of the self; the other as *other*; and the other as complement, as the other half of the androgyne unity of coupling."[13] In the process of her inner dialogue with Lawrence, Julia considers his ideas about male-female polarity insufficient because they do not encompass the last factor in this equation. Instead, drawing on the insight gained from her trauma in pregnancy, Julia terms the source of creative inspiration "child-consciousness," a mood inspired by love that is yet "sexless, or all sex" (*BML*, 62). Born of her war-torn marriage with Rafe, the "Christ-child of their battered integrity," such a psychic state depended on connection with the blissful realm of the unborn, a realm anterior to the conflict and blight resulting from the internalization of pernicious social norms: "This mood, this realm of consciousness was sexless, or all sex, it was child-consciousness, it was heaven. In heaven, there is neither marriage nor giving in marriage" (*BML*, 62). On the basis of child-consciousness then, Julia asserts that Rico's "man-is-man, woman-is-woman" theory is "false." Though he is right that "it is the intuitive woman-mood that matters," he is wrong and oppressive to insist that she cannot empathize with the predicament of men: "She understood Rafe, really understood that he loved her—that he desired *l'autre*" (*BML*, 62).

Julia delineates the meaning of child-consciousness more fully, distinguishing between it in life and in art, after Rafe has left her for Bella because Bella "wants a child," and after Rico ("correct, even puritanical") has disapproved on moral grounds of her decision to go to Cornwall to live temporarily with Vane. Drawn to Vane "by some law of emotional dynamics," Julia recalls the ludicrous "charade" they had all played in her flat, a game that Rico, playing Jehovah, had orchestrated (*BML*, 107). Elsa was the growling serpent, Rafe and Bella were Adam and Eve, Vane was "the angel at the gate," and she was "the tree of life" (*BML*, 111). She was supposed to dance, Rico had said, "the Tree has got to dance" (*BML*, 112). Therefore, in keeping with their pairing in Rico's game, she would take Vane's gift of respite from the war in Cornwall. Ironically, despite his disapproval, Rico had precipitated this: She and Vane were "the Tree of Life and the Angel at the Gate, *for all eternity*" (*BML*, 120).

Julia continues to reinvent Rico's rejection of her, turning it instead into acceptance on a mythic plane. She remembers her first meeting with Rico at the beginning of the war when she was pregnant.

For a brief moment he had "touched her on the quick," making "that child his child" (*BML*, 140). Recalling his tenderness toward her when the child died, his intuitive understanding of the sorrow in her early flower poems, she renames him Dis of the underworld, "the husband of [herself] Persephone" (*BML*, 140). Alone among her friends, Rico had understood that she herself "projected out in death, was that dead child actually" (*BML*, 141). Julia reinterprets his appearance in her flat, just as she was about to go with Vane to Cornwall, as another such gesture of empathy. Rico was an agent, a "medium" who bid her to live as an artist: "something had been arranged" that something might "come of this, of this war" (*BML*, 142).

At the end of the novel, in a letter from her room in Cornwall, Julia returns Rico's compliment. Continuing her debate with him about creativity, she offers a freshly empathic reading of his work from her new perspective of child-consciousness. After she savors the salt in the invigorating sea air, after her lungs drink in "mist and salt-mist," after she lifts to her nostrils the "new fragrance" from a "ragged new leaf," the novel's tone and imagery alter (*BML*, 143). When Julia gathers indigenous plants from this legendary landscape of "rock and steep cliff" to send to Rico, she feels, like him, that this place is "not England" (BML, 145). With its "Druid sun-circle," the sea coast at Cornwall represents both a land with which she is "perfectly at one" and a vibrantly lucid inner space (*BML*, 145). In the last three chapters of the novel, completed after the *Sword* cycle, the grim irony and the allusions to tragicomic charade prevalent earlier gradually give way to pellucid lyricism (fire burning clear in crystal) and to references to painting. For example, Julia's description of the scenery at Cornwall, which foreshadows the Leuké section of *Helen in Egypt*, is reminiscent of H.D.'s mention in *Tribute to Freud* of Böcklein's *Toteninsel*:

> The scene displayed, the first morning after her arrival, was so clear, so vibrant that it had for a moment struck her as, not so much a dream, but part of the series she had called magic lantern slides, when her memory back in town, had suddenly appre-

hended (not seen but so suddenly apprehended) the separate cypress-tree or ledge of island within her, yet seen projected on the Spanish screen, in too bright colour. So this. (*BML*, 145)

In her room "to work" in Cornwall, Julia feels redeemed — like "Medea of some blessed incarnation, a witch with power, a wise-woman. She was seer, see-er" (*BML*, 146). Though it would take her a long time to get over the trauma of these war years, this room represented "space and time to do it" (*BML*, 157). Here "where the salt seemed visibly to sputter," it was safe to realize that the "sex-union" Rico so vaunted was important "in another mode" (*BML*, 158). As in the game they had played as children — "birds, beasts, fishes" (compare Lawrence's *Birds, Beasts and Flowers*) — her mode was "not beasts so much as birds or fishes" (*BML*, 149). He had been right that she should kick over her house of life in London. This stone cottage in Cornwall could better sustain an embattled man or woman: "man, woman could face wind pounding at a wall, find delight in it" (*BML*, 159). Here she would be both "self-effacing" and "flagrantly ambitious"(*BML*, 162). Knowing that "words themselves held inner words," she would brood over each word "as if to hatch it" (*BML*, 163). Like a blind woman, "reading the texture of incised letters" with her fingers, she would rejoice in the discovery of an "inner light," a reality that "the outer eye" could not grasp. A translator of the palpable into language, she would "coin new words" (*BML*, 163).[14]

When she argues with Rico for the last time, alluding to his views about sex roles only to rejoin that "it's no good," Julia feels relieved of tension. When she asserts that she will continue despite his jeers at the "graven images" in her work, she experiences a final illumination. Through tears of joy she discerns a Devonshire jug near the door of her room, "placed there for an easy drawing lesson," as out of Veronese's "the *Marriage of Cana*, touched with the aura of miracle" (*BML*, 165). Deciding she will not reread what she has written about Rico, she thinks, "I'll get some fresh flowers for that jug" (*BML*, 166).

But the flowers Julia alludes to last in *Bid Me to Live* have no association with the biblical motif celebrated in Veronese's painting.

For the "dead Dutchman," Van Gogh, with whom she compares Rico and by implication also herself, was famous not for his rendering of a sanctified marriage banquet but for his glorious sunflowers and his dynamic landscapes. Julia realizes that, like Van Gogh's wheat fields, the celebration of nature's vitality in Rico's vivid landscapes was all "self-portrait" (*BML*, 167). His dogmatism about sex roles masked a profound repressed connection with the female principle.

Thus, though she vows never to see Rico again because she fears that his criticism might prevent her from writing her own book, Julia attempts first to thank him by explaining such anomalies as his "*gloire-de-Dijon* roses": "how it is that the rose is neither red nor white, but a pale *gloire*" (*BML*, 176). Feeling that perhaps she "caught the *gloire*" from Rico, she must find words to explain it to him. She could be Orpheus as well as Eurydice, because the *gloire* is "both and neither." Unable to share this insight with him in person, she writes:

> The child is the *gloire* before it is born. The circle of the candle on my notebook is the *gloire*, the story isn't born yet.
>
> While I live in the unborn story, I am in the *gloire*. I must keep it alive, myself living with it. (*BML*, 177)

But no merely discursive explanation of the *gloire* really suffices. Julia finally abjures explanation and chooses instead utterance, an intuitive kind of *mutter*ing, to which she feels her ego submit: "No, I am forcing this. I am trying to explain it. When I try to explain, I write the story. The story must write *me*, the story must create *me*. You are right about that great mother, Elsa is like a wheat-field" (*BML*, 181). Referring to his physical resemblance to Van Gogh, to the "luminous phrases" in his first books and in his letters to her, Julia bids Lawrence to write as Van Gogh painted—from an unabashed connection with this female life-force:

> He would draw that magnetism up out of the earth, he did draw it. His wheat stalks are quivering with more than the wind that bends them.
>
> There is peace in the centre of the cyclone. (*BML*, 183)

Julia's comments to Rico about "the *gloire*" in Van Gogh's paintings best show us what she means by child-consciousness—the vision of eros that informs her own work. Referring to Van Gogh's extraordinary cypress trees, she writes that "he would get into the cypress tree": "Because of him alive in the cypress tree, alive in his mother, the cypress would be deified" (*BML*, 182). This is love of a very profound order; it is "worship, such as the Druids felt . . . [Unlike Rico's concept of "the dark god"] there is nothing dark about it" (*BML*, 182). Propelled by movement toward the beloved object, one simultaneously regresses and goes forward, to a place where one is "not yet born" (*BML*, 183). Here H.D.'s original title, *Madrigal*, reveals its inner meaning. As John Walsh has written, H.D. refers not only to the part-song popular in the Renaissance, to the "contrapuntal dance," the "dialogue of contrasts and affinities"; she also refers to the new "matrix" that issues from such juxtapositions.[15] Herself released into the *gloire*, she reminds us of the root of the word *madrigal*, from the Latin *matricalis*, "of the womb," newly sprung from the womb.[16]

H.D.'s lyrical finale to *Bid Me to Live* represents a major departure from her first attempt to fictionalize her thoughts and feelings in Cornwall, the setting of her second pregnancy. More than twenty-five years earlier, in *Fields of Asphodel*, she had depicted the distraught Hermione imagining herself as the passive receptacle of a Druid god in an effort to discharge the conflict she felt between creativity and procreativity. In letters to Bryher written after she had completed *Bid Me to Live*, H.D. implies that her substitution of "an unusual appreciation" of Lawrence for this distortion represented a better resolution. She had omitted Bryher and Perdita from her *roman à clef*, she wrote, because life with them represented a stage beyond the turbulent war years: "a new *Vita* [that] began with the first Greek trip."[17] Thus she implies that her new understanding of the bond between mother and child, acquired in the aftermath of painful maternal loss, had given her a woman-centered theory of the emotional source of creativity with which to counter the restrictive phallocentrism of her male contemporaries.

Finally, the vision of eros at the end of *Bid Me to Live* is particularly poignant, given Lawrence's and Van Gogh's untimely deaths — and the unforgettable trauma in H.D.'s long life. Like the works of these men, H.D.'s art grew out of an extremity of anguish, out of her resistance to inner disintegration; yet art seemed to her, as it did to them, healthful and strengthening.[18] Unlike Lawrence or Van Gogh, however, who did not live long enough to fulfill themselves, H.D. saved herself through her art. I think of Van Gogh's painting *The Starry Night* when I think of the relation between H.D.'s poetry and the crucible of maternal loss that she portrays in *Bid Me to Live*. Van Gogh's dark, flaming cypress tree and his golden stars whirling in purple express a tormented desire for mystical union and release that H.D. also felt and expressed. Transformed in her last poem to encompass the peaceful homecoming of the imagination that she had described in her tribute to Shakespeare, this night vision ultimately became, in her words, a "Star of Day."[19]

6

"Not One Child but Two"

The Counterforces in Helen in Egypt

The poet represses the outright narrative of his life.
He absorbs it along with life itself. The repressed
becomes the poem.

—Louise Bogan

IN HIS FOREWORD to the posthumous publication of "Winter Love," H.D.'s final group of Helen poems, Norman Pearson mentions that she often referred to this lyric sequence as a coda to her epic poem *Helen in Egypt*. Her letters to him in 1959 further indicate that she expressed explicitly there the long-standing emotional conflict that lay behind her epic heroine's "self-seeking quest" (*HD*, Foreword). Recognizing the value of such clarification to her readers, Pearson suggested that "Winter Love" be an actual coda when *Helen in Egypt* was published in 1961, to "show how she herself had always figured in her own poems" (*HD*, Foreword). But after first agreeing, H.D. at the last moment demurred, fearing that publication in the same book of this more "earthbound" poem would "mix the dimensions" and undermine the larger work's mythic stature.[1] She wrote: "We must omit it. Later it could be brought out perhaps with some additions as *Helen After*. The whole atmosphere of the *Coda* somehow contradicts the real psychic or spiritual achievement of *Helen in Egypt*."[2]

Both H.D.'s acknowledgment of the important connection between these works and her wish to delay publication of "Winter Love" on aesthetic grounds are provocative. When she calls the latter a coda in a more "earthbound" key, she suggests that the emotional issues embodied in it are relevant to an understanding of *Helen in Egypt* as well, though her handling of them is more openly self-revealing in "Winter Love." Both poems are love stories of a sort; that is, both make love the vehicle of the heroine's quest for self-knowledge. But though "Winter Love" begins as a potential "romance" between Helen and Odysseus (a former suitor whom she recalls), H.D. gradually shifts the focus away from the romantic interaction, away from sexuality in that context, to a related aspect of erotic experience more fundamental to her sense of self: the meanings and emotions of reproduction. At the end of "Winter Love" Helen nurses a poem-child "Espérance," who represents the ideal product of her (pro)creativity, "the hope of something that will be // the past made perfect."[3] But the operative force in this birth is not Odysseus or any other of Helen's other traditional male lovers; it is the memory of her aged "grandam" who acts as midwife.

Further, Helen differentiates this symbolic child from her historical daughter Hermione, from whom she is separated in conventional myth, on the basis of its having been engendered by "Song . . . the Sun" and therefore impossible to lose ("WL," 105). Rejecting traditional myths that inflate the importance of the father in childbirth and relegate the mother to a passive role, she draws on her memory of having experienced life in her womb to describe this symbolic child's significance for her:

> they said there was a Child in Leuké,
> they said it was the Child, Euphorion,
>
> Achilles' Child, grandam
> or fantasy of Paris and a Child
> or a wild moment that begot a Child,

when long ago, the *Virgo* breasts swelled
under the savage kiss of ravening Odysseus;
yes, yes, grandam, but actually and in reality;

small fists unclosed, small hands fondled me,
and in the inmost dark,
small feet searched foot-hold;
Hermione lived her life and lives in history;
Euphorion, *Espérance*, the infinite bliss,
lives in the hope of something that will be,

the past made perfect;
this is the tangible
this is reality. ("WL," 112)

However, "Winter Love" does not end on this note of transcendent ecstasy. In an inspired series of ironic turns, H.D. depicts Helen's act of nursing this poem-child as fraught with displaced feelings of ambivalence that she is unable to escape. "I die in agony whether I give or do not give" ("WL," 117), Helen complains, describing her charged experience of creative release. In the final strophes of "Winter Love" Helen is dragged back to life involuntarily by the soft touch of the poem-child that has been thrust upon her by the "cruel *Sage Femme*" whom she alternatively recognizes is "wiser than all the regents of God's throne" ("WL," 117). Finally, she acquiesces to her own sacrifice in lines that enigmatically suggest gnosis and regeneration at another level of existence:

Come, come, O *Espérance*

Espérance, O golden bee,
take life afresh and if you must
so slay me. ("WL," 117)

The ending of "Winter Love" is inspired because it draws on a deep, subliminal reserve of emotion and moral response that has been virtually unexpressed before in poetry. Even in this poem of self-empowerment, Helen's experience of creativity is fraught with feelings she associates with procreation, with psychological pain connected with the social institution of motherhood, which has reinforced a division of labor based on reproductive sex differences. By using the childbirth metaphor in a way that exposes the cultural inequity it masks, H.D. explores the role of language in the internalization of damaging sex-role stereotypes.

Part of H.D.'s elaboration of the childbirth metaphor in "Winter Love" involves a charged use of the word *Child* (which she often capitalizes). In the first passage quoted above the word refers to more than what it customarily denotes, the human product of a conventional coupling (in this case Helen's daughter Hermione); it also refers to the psychic state, alternately "bliss" or "hope," which the speaker associates with her created poem and which she equates with a revised valuation of woman's role in the reproductive process. In this context the word *Child* asks us to question our assumptions about the power structure in the patriarchal family: it functions as a constitutive symbol through which the poet reorders the world.[4]

Whether the coda is published in the same volume as *Helen in Egypt* or not, it calls into question the design and motives of the longer poem. The very fact that H.D. returned to the Helen theme suggests that the emotional issues raised by the epic were not fully resolved and therefore remained compelling. How does the coda illuminate the submerged themes and counterforces in the epic that preceded it? Since "Winter Love" eloquently links sexuality with reproduction, is there an implied link in *Helen in Egypt* as well? How does the symbol of the child adumbrate this linkage in the longer poem? These are questions I explore in this chapter.

Helen in Egypt is about the psychological effects of patriarchy and war. H.D. employs the constellation of myths surrounding Helen of Troy—that irresistible avatar of female beauty who became the despised symbol of the Trojan War—to explore the female psyche's response to a history of male domination. She takes her moral direction from Stesichorus and Euripides, post-Homeric poets who were "restored to sight" after they recanted their earlier indictment of Helen and exculpated her in their late work: she, too, is writing a "pallinode" — a "defence, explanation or apology."[5] Just as Euripides had once connected the fall of the Athenian empire with the disparagement of women, so H.D. was convinced that the negative values associated with archetypal woman, with Helen, must be reassessed in order to end modern civilization's recent history of warfare. Having survived two world wars only to find herself in an age of potential nuclear holocaust, she wrote that her artistic mission was one of reclamation: "I am living this Eleusinian cycle" (*CF*, 70).

Because H.D. thought that society could not be reconstructed "from outside," but that first one must "try to grapple with the forces inside," *Helen in Egypt* is both a meditation on the causes of social violence and an intricate psychodrama (*Sword*, I, 140). In it H.D. retells the story of Helen of Troy from Helen's perspective. In the Homeric tradition Helen's beauty is the cause and symbol of a terrible war: her seduction by Paris is the reason Achilles leads the Greek army to Troy. Homer does not clarify whether she leaves voluntarily or whether she is abducted (that is, whether she is guilty or innocent), but later she becomes the stock promiscuous woman who is vilified for provoking the rape that leads the Greeks to battle and death.[6] *Helen in Egypt* questions this justification of rape and incursion implicit in traditional mythology by substituting a meditative return to female primacy. As Albert Gelpi has written, the three important men in the poem (Achilles, Paris, and Theseus) represent "areas of [her] psychological experience of the masculine"; Helen's is the "subsuming consciousness."[7] Further, to the extent that she achieves spiritual regeneration, it is by recovering the meaning of a repressed female inner object. As in the ancient mysteries at Eleusis, where initiates participated in the mourning mother's "finding again" of her lost daughter who had given birth among the fires of Hades, Helen descends into the darkness in order to redirect her life. For her the Trojan War becomes an initiation ritual.

H.D. begins with an allusion to Euripides and Stesichorus. Helen, we are told, did not go to Troy; she was "transposed or

179

translated from Greece into Egypt. Helen of Troy was a phantom. . . . The Greeks and the Trojans alike fought for an illusion" (*HE*, 1). But unlike the revisions of her ancient predecessors, whose exculpations posit an alternative Helen who is faithful to Menelaus but asexual, H.D.'s poem has a more radical objective. For H.D.'s alternative Helen is not the chaste wife whom we find in Euripides' play, nor is she a harlot. She is a grief-stricken ghost, traumatized and pathetic, who has met Achilles after death in a mysterious romantic encounter that she does not understand. By making Helen's consciousness her subject, H.D. shows the painful self-division, the loss of a part of the soul, caused by woman's internalization of culture's traditional ambivalence toward her sexuality; and she dramatizes the obsessive convolutions of the slow process of recovery. As Horace Gregory has written: "The conflicts of Helen's guilt are the springs of tension throughout the poem."[8]

In its assumptions about beauty, its structure, and its characterizations, *Helen in Egypt* transvalues the main tenets of the epic tradition. In the Homeric epic the heroic code concerned men alone. That is, the attainment of glory (*areté*) through valorous death in battle was a male prerogative, a male version of essential reality, of the means "to take possession of the beautiful."[9] Reflecting the priorities of a historical age of migration and conquest, the heroic ideal exalted the warrior's courageous behavior in battle as the moment of his potential preeminence, his *aristeia*. Therefore, though it offers a critique of this value system, as Charles Beye has written, "the central fact of *The Iliad* is battle and war; Achilles functions within and through it."[10] H.D. updates this view of heroism by valorizing the apparent motionlessness of dream, the "timeless time" during which significant inner conflicts are resolved. Giving us Helen's perspective after the devastation of war, she emphasizes the moment of mourning, traditionally a woman's moment. Though, like *The Iliad*, her poem considers "Achilles' wrath," her perspective of psychological postmortem, a survivor's consciousness, permits her to challenge the exigencies of fighting men by asserting the equal value of a woman's solitary subjectivity. Ironically, she offers a modicum of hope by implying the ghostliness of both: "Do not despair, the hosts / surging beneath the Walls, / (no more than I) are ghosts" (*HE*, 1).

In mode also, *Helen in Egypt* is first of all a "pallinode," a "defence, explanation or apology," literally a "song against" the tradition (*HE*, 1). Like *The Odyssey*, which introduced the theme of quest in western literature, it emphasizes human responsibility more than heroic fatalism.[11] But unlike this Homeric precursor, in which the wandering hero's return culminates in a fight for repossession of his physical property, the goal of Helen's quest is psychological hegemony. Composed of a precisely organized series of semidramatic lyrics (mostly monologues), each introduced by a passage of narrative prose, *Helen in Egypt* is constructed like rippling water—with reactive psychological responses to a single emotional issue providing the means of progression. As Susan Friedman has written, H.D. adapts the reflective, associational methods of psychoanalysis and the modernist novel of consciousness to epic form.[12]

H.D.'s characterizations of Helen and Achilles also deliberately challenge the traditional heroic formulae. This Helen is "not to be recognized by earthly splendour," she states near the beginning, "nor this Achilles by accoutrements of valour" (*HE*, 7). Rather, she is "alone, bereft" and he is "shipwrecked" (*HE*, 7). Their encounter has been conditioned by the "lost legions" and "the sea-enchantment in his eyes / of. Thetis, his sea-mother" (*HE*, 7). Though historically Achilles was Achaean, a member of the race that gave the "warrior-cult" to Sparta, in Egypt after death "values are reversed" (*HE*, 9). No longer the invincible "hero-god," here his Achilles heel identifies him as the "new Mortal" and his wound is the token of their mutuality: "This was the token, his mortality, / immortality and victory / were dissolved" (*HE*, 9). Similarly, Helen will not use her divine inheritance in the service of forgetfulness and superficial solace, as she did in *The Odyssey* when she drugged Menelaos' wine with a painkiller.[13] Transposed to Egypt, she will employ her powers to achieve "everlasting memory" in order to understand the meaning of the historical "anathema or curse" (*HE*, 3). She equates this feat of memory, during which she must confront the damage done by a misogynist patriarchal tradition, with the heroism of the Greek sea journey.

Helen in Egypt is divided into three main sections that correspond to the stages of Helen's developing consciousness: "Pallinode," in which Helen remembers her central emotional dilemma and intuits its cause; "Leuké," in which she recalls her "first rebellion" and contacts a guide to help her understand her shattered integrity; and "Eidolon," in which she identifies and gives voice to an image of female devaluation that has held her in its grip. Secluded in the "Amen-temple," where "space and leisure" distance her from the battle surging beneath the Trojan ramparts, Helen has divine sanction to reconstruct the meaning of the debacle. She forgives the proponents of the Homeric warrior ethos who cast her in the role of "anathema or curse," after asserting that, instead of ruin, her suffering has brought reconciliation with the "new Mortal," Achilles, and a deeper dimension of consciousness conditioned by loss.

This climactic event that occurs at the outset, the explosive meeting between Helen and Achilles after the war on a desolate beach in Egypt, provides a hieroglyph of her condition and poses the poem's central problem. For though Helen implies that it is ultimately beneficent, a union between soul mates that produces a "Star in the night" of illumination, H.D. first describes the encounter as an attack that would strangle Helen and efface her identity. The meeting is highly "romantic" in the popular sense; without H.D.'s restraint and skill it would be indistinguishable from the stuff of soft pornography. Helen remembers love at first sight, a flame kindled, a few words exchanged, a misunderstanding. Then, her focus narrowing, she recalls Achilles' brutality, a debilitating loss of consciousness, and finally, rhapsodically, memory and an illumination that suggests conception and divine birth. Instrumental in her dramatic shift of perspective has been an appeal for protection to Thetis, the "sea-mother":

> O Thetis, O sea-mother
> I prayed, as he clutched my throat

with his fingers' remorseless steel
let me go out, let me forget
let me be lost . . . .

O Thetis, O sea-mother, I prayed under his cloak,
let me remember, let me remember,
forever, this Star in the night. (*HE*, 17)

By beginning with rape, the most repugnant element of the
Helen tradition, and then by implying that Helen's meditation is a
kind of psychological accommodation of it (even a transformation),
H.D. raises important questions about the moral center of her poem.
To what extent is she, the poet, identified with her heroine? Does she
endorse Helen's reaction? Does the poem oppose the patriarchal
social arrangement in which rape is an extreme form of men's pervasive
power over women, or does it condone the status quo? How does
Thetis, Achilles' mother, contribute to the shift in perspective that
Helen experiences after her momentary obliteration (the lacuna in
consciousness indicated with seven periods in the text)? H.D.'s remark
about the Eleusinian tenor of her life and her revision of the myth of
Demeter and Persephone in the poem suggest an approach to these
questions.

As a writer-daughter (Helen was her mother's name), H.D.
regarded the exposition of woman's suffering and loss in patriarchal
culture in an intensely personal way. Comments in her journals and
letters indicate that she considered writing this text as a means of self-
discovery involving a process of vicarious introspection. In her words:
"I had found myself. I had found my alter-ego or my double — and that
my mother's name was Helen has no doubt something to do with it"
(*CF*, 17). That her mother was her muse was an exhilarating
experience for H.D. (The only girl among five boys, as a child she had
felt chagrined that her mother preferred one of her brothers, while she
was her father's favorite. As I have written earlier, her early fiction
depicts the pain of feeling unmothered.) But this close identification
with her mother may have also presented a problem. Although she
could invest her heroine Helen with her own values and perspective,

on one hand, fear of betrayal may have inhibited her, on the other, making the poem conform to what she imagined her mother, a more conventional woman, would feel and wish. In *Helen in Egypt*, Helen's own mother, Leda, is not mentioned; rather, Thetis, Achilles' mother, the mother who fosters the patriarchy, is chosen to replicate the poet's conflicted relation to Helen Doolittle and the cycle of self-abnegation and sacrifice she represented. Anticipating Jessica Benjamin's recent analysis of how domination is anchored in the hearts of the dominated under patriarchal gender arrangements, H.D. thus simultaneously dramatizes and critiques the psychological mechanism through which submission to male power allows a woman to reenact her early identificatory relationship with her mother, to replicate the maternal attitude itself. [14]

Though they appear totally different, Helen's two responses to Achilles' attack (each orchestrated by an appeal to Thetis) dramatize the alternatives of losing herself or glorifying the unpleasant facts of her experience, a flip-flop in which the context changes from forgetting to remembering but the structuring factor remains the same: masochistic submission to male power. This disclaimed emotional issue, which H.D. conveys with a gap in the text, sets up a powerful thematic counterforce. Helen attempts to accommodate male brutality, not because H.D. condones it, but because she finds it a disturbing element of personal as well as historical reality that she wishes to control imaginatively. The obsessive convolutions of the poem, the frequent tentative questions and admissions of quandaries, eloquently document the difficulty she experiences. In this way H.D. embeds a narrative of problematic female affiliation into the romance of Helen and Achilles, which enriches its meaning.

Further, H.D.'s revision of the myth of Demeter and Persephone more explicitly counters Helen's tendency toward capitulation. In a step toward freeing female sexuality from the strictures of the institutions of marriage and motherhood (and herself from identification with her mother's role), she revises the imaginative import of the birth of a divine child that is central to this myth. As Susan Gubar has noted, H.D. is part of a tradition of women writers, such as Mary Shelley and Elizabeth Barrett Browning, who interpret Persephone's marriage of death as a brutally sexist explanation of the seasonal death of nature, whereby "male domination in sexual relationships becomes a synecdoche for a culture based on acquisition and brutality."[15] To such writers, the tragedy of the separation of mother and maiden dramatized in this myth, which results in woman's debilitating self-division, is not canceled out by the birth of a divine son, as the myth implies.

Like these women writers, H.D. dismisses the palliative effect of the birth of a divine son in *Helen in Egypt*. She alludes to the story of Helen's marriage to Achilles and the birth of a son Euphorion once in the prose introduction to "Leuké," only to underscore its inadequacy by then depicting something else in the poetry. Recognizing that, like Persephone's marriage of death, the sentimental Leuké story masked patriarchy's channeling of women's procreative power to serve its own interests, she dramatizes the emotional issues behind Helen's self-division instead. On Leuké Helen reconsiders the meaning of her seduction by Paris. Then, with Theseus' help, she recovers an earlier heroic self who acknowledges the pain of identification with, as well as estrangement from, her mother. Here she experiences a moment of self-confrontation that foreshadows her later realization, in "Eidolon," that "the promised Euphorion is not one child but two," a girl as well as a boy (*HE*, 288). Thus (anticipating "Winter Love"), H.D. calls our attention to the need for a new concept of renewal based on an expanded consciousness of the strength and well-being of both sexes.

As in *Bid Me to Live*, where she used the term *child-consciousness* to describe the source of her creativity, in *Helen in Egypt* H.D. uses the gender-free word *child* to signal this concept of renewal. In the first section of the poem (and in flashbacks later), it refers to a disturbance in self-concept caused by internalized sex-role stereotypes. In the second section, as Helen gains insight, it designates the inherent modifiability of psychic reality. Finally, in the third, it comes to represent an area of future psychological experience in which woman's procreative power is not turned against herself, a blissful psychic state where the distortions of sex roles are vitiated.

Helen gradually recovers her subjectivity by becoming increasingly aware of her relationship with Thetis. In "Pallinode," the first section, H.D. identifies Thetis as the unconscious force behind the charged meeting of Helen and Achilles. For though Helen presents herself ironically as a "woman of pleasure" when Achilles builds her a fire on the beach, she is really a grieving mother who is "stricken, forsaken" (*HE*, 12, 5). Unfortunately, however, her historical role as a sexual object, a victim of male autocracy, has caused her to doubt the validity of her own maternal loss. Denying the ignominy of "Helen on the ramparts," she also questions the reality of her existence in Egypt: "Are they both ghosts?" (*HE*, 15). Having been divided from her home and family once and then accused of illicit sexuality, she fears that this new attraction may result in further damage to her integrity and in additional blame. Therefore, she invokes the "protective mother goddess," a traditional Demeter figure who represents female experience as a source of virtue, to protect her from acrimony and guilt: "*let me love him, as Thetis, his mother*" (*HE*, 14).

Her invocation of the mother goddess does not protect her, however. For though Paris's arrow has released Achilles from the "iron casement" of heroic invincibility to a new capacity for feeling, his vulnerability has a negative dimension. Having just arrived from the carnage of the Trojan battlefield, he is startled when a vulture swoops toward them, interpreting this ancient Egyptian symbol of woman as the Great Mother in its negative aspect as "a carrion creature" that feeds on the dead (*HE*, 17). Grief for his "lost legions," a generation of young men who perished because of the violence of a mass delusion, becomes rage at Helen, whom he perceives (according to tradition) as the cause: "you stole the chosen, the flower / of all-time, of all-history, / my children, my legions" (*HE*, 17). The "burning ember" that flames between them is at once the funeral pyre of the Greek heroes and the spark of his anger.

Helen's parallel refusal to forget this "unnumbered host" marks the beginning of insight. In lines that evoke the passage in *Magic Mirror* (quoted earlier), where H.D. equates the dead RAF pilots with her stillborn child, the Greek heroes become as a single child to

Helen: "They are not many, but one, / enfolded in sleep" (*HE*, 21). This sense of a maternal relation to them enables Helen to comprehend a deeper reason for Achilles' hostility. For simply because he is a man (whose role in the process of procreation is limited to intercourse), the positive dimension of the Great Mother, woman's capacity to bear and foster new life, is also alienating. Thus Helen attributes Achilles' hostility to sexual jealousy produced by his fear that the "spread of wings," a symbol of procreative power, is hers, not his:

> I read the writing when he seized my throat,
>
> this was his anger,
> they were mine, not his
> the unnumbered host. (*HE*, 25)

To counter Achilles' hostile reaction to the vulture (a response to women shared by "the whole powerful war faction"), Helen claims to have become what his anger made her: "Isis, forever with that Child, / the Hawk Horus" (*HE*, 23).

By identifying Helen with the Egyptian Great Mother, H.D. is able to connect the Greek warrior ethos that has victimized her heroine with the patriarchal family drama. She sees that just as the masculine sex role requires the son to repress connection with his mother in a patriarchy, so the warrior must devalue eros and the woman's world to survive on the battlefield. The result is an unacknowledged inner schism that manifests itself violently. Like Osiris, who was "torn asunder" by his brother Typhon in Egyptian resurrection myth, Achilles has lost "his very self," the child in him, by his commitment to "chariot-wheels, / the clang of metal / and the glint of steel" (*HE*, 26, 27). As the Egyptian vulture Isis devoured her dead brother-consort Osiris, reincarnated him in her own body, and then gave him rebirth as the child Horus, so Helen will "gain spiritual recognition and ascendancy" over the whirlwind Typhon, with the aid of the "unnumbered host" (*HE*, 28).

In the process of understanding Achilles' attack on Helen, and in order to reclaim him, H.D. exposes the brutal inner sacrifice implicit in masculine psychosexual development in a patriarchy committed to the necessity of war. Her poem implies a critique of the social foundation of oedipal theory: socialization of the male child is a destructive act that results in estrangement from the mother and perpetual sexual antagonism. Her criticism of this system takes the form of an apostrophe to the essential "Child" within Achilles, the victim of a socialization process that links adult masculinity with the machismo of the warrior and devalues the woman's world. Implying a related distortion in Helen's development when she alludes to Persephone's experience of childbirth in Hades, H.D. would reclaim a condition of psychic wholeness for each in order to achieve personal and social renewal:

> O Child, must it be forever,
> that your father destroys you,
> that you may find your father?
>
> O Child, must the golden-feather
> be forever forged by the Spirit,
> released in the fury of war?
>
> O Child, must you seek your mother
> while your father forever
> attacks her in jealousy,
>
> "I begot them in death, they are mine";
> must death rule life?
> must the lily fade in the dark?
>
> . . . .
> who but Helen of Troy
>
> and Achilles, shipwrecked and lost,
> dare claim you and know the Sun,
> hidden behind the sun of our visible day? (*HE*, 28, 29)

When H.D. considers the spiritual price of Achilles' socialization as a warrior, she begins to regard his anger at Helen as a defense mechanism. Seeing herself on the walls from the perspective of his battle fatigue, Helen realizes that, at least half-consciously, he had died willingly at Troy. For Achilles had come to distrust the "purely masculine 'iron-ring'" with its constant jockeying for power and position; she had seemed like a "mist / or a fountain of water" to a man dying of thirst (*HE*, 55, 48). When the fatal arrow pierced his heel while he was distracted by her glance, Greek victory had already seemed a "small matter" (*HE*, 55). Dimly remembering a more primitive "Power" that he seemed to have lost, he found himself transported to the "ledge of a desolate beach" after death (*HE*, 59). The "evil words" he had spoken to her earlier were a product of inner conflict. Like her he was haunted by the question "how are Helen in Egypt / and Helen upon the ramparts / together yet separate?" (*HE*, 63). Like her, he was dedicated to the "thought of reconstruction" (*HE*, 63).

H.D.'s criticism of Achilles' socialization leads to potentially liberating insight into the causes of Helen's victimization as well. As Helen continues to decipher the mysterious "pictures" on the temple wall, she sees that in order to survive in a patriarchy, *both* she and Achilles have had to falsify themselves. Helen, too, had been "crowned with the helm of defence"—in that her "defencelessness" had masked suppressed rage (*HE*, 66). Delving back into family history to counter the "overwhelming fact" of her meeting with Achilles, she finds it helpful to visualize her fate "in terms of that of her twin-sister" Clytemnestra (*HE*, 68, 74). By reconnecting herself and her abandoned daughter Hermione with Clytemnestra, who had murdered her husband to revenge the sacrifice of her daughter Iphigeneia, Helen recovers her anger at the expendability of women's lives in a patriarchy. Helen now acknowledges that Clytemnestra is a split-off part of herself; for Clytemnestra could never forget "the glint of steel at the throat / of her child on the altar" nor the deceptive bridal pledge that led to death (*HE*, 73). Implying that her desertion of Menelaus was comparable to her sister's murder of Agamemnon, she wonders if they "share Nemesis together" (*HE*, 75).

Although Helen's admiration of Clytemnestra's bravery on behalf of Iphigeneia almost enables her to transcend the war and its consequences, she does not succeed. Helen compares her sister to an angry swan fighting for her cygnet, who achieves a divinity that makes her "stronger than all the host" (*HE*, 76). But because this line of thought threatens to preclude a conciliatory solution to the problem of Achilles' attack, H.D. does not allow her to pursue it. Instead, she uses typographical devices (ellipsis, space, a solid line) to convey the mechanism of denial operative in this first phase of her heroine's memory:

> surely, she must forget,
> she must forget the past,
> and I must forget Achilles . . .
>
> ———————————
>
> . . . but never the ember
> born of his strange attack,
> never his anger,
>
> never the fire,
> never the brazier,
> never the Star in the night. (*HE*, 77)

Because it ultimately stirs up guilt, Helen's recollection of Clytemnestra's angry revenge does not liberate her.

At the end of the poem's first section H.D. brings Helen into "complete harmony" with the "Image or Eidolon of Thetis," ironically suggesting the reason for her heroine's block. Appearing as a choric inner voice, Thetis's claim, that "Phoenix, the symbol of resurrection has vanquished indecision and doubt," seems magical and without emotional coherence (*HE*, 93). In interpreting Thetis's appearance thus, I differ with Susan Friedman and Albert Gelpi, both of whom find her a positive influence on Helen here. According to Friedman, Thetis's voice speaks in the "Pallinode" to "help Helen define the nature of women's power more precisely," as an agency that is not "violent or aggressive," but rather "invisible, tangible and omniscient."[16] Thetis does advise that Helen cease to grieve for Clytemnestra because the latter "struck with her mind, / with the Will-to-Power," a course of action that, by imitating the masculine model, simply repeated her "husband's folly" (*HE*, 97). But what she proffers instead is an equally inadequate solution to the emotional issues raised. According to Thetis, Helen should employ a woman's "wiles" as weapons; she should "fight by stealth // with invisible gear," seek "not to know too much," nor strive to annul "the decree of the Absolute" that she be united with Achilles while her sister is "called to another star" (*HE*, 97, 105, 102). Thus, though her admonition to "let rapture summon" seems life enhancing (*HE*, 108), the conventional masochism implicit in her advice leads the poet to a deeper level of meditation.

In the second section of the poem H.D. makes more explicit her submerged concern with how the myth of Demeter and Persephone reinforces male power and cultural hegemony. Having been directed to "come home" by Thetis, Helen finds herself on Leuké, the paradisiacal white island where traditionally "Achilles is said to have married Helen who bore him a son Euphorion" (*HE*, 109). But in H.D.'s poem Leuké is a liminal psychic space where remembrance takes the place of dream. No such romanticized birth takes place here. Instead, Helen reconstructs the Greek past, retelling the early story of love and discord that surfaces when she ceases to suppress the memory of Paris. When she considers the "old dilemma" of who caused the war, herself or Paris, she recalls that neither of them was at fault. Thetis, Achilles' mother, a goddess who married a mortal, had unintentionally precipitated the war when she neglected to invite Eris (Discord) to her wedding banquet. Paris was simply an "agent, medium or intermediary of Love and of Troy's great patron, Apollo, the god of Song" (*HE*, 112).

On the island of Leuké the Egyptian temple where Helen wandered in a partial trance in the first stage of her meditation is replaced by a "finite image" (*HE*, 114). A "delicate sea-shell" given to her by Thetis tells an enigmatic tale of moral equivalency between the fall of the Greek heroes at Troy and her own fate: "the thousand, thousand Greeks / fallen before the Walls / were as one soul, one pearl" (*HE*, 114). For with Helen's memory of her "first rebellion," her seduction by Paris, comes the bitter realization that she has learned to associate her sexual feelings with an evil, with death—a tragic by-product of the threat of rape on a young girl's life. But instead of blaming the patriarchy for permitting this curtailment of her liberty, she has turned her anger inward into guilt.

At first Thetis is again the unconscious force behind Helen's self-sabotage. When Helen remembers the springtime enchantment she associates with Paris (laughter, roses, the possibility of love without rancor, escape from Achilles), she experiences anxiety about the approval of the sea-goddess. This is the island of Thetis, who had called her from Egypt to a Greek marriage with Achilles. Therefore, having found Paris instead, Helen wonders, "will she champion? / will she reject me?" (*HE*, 117). Because male experience has defined reality (the only mother in the poem is a mother who perpetuates the patriarchy), Helen has been conditioned to see herself as men see her and cannot imagine a direct answer. As in "Pallinode" where she identified with Achilles to apprehend her own rage, in "Leuké" she gains access to her depression by seeing her degradation and death through Paris's eyes.

Though he also remembers a vibrant earlier Helen, the image that haunts Paris is one he saw before his death—Helen vilified as an adultress, limping and hesitant at the stair-head, preparing to leap from the burning towers of Troy. Helen died when the walls fell, Paris asserts. The stories told by the harpers, that she was "rapt away by Hermes, at Zeus' command," that she met Achilles, are mere compensatory lies (*HE*, 129): "I am the first in all history / to say, she died, died, died / when the Walls fell" (*HE*, 131). Therefore, Paris would convince Helen that Achilles was never her lover; he offers a partial emotional truth that takes her further inward to Theseus.

Thetis changes from being the unconscious force behind Helen's self-sabotage to the consciously apprehended means of her psychological recovery after this restorative meeting. Although in traditional myth Theseus is the Athenian king who stole Helen from Sparta when she was a child (as Dis stole Persephone), H.D. makes him an enlightened father-analyst (another fantasy version of Freud) who has long since resolved his own insecurities. Helen arrives in his presence "baffled, buffeted and very tired," in need of psychic "readjustment" (*HE*, 153). After reassuring her that he will not "immolate" her on an altar of unduly sacrosanct beliefs, Theseus offers comfort, warmth, and the possibility of re-creating her own myth. Having noticed that her feet are wounded by ill-fitting huntsman's boots (an allusion to the virgin goddess Artemis), he compares her to the lost Persephone:

> This is Athens, or was or will be;
> do not fear, I will not immolate you
> on an altar; all myth, the one reality
>
> dwells here; take this low chair;
> so seated you are Demeter;
> it was her daughter, your sister
>
> that lost me Helena; all, all the flowers
> of Enna are in your tears;
> why do you weep Helen?
>
> what cruel path have you trod?
> these heavy thongs,
> let me unclasp them;
>
> did you too seek Persephone's
> drear icy way to Death? (*HE*, 151)

Helen's interaction with Theseus recapitulates the outcome of H.D.'s analysis with Freud: she integrates achievement with nurturance by identifying with her mother while rejecting the latter's devalued role. Like the mage Kaspar, who validated Mary's vision of female godhead in "The Flowering of the Rod," Theseus urges Helen to compensate for a "too intense primary experience" by returning to "the Shell, your mother, Leda, Thetis, or Cytheraea" (*HE*, 162, 165). In order to help Helen to "reintegrate," he tells the story of his own "primeval terror" (*HE*, 167). In retrospect, after Theseus acknowledged the private source of his monster, the Minotaur proved to be merely "an idle fancy, / a dream, a Centaur, / hallucination of infancy" (*HE*, 168). Similarly, he invites Helen to recall "the shock of the iron-ram, / the break in the Walls, / the flaming Towers" (images that suggest sexual violation) in order to progress beyond them (*HE*, 170). H.D. dramatizes the dynamics of the therapeutic process, specifically the operation and analysis of layers of resistance, in order to uncover Helen's hidden emotional issues. When Helen, "half in a trance," refuses to forget Achilles, Theseus deliberately steps outside of her stream of consciousness to confront her (*HE*, 172). Recognizing anxiety and self-denial behind her overwrought refusal to forget, he recalls stories of other women who were "sacrificed" to Achilles, advising Helen to "leave him with the asphodels" in favor of "life here with Paris" (*HE*, 173). At first Helen disavows his advice, claiming that she has been drawn to Athens by an emotion other than sorrow. But her disavowal disguises an affirmation of the essential issue that he has isolated. As she lies "quietly as the snow," she recovers a heroic voice buried deep within, "the voice of Helen of Sparta," which admits to desiring a bond with Achilles, a connection with the masculine, different from that of self-abnegating love (*HE*, 176). This heroic voice declares that "the loves of Achilles, the loves of Helen of Troy seem ephemeral and unimportant beside their passionate devotion and dedication to " 'the rage of the sea, the thunder of battle, shouting and the Walls' " (*HE*, 176). Then, as if confused by this evidence of her own aggression, she asks diffidently: "Do I love War? / is this Helena?" (*HE*, 177).

As if to comply with her discomfort, the "heroic voice" speaks again for Helen, this time in a more conventional feminine mode that she thinks will better please Thetis: "What does she want, this Cypris" (*HE*, 178). In a "song rather than a challenge," the Spartan Helen offers a way in which to reconcile Achilles and Paris, to balance love and death, by exchanging the values they represent and blurring the distinction between them (*HE*, 178). To avoid owning her own anger at being a disenfranchised daughter in a patriarchy where identification with the mother is problematic, Helen construes an oedipal relation between Paris and Achilles: she makes the slayer (Paris) the son of the slain (Achilles): "he, the fire-brand, was born of the Star, / engendered under the cloak / of the new mortal Achilles"

(*HE*, 185). But because this solution, too, is based on self-denial, the conflict is raised to a new pitch, and she turns to Theseus for further clarification.

With Theseus' assistance Helen gains insights that open the resolution of the poem. Recognizing that Helen risks losing herself by adhering too rigidly to patriarchal myths of regeneration associated with Achilles, Theseus recalls her from "her abstraction, her Absolute, the 'Star in the Night' " (*HE*, 187). He bids her to remember other people in the years before Troy who affected her inner world (she and Clytemnestra were the twin sisters of twin brothers), and he stresses the inherent modifiability of psychic reality: "the child . . . takes many forms" (*HE*, 187). Most important, he helps her to make conscious her own unacknowledged preoedipal relation to the mother ("the child-mother, yourself"), lest she remain oppressed by a frightened construction of reality and "flame out, incandescent":

> Helen — Helen — Helen —
> there was always another and another and another;
> the rose has many petals,
>
> or if you will, the nenuphar,
> father, brother, son, lover,
> sister, husband and child;
>
> beyond all other, the Child,
> the child in the father,
> the child in the mother,
>
> the child-mother, yourself;
> O Helena, pause and remember,
> lest you return to that other
>
> and flame out, incandescent. (*HE*, 187)

As Rachel Blau DuPlessis has written, the mystery of the nenuphar or water lily that Theseus gives Helen to decode here comprises a "subtle genealogy" of both sibling pairs and parent-child dyads.[17] Theseus emphasizes the value of relationship rather than difference as the basis of true psychological independence and growth. Differing with DuPlessis on the extent to which these values are fully realized in this poem, I would argue that they remain nascent here and not fully developed until H.D.'s last lyric sequences. Theseus' counsel leads Helen to modify her view of Achilles and to confront the fear of motherhood at the root of her anxiety. As she had seen herself and Clytemnestra as counterparts in "Pallinode," now Helen sees Theseus and Achilles as "twin-stars" who meet "as opposites" or complementary forces in her own psyche (*HE*, 190). This emotional maneuver, in which she tempers Achilles' wrath with Theseus' compassion, enables Helen to confront her fear. At this point the poem becomes obscure, as if H.D. could not fully claim the insight that she dramatizes in the ensuing lyric. After the narrator tells us that "Helen understands, though we do not know exactly what it is that she understands," Helen voices a pained disavowal of the conventional woman's self-abnegating role:

> Isis, yes Cypris, the cypress,
> the Tomb of Amor,
> the Tomb of Love;
>
> yes—it breaks, the fire,
> it shatters the white marble;
> I see it, suddenly I see it all,
>
> the Shell, the Tomb, the Crystal,
> Tyndareus, my earth-father, and Zeus
> or Zeus-Amen in heaven,
>
> and I am only a daughter;
> no, no, I am not a mother,
> let Cypris have Amor,
>
> let Isis have Horus,
> let Leda have Zeus,
> and Hecuba, Priam. (*HE*, 191)

In the passage above Helen intuits why the transformative power of the mother, Isis, has been devalued in patriarchal culture. Because birth reminds men of death, Isis is associated both with Cypris (Aphrodite) and with the cypress tree from which coffins are made. Feeling maternal love as a flame that shatters her integrity ("the white marble"), Helen connects the shell (given to her by Thetis) with the tomb (her experience of love in patriarchy) and the crystal (her capacity for vision).

Voicing this insight brings both Helen and the author "peace." In a letter to Norman Pearson, in which she enclosed the sections quoted from above ("Leuké," VI, 5–8), H.D. described the sense of self-discovery she felt while she was writing them: "I must tell you now and forever that the writing of the poems, this *Leuké* has given me 'answers.' . . . It is mysterious and really funny to me, to find the clues unravelling as I go along rather scrappily, now and again. Treat this *Leuké VI* and all of it in this manner. I just feel with Theseus that 'myth, the one reality dwells here.'"[18] Her rejection of woman's devalued role enables Helen to redefine Thetis, to transform her from the "sea-mother" who fosters the patriarchy to "Artemis, the Moon-goddess," an island-mother in whose white sphere she feels secure (*HE*, 193).

As if to acknowledge that feminine identity first becomes problematic after male cultural hegemony gives sex differences a transformed value at the oedipal stage of development, H.D. refers to that phase to describe Helen's final refusal to forget Achilles. Rather than rival "either the earth or the heaven mother" for "union with her Absolute" (Zeus), Helen claims to have chosen "the Absolute of negation" (*HE*, 195). She has preferred "immaculate purity," one kind of death, to a psychosexual pattern that would repeat the cycle of self-sacrifice that has constituted her mother's life. As Persephone who embraces Death (Dis or Achilles), she remains "only a daughter" (*HE*, 191). In H.D.'s revision of Persephone's abduction, then, Helen embraces Dis (or Achilles) in order to recover a preoedipal connection with a powerful mother, a mother whose ability to model autonomy is not debased by the present gender system. Whether "Achilles waits" is a secondary matter: "only let Thetis, / the goddess hold me for awhile / in this her island, her egg-shell" (*HE*, 197).

Helen's acknowledgment of the pathos of this wish completes her task on Leuké, and the poem circles back with deeper comprehension to the charged meeting between Helen and Achilles with which it began.

In the final section of the poem Achilles becomes, more self-consciously, a means of connection with this longed-for maternal presence. "Eidolon" opens with the image of Achilles calling Helen back to Egypt, not as "Lord of Legions" but as one commanded to a new order of love:

> You ask how you came here;
> Theseus' servants bore your couch,
> silently set down the lion claws
>
> on the steps; softly
> as those lion-paws on sand,
> Theseus and Achilles
>
> lifted the catafalque, the bier
> and you sleeping, exhausted
> with the fight, your struggle
>
> to understand *Leuké*, the light;
> silently, Thetis commanded,
> Thetis in her guise of mother
>
> who first summoned you here
> with *Achilles waits*. (*HE*, 210)

But before Helen can fully understand the true basis of her reconciliation with Achilles, this "innermost mystery of 'life-in-death,' " she must undergo a reprise of Paris's seduction and Theseus' rescue, because in traditional myth Paris is associated with Helen's sexuality as it is divorced from motherhood. Early in "Eidolon" the image of Paris reappears to question her choice of Achilles. "Pluto-Achilles" represents a "death-cult," Paris argues, "to drag you further and further underground" (*HE*, 216). Unwilling to repeat the old oedipal story of the son's abandonment by his mother, Paris will accept the position of son in her new "spirit-order" only if Helen replaces Hecuba. Then, provocatively turning from his own child-hood history to hers, Paris reminds Helen of daughters who were sacrificed to "propitiate a ghost" (particularly his sister Polyxena), and he wonders if he and Achilles "stand over / a new victim" (*HE*, 219). The anxiety Paris arouses about the relationship between mother and daughter in a patriarchy causes Helen to call again on Theseus to reconcile disparate parts of herself.

Because he provides a new perspective from which to understand her actions, her recollection of Theseus enables Helen to touch on the deepest ironies of her flight with Paris. Back in Sparta "for the first time in our sequence" (*HE*, 227), Helen recovers the suppressed memory of the painful moment when she left her daughter Hermione. As Susan Friedman has written, she had repressed this flight because it violated patriarchal "norms for devoted motherhood that she had internalized."[19] "What has she lost? What has she gained?" the narrator asks (*HE*, 227). Her answer conveys the sorrow and alienation of the woman who rejects conventional roles: "She had lost her childhood or her child, her 'Lord's devotion' or the devotion of the conventional majority" (*HE*, 227). In the striking lyric that follows, H.D. portrays Helen's entrapment in a supposedly ideal marriage, where her very autonomy, the decision to pursue her own impulses, makes her a "stranger" in her own household. The focal point of her leave-taking is a glance exchanged between mother and daughter. Because H.D. shows Helen's agony mirrored in the "wide eyes and white face" of Hermione (*HE*, 228), the scene has an eerie resonance. It also poignantly conveys the poet's own feelings of motherlessness at the beginning of her career when she lost her first child, and perhaps her fear of having abandoned her daughter Perdita while she worked:

> Sparta; autumn? summer?
> the fragrant bough? fruit ripening
> on a wall? the ships at anchor?
>
> I had all that, everything,
> my Lord's devotion, my child
> prattling of a bird-nest,

playing with my work-basket;
the reels rolled to the floor
and she did not stoop to pick up

the scattered spools but stared
with wide eyes in a white face,
at a stranger — and stared at her mother,

a stranger — that was all,
I placed my foot on the last step
of the marble water-stair

and never looked back;
how could I remember all that?
Zeus, our-father was merciful. (*HE*, 228)

"What has she gained?" This memory enables H.D. to perceive a related irony. Helen has suffered because of "Apollo's snare," because of a male-devised story that is still incomplete. The question of her integrity is a false issue: neither "daemon or goddess" she has been merely a "player" in an "already written drama or script," who learned the part of vilified harlot "by rote" (*HE*, 230). Her means of breaking from this "recorded drama" is to reconstitute "the unre-corded . . . her first meeting with Achilles, 'on the ledge of a desolate beach'"(*HE*, 235). As Albert Gelpi has pointed out, "in writing her own Helen-text, H.D. arrived at a reading of identity which resumed and surpassed the past."[20]

Because it brings into vision the source of her pain, the empathic glance Helen recalls in the scene above precedes her ability to understand "the human content" of her encounter with Achilles (*HE*, 255). Like her own history, his career as a warrior and a lover had been distorted by a repressed image:

I say there is one image,

and slaves and princesses
and the town itself are nothing
beside a picture, an image, an idol

or eidolon, not much more than a doll. (*HE*, 244)

Originally his mother's son, Achilles had forgotten her "simple wish / that he learn to rule a kingdom" in the process of becoming a warrior (*HE*, 287). When the "heroes mocked," he had replaced her with a wooden doll, a figurehead to decorate the prow of his ship. He had forgotten his mother "and that is where her power lay" (*HE*, 295). Here H.D. graphically depicts the legacy of the Oedipus complex as it reflects patriarchal socialization. Anticipating contemporary revisionist psychologists, she shows that to repress one's connection with the mother, to define masculine as not feminine, is to produce a rigid, defensive, ultimately inadequate criterion of the strength of the self.

When Helen shares Achilles' childhood memory of bitter loss and abandonment, she experiences a "miraculous birth" quite different from that suggested by the traditional image of "the Star" associated with male divinity in western tradition. She realizes that "the promised *Euphorion* is not one child but two. "It is 'the child in Chiron's cave' and the 'frail maiden,' stolen by Theseus from Sparta" (*HE*, 288). A lost dimension of herself reborn to consciousness, Euphorion represents human nature (female as well as male) in a transformed state. Euphorion is a psychic state that transcends the limitations of sex roles. H.D. contrasts Helen's blissful "ultimate experience" with the pain of having a child (or being one) in a culture where adult femininity and masculinity (the roles of mother and father) require self-division and alienation:

> it was epic, heroic and it was far
> from a basket a child upset
> and the spools that rolled to the floor;
>
> and if I think of a child of Achilles
> it is not Pyrrhus, his son,
> they called Neoptolemus
>
> nor any of all the host that claimed as father,
> the Myrmidon's Lord and Leader,
> but the child in Chiron's cave;
>
> and if I remember a child that stared
> at a stranger and the child's name is Hermione,
> it is not Hermione

I would stoop and shelter,
remembering the touch on my shoulder,
the enchanter's power. (*HE*, 289–90)

Thus, by revising the psychological import of the birth of a divine child in *Helen in Egypt*, H.D. incorporates a critique of the institutions of marriage and motherhood into the romance of Helen and Achilles. This is the epic's connection with "Winter Love." On one level the poem dramatizes the inner process of romantic quest, a process in which the desiring self finds a fulfillment that will deliver it from the anxieties of reality while still containing that reality.[21] Like popular romances, which end in complicity with patriarchal domestic arrangements, it portrays and appears to ratify what Janice Radway has called "a woman's journey to personhood *as that particular psychic configuration is constructed and realized within patriarchal culture.*"[22] But on a deeper level, to the extent that fundamental emotional issues remain unresolved, the poem questions the serious imbalances created by that culture. Helen's memory of Achilles' attack leads to an exploration of an ambivalent relationship with his mother Thetis, the mother who is a product of and fosters the patriarchy, and to a revision of the myth of Demeter and Persephone. Her acknowledgment of Achilles' repressed connection with Thetis enables Helen to realize the ambiguities of her own, a necessary step in the poet's task of authentic self-representation.

At the end of *Helen in Egypt* Helen chooses Achilles instead of Paris, "La Mort" instead of "L'Amour," because only through "constant preoccupation" with a moment of maternal loss can she relieve herself of an unconscious burden. Instead of reconciling Trojan and Greek, H.D. makes palpable the veracity of Helen's pain. (Here I differ with Susan Friedman and Rachel Blau DuPlessis, who posit a transcendence of conflict in "Eidolon."[23]) For even at the very end, the poem's resolution is accomplished by fiat: "One greater than Helen must answer," the narrator tells us, "though perhaps we do not wholly understand the Message" (*HE*, 303). Helen claims that Thetis enables her to reconcile Paris and Achilles. But though Helen's

reference to the "Phoenix-nest" in the final lyric implies resurrection
and transcendence, her final veiled allusion to Persephone's marriage
of death ("the seasons revolve around a pause") emphasizes the pathos
usually overlooked in conventional conceptions of renewal:

> so the dart of Love
> is the dart of Death,
> and the secret is no secret;
>
> the simple path
> refutes at last,
> the threat of the Labyrinth,
>
> the Sphinx is seen,
> the Beast is slain
> and the Phoenix-nest
>
> reveals the innermost
> key or the clue to the rest
> of the mystery;
>
> there is no before or after,
> there is one finite moment
> that no infinite joy can disperse
>
> or thought of past happiness
> tempt from or dissipate;
> now I know the best and the worst;
>
> the seasons revolve around
> a pause in the infinite rhythm
> of the heart and of heaven. (*HE*, 303–304)

At one level, "the dart of Love / is the dart of Death" refers to an ideal
of the sex act that haunts the adult psyche: the dissolution of psychic as
well as physical boundaries and the merging of two individuals into
something like a single transcendent entity. At a deeper level,
however, H.D. reminds us that our capacity for feeling and symboliz-
ing dimensions beyond our finiteness is inseparable from our painful

awareness of death, separation, and disintegration—an awareness that is also culturally defined.

Indeed, the "Eidolon" itself (printed in italics) replaces a whole book in the third section, altering the epic's otherwise parallel structure. This foreshortening also underlines and undercuts the complacency inherent in traditional ideas of resurrection and rebirth, and in some standard readings of the poem. By giving voice to Helen's "eidolon" and thus creating an auditory counterpart to the little wooden doll that Achilles made to replace his mother, H.D. draws upon a classical model even older than the deceptive wraith employed by Euripides. As William Prost has pointed out, H.D.'s eidolon is a "shade-eidolon," like that of Odysseus' mother in *The Odyssey*. A ghost that survives the destruction of the body, she is that aspect of the psyche that "cannot know or perceive anything without some contact wth matter, ie. drinking blood, the essence of life."[24] In more modern terms, by giving Thetis voice, H.D. evokes the whole psychosocial script that has unconsciously determined Helen's response to life, the inchoate image that must be acknowledged in order to be outgrown.

Finally, when the Eidolon of Thetis is given the last words, there is a drop in musical pitch: H.D. shifts from the operatic to the homely, to the rhythm of sorrowful lullaby to underscore the pathos of Helen's choice. Having fished an image of female devaluation out of the depths of her unconscious, Helen hears the "beat and long reverberation" of the sea and feels the emotional residue, "again and again the sand" (*HE*, 304). Thus H.D. conveys the terrible beauty of the imaginative journey when one is haunted:

> the crash and spray of the foam,
>
> the wind, the shoal, the broken shale,
> the infinite loneliness
> when one is never alone. (*HE*, 304)

Since such pain informed Helen's union with Achilles, no wonder H.D. returned to her in "Winter Love."

7

The Childbirth Metaphor in
H.D.'s Late Poetry

*She showed a way to penetrate mystery; which means,
not to flood darkness so that darkness is destroyed,
but to enter into darkness, mystery, so that
it is experienced.*[1]

—Denise Levertov

AN EXHAUSTIVE SELF-ANALYSIS and a penetrating social critique, *Helen in Egypt* is the zenith of H.D.'s career. Her four late poems, "Vale Ave" and the three lyric sequences of *Hermetic Definition*, consolidate and refine the mature legend presented there with the clarity of a radiant finale. Compressed in scale and mellower in tone, they offer a definitive self-representation and a major aesthetic statement. In her earlier poetry H.D. explored the discrepancy between received myth, the product of collective male fantasy, and her own experience by giving traditional mythic female subjects interiority — thus masking the personal dimension of her work. In these late poems she increasingly subordinates references to the usual mythic pantheon to explicit allusions to her life, suggesting that her subject here is not so much received myth as her own power as mythmaker. By objectifying intimate, personal material in symbolic language, which then itself becomes social fact, she intends to influence the transmission of culture, not simply reflect or explore it.[2]

In their self-conscious examination of the relationship between female experience, as it is interiorized, and language, H.D.'s late poems anticipate the flowering of contemporary feminist poetry and theory in Europe and America. Like Hélène Cixous and Julia Kristeva, she regards writing as an activity that liberates the writer from constraining linguistic, psychic, and social networks.[3] In these poems H.D. is concerned with revising myths about the relation between gender and language. Like Denise Levertov and Adrienne Rich, she utilizes previously neglected female moments of procreative process, such as gestation and lactation, to articulate a vision of creativity that invests female experience with new moral and social value.

Though H.D. could not walk without crutches after she broke her hip in 1956 and rarely left the environs of Dr. Brunner's Nervenklinik in Küsnacht, she did not languish in her "confinement" there. Rather, she regarded the beauty and peace of the Swiss Alps to be perfectly conducive to meditation and to poetry. A place where psychotherapy was conducted in an atmosphere of music and art, the clinic provided a kind of "sanctuary"; its views of the lake and the mountain forest hushed with snow in winter reminded her of scenes from Japanese prints.[4] Besides serving as confidante and auxiliary therapist to some of the patients, she established a close friendship with Dr. Erich Heydt, a young psychiatrist who was interested in her work. As she anxiously awaited the births of her third and fourth grandchildren, Heydt helped her to recall and re-create the experience of her own first "confinements." A delighted grandmother, she returned in her late poetry to the scenes of her youth.

H.D.'s Küsnacht memoir, *Compassionate Friendship* (1955), and her novel, *Magic Mirror* (1956), document her relationship with Erich Heydt and provide an important meditative prologue to her four last poems. She had come to the clinic first in 1946 after the emotional breakdown engendered by World War II; then again in 1954 to recuperate from a serious stomach operation. In these two accounts of her later stay there she stresses that her friendship with Heydt helped her to bridge the two wars. With his guidance she realized that her "second [emotional] illness had been a repetition of the first shock," the death of her first child *in utero* when her husband told her (in a brutal manner) that the *Lusitania* had been sunk, bringing America into World War I and ensuring his recruitment. She wrote, "Noone had ever palliated the shock of that disaster" (*MM*, III, 7). Therefore, when Air Marshal Hugh Dowding refused to participate in her alleged communications with the spirits of dead RAF pilots thirty years later, she felt that the two wars "were exactly superimposed on one another" (*MM*, III, 7). In her fantasy the spirits of the dead pilots, who signaled to her from their "totenschiff," had merged with that of her lost child, and the air marshal's repudiation of them (and her) had evoked her husband's earlier apparent repudiation, when a few days before their baby was due, he burst upon her with "don't you realize what this means? Don't you feel anything? *The Lusitania has gone down*" (*MM*, III, 7).

H.D. had never discussed her feelings about this first loss with anyone until her talks with Heydt in 1956. Nor had she realized that she had been "driven on to the illumination" of her later poetry by something too terrible to face (*MM*, III, 8). As she put it, "the deepest depth of desolation was balanced by the spirit-ship, the Child of the second war, the composite or symbolical child" that led to the Helen sequences (*MM*, III, 12). After she remembered her despair when the first child perished under her heart, she felt "a strange new lightness"; retrojecting that lightness back into the past, she recovered the happiness of her marriage before the war:.

> But there was that dark curtain and the lost image; she never "resolved"—Aster or Amor—shall we call him? It is Amor that Eric calls back and the spirit *Totenschiff* of the second war, that Ship, described in the series, in *Magic Ring* and the other records, becomes the *Lusitania*, an actuality, too terrible to face. Only in facing it, recalling the exact second that the heart under her heart stopped beating, she recalls those years, banishes for the time, all the other years. (*MM*, III, 8)

When she connects the recovered image, "Aster or Amor" with the memory of a literal child, whose loss she had repressed, H.D.

provides the crucial nexus between her life and her late poetry. In her conversations with Heydt, H.D. came to understand how her trauma in pregnancy had revived earlier conflict around motherhood and authorship that reflected the internalization of a socially constructed reality damaging to herself as a writer. She uses symbolic language here, as she does in her late poetry, to incorporate the reality of her dreams into the common stock of knowledge in order to unmask the strictures of woman's role in everyday life and to transcend them. By conflating writing with discrete moments of the procreative process, she thematizes the problem of women's speech in a society that has excluded mothers from discourse.[5]

In *Thorn Thicket* (1960), the diary in which she recorded her reaction to Erich Heydt's wedding engagement, H.D. calls "Vale Ave" her "*Madrigal* poem sequence," referring to the persistent "theme of departure, desertion, death" in her life, which she traces back first to her wartime marriage, and then to her psychosocial development in a traditional male-dominated family.[6] She asserts that she has counterbalanced or "redeemed" this debilitating psychological archetype in "the magic . . . of the actual writing" (*TT*, 8). Surrounded by adoring female patients who were upset by his engagement, Heydt was continually "going-coming, coming-going," behavior that recalled Richard Aldington's dallying with a number of women before finally leaving H.D. for Dorothy Yorke (*TT*, 16). H.D. had seen him and the *Madrigal* Bella in bed together, but she had repressed that sight: the feelings that she should have had in 1917 "were awakened or invoked some forty years later, *through other people*" (*TT*, 15).

H.D. compared her repression of this scene with that of a child who represses the "primal scene" of classical analysis—the "consciousness or actual 'picture' of father-mother in the act of creating"—in order to safeguard the idealization of the parents (*TT*, 19). Just a couple of months before writing this poem, she had recorded a "terrible" dream of her mother's being raped by a father-figure, which she interpreted as a sadomasochistic version of the primal scene fantasy typical of children in a patriarchy.[7] Her remarks indicate that she probably knew Freud's view that children will "inevitably regard the sexual act as a sort of ill treatment or act of subjugation."[8] She thought that both her writing and her concept of herself as a writer devolved from the need to revise the degraded image of victimized womanhood implicit in this fantasy: "I must repeat the heart-break, the 'primal scene,' to regain the marriage image or imago" (*TT*, 16).

Because Air Marshal Dowding was interested in psychic research and shared her belief in the existence of the soul after death, H.D. connected him with her attempt to reconstruct this phallocentric model for (pro)creativity. Though he ultimately repudiated the "messages" she received, the air marshal (whose initials were also "H.D.") had also been deeply affected by the loss of a child in battle. Believing that they met on an "astral" plane, H.D. made him the model both for Achilles in *Helen in Egypt* and for Lucifer, Lilith's counterpart in "Vale Ave."

As Susan Friedman has pointed out, H.D. drew increasingly upon mystical religious tradition and the occult sciences of astrology and alchemy to find alternatives to the patriarchal conceptual machinery that reified a sexist version of the "primal scene" to legitimate the subjugation of women. Unlike orthodox religious tradition, which created a masculine imagery of God and then used it to justify taboos against women, mysticism posited the "primal existence of a divine One, a latent androgynous whole that incorporates equally both masculine and feminine potential."[9] Such documents as Robert Ambelain's *La Kabbale Practique* and *Dans l'ombre des cathédrales* and Jean Chaboseau's *Le Tarot* and *La Voyance* were increasingly helpful because they offered a secret wisdom and a fresh imagery of creativity unavailable in the official texts of established religions.

To explain how her meetings and parting with Dowding mediated the pain of the original London scene by providing a new degree of detachment, H.D. drew upon the practice of casting Tarot cards in a figure eight, signifying eternity. Drawing upon Chaboseau, she describes the creative process in terms of three phases or circles, in which the first circle represents the realm of matter or worldly affairs (male) and the second, the realm of spirit and inward meanings (female). Inspiration or poetry (the child) is a third circle, or neutral linguistic core, which runs through the other two, simultaneously uniting them and providing continuity, while existing independently:

> There are the three phases: *"militante* (terrestre), *suffrante* (astrale), *triumphante* (céleste)."* There is *"un corps,* un *double,* une *âme."* This is the circle in which the *Madrigal* War I marriage is the *corps,* the Lord D. contact in War II, the *double,* & the inspiration, the poetry, running through this, before it and after, the *âme.* (*TT,* 20)

In H.D.'s psychic economy, her relationship with Dowding represented a marriage on the rocks and a child born at a level beyond fury and fear. It created a third entity that compensated for the child she had lost: the blessing of the spirit-ship, the "messages," the new words that were her salvation.

In "Vale Ave" H.D. re-creates the meaning of the primal scene by shifting from the literal to the figurative and back again. She superimposes the redemptive meeting of the prelapsarian lovers, Lilith and Lucifer, on the destructive meeting and parting of a *"processus"* of human lovers from key historical epochs; she shows how "the alchemy of memory" enables her to transmute a debilitating cultural pattern abstracted from everyday experience. More specifically, she shows how symbolic language itself, the tradition of *"la parole,"* can "appresent" such a pattern, bringing it back reformed, as an objectively real manifestation of personal resurrection and as a harbinger of social change.[10]

Though Elizabeth Dyer, the niece of an Elizabethan poet and alchemist, is her primary persona in "Vale Ave," H.D.'s choice of Lilith and Lucifer as the primordial protagonists indicates a more openly subversive intention than in *Helen in Egypt.* She introduces Lilith, Adam's first wife, as "the Serpent who tests the *androgynat primordial,"* asserting that as the word *Serpent* has "the same root derivation as Seraph, so Lilith may be Serpent or Seraph, as Adam, whom we invoke as Lucifer, the Light-bringer, in his pre-Eve manifestation, may be Angel or Devil."[11] The poet invokes Lucifer in his original incarnation as the "Light-bringer" who knew Lilith, before she was cursed, to be "a being, an entity / born of no man-rib but a Tree" ("VA," 19). Neither asleep nor awake, she is in a trance state when she invokes the infernal pair, whose privilege it is "to taste no bitter fruit, / nor toil nor bear children, / but to remember, only to remember . . ." ("VA," 19). Such an invocation causes "a monstrous fissure / in time, a breaking of law"; God's curse gives way to a new "enchantment" rising out of the sea ("VA," 20).

Though it manifests itself primarily through the parting and meeting, *vale ave*, of Elizabeth Dyer and Sir Walter Raleigh, the Lilith and Lucifer "formula" may also be applied to various women and men throughout history, to other prototypical lovers from late Rome, dynastic Egypt, legendary Provence, and contemporary London. H.D. extends the associational method of psychoanalysis across history, creating a palimpsest in which essential imagery from the lives of each pair continues to influence those of all the others. For example, the penitent nun in Provence, prostrated in adoration, remembers a vow made in ancient Rome when her counterpart's lover, upon returning from the "burning village," shows her a peaceful vista before her "purple tent." Similarly, Lady Elizabeth, whose loss of husband and child have been balanced by recalling Sir Walter Raleigh to her, remembers the "stark eyes" of a protector in Egypt who prevented the threatened rape of a young girl. The "same / hunger, the same desire, the same appeasement" experienced by all these prototypes affects the poet herself in contemporary London as she contemplates her most recent meetings and partings with other spiritual "*semblables*" ("VA," 48, 49).

Besides illustrating her palimpsestic vision of history, H.D.'s "*processus*" of lovers recapitulates major motifs from her earlier poetry and fiction, which she then weaves seamlessly into the fabric of world literature. For example, the nun who wears "the rose with nails for petals" underneath her robe, whose "swollen eyelids burn" with tears before the candle flame ("VA," 21, 22), recalls the self-lacerating passion of H.D.'s early poetry, as well as her designation of Provence (in *By Avon River*) as the source of a religious mysticism, disguised in the language of sexual passion, which was inherited by the Elizabethans. The nun's wish for "revolatizing" new prayers that will revoke "decrees made long ago" evokes both an allusion to Octavius, the warrior contrasted with Antony in Shakespeare's romantic tragedy, and Hipparchia's longing for an empathic lover in the decadent Rome of H.D.'s *Palimpsest*. Is it Shakespeare's Antony and Cleopatra, united after the battle at Actium, who seem "*one flambeau for the world to see*" ("VA," 25), or is it H.D.'s Helen and Achilles huddled together over a flaming brazier after the Trojan War?

In order to demonstrate the dialectic between the personal and the mythic more specifically, H.D. gives her persona, the Renaissance lady, Elizabeth Dyer, a name that alludes both to the primordial Lilith ("Lizeth") and to the capacity for spiritual rebirth (die-er). Through Elizabeth, H.D. appresents the chief components of her own biography, indicating emotional and intellectual stratagems necessary for the poetic re-creation of identity. Like H.D., Elizabeth remembers opposing masculine figures, a husband (Hugh) whose departure she has repressed, and a lover (Sir Walter Raleigh), whom she recalls after his death through the practice of craft (alchemy). Like H.D., Elizabeth remembers "a dead child" and a faithful nurse who rescued her from death, enabling her to write a "precious book" in which she "strives to save identity" ("VA," 38). Like H.D., Elizabeth asserts that anger "drew her back and out of time," ultimately empowering her to see "in-time and passionately" and to dare to "recall the symbols, name the Powers" that would effect a transformation ("VA," 30). Like H.D., Elizabeth draws on the spiritualist séance and the imagery of the kabbalah to find a new paradigm for creativity.

Just as she asserts the rehabilitative power of her own anger, H.D.'s Renaissance persona distinguishes between the integrity of her lover, Sir Walter, and the complacency of her husband on the basis of the former's rebellion against a social system in which the brutality of war and the rape and silencing of women are inextricably linked. Elizabeth's memory of Sir Walter's anger leads the poet back first to Julia and Julius, Roman lovers who "stood alone" in their desire to "forget / anxiety and ceaseless threat and war," and their determination to "found a City, greater / and with more power, even than ancient Rome" ("VA," 41). Then, when she questions the destruction implicit in building again, she remembers even further back to ancient Egypt, when "stark, hypnotic eyes" that blazed "amber and fire" enabled her to regain

> an image in the sacred lotus pool,
> a hand that hesitates to break
>
> the lily from the lily stalk and spoil
> what may be vision of a Pharoah's face. ("VA," 44)

Recalling this ancient image of a divinity not inimical to women permits H.D. to further imagine a sympathetic protector who forestalls the rape of a young girl by one of the Pharoah's warriors. She remembers a moment when "time paused," when she found herself "standing on a mosaic floor," the pattern of which is familiar and natural, in the presence of a lover who values, not female defloration, but the singular beauty of "one purple lily / in an alabaster vase" ("VA," 46). Unlike the subjugation of women under the shadow of "Eden's tree," intercourse with this lover suggests both sexual equality, when woman's sexual hunger is satisfied simultaneously with man's, and poetic liberation: a view of inspiration wherein the male principle "releases" the female, thus contributing to her "appeasement." Amenti, the Egyptian land of the dead, where there is "urgency" but "no fear," elicits one of H.D.'s most erotic lyrics:

> If there is urgency, there is no fear,
> hail, yes, but not farewell,
>
> *Amenti* flowered long before Eden's tree;
> his hand invites the *delta* underneath
>
> the half-transparent folds of the soft pleats,
> and does not tear but draws the veil aside,

then both his hands grasp my bare thighs,
and clutch and tighten, bird claws or a beast

that tear open, tear apart, but keep
the appetite at bay, to gratify a greater hunger

or to anticipate greater enjoyment;
yet his commanding knees keep my knees locked,

even while his virility soothes and quickens,
till in agony, my own hands clutch and tear,

and my lips part, as he releases me,
and my famished mouth opens

and knows his hunger and his power;
and this is the achievement and we know the answer

to ritual and to all philosophy,
in the appeasement of the ravished flower. ("VA," 46, 47)

H.D.'s Renaissance persona, Lady Elizabeth, further conflates female sexual satisfaction with poetic inspiration when she distinguishes her husband Hugh, who sailed off to sea and her cousin, who bid her "laugh and forget," from her true lover, Sir Walter, who defied the existing system by honoring his "*parole* . . . his personal word, his honor" ("VA," 65). Though he could have "ruled the realm, the world," he chose instead an alternative "way of love," an Elizabeth "not the Queen" ("VA," 37). Having died in the Tower, he returns to her as an angel or devil who paces the corridors about her bed as she struggles to give birth. A demonic lover, part of herself, he will be restored, like her dead child, through the magic of her art: "I do go back and clutch my precious book / and warm it at my breast, / it is the child I lost" ("VA," 38).

Lady Elizabeth's memory of the "purple lily" of herself, which signifies the restoration of eros, brings the poet to contemporary London and the task at hand. In old age it is insufficient simply to decipher and transcribe "the Mystery, the Writing and the Scroll" ("VA," 50); she must show how her writing re-creates it. In the

214

decipher and transcribe "the Mystery, the Writing and the Scroll" ("VA," 50); she must show how her writing re-creates it. In the penultimate lyrics H.D. turns her historical personae inside out to show how her own meetings and parting with Lord Dowding during World War II, recollected later, inspired her to write this poem. She connects the underlying pattern of her emotional dynamic with specific elements of her poetics. True to her imagist beginnings, H.D. first invokes "infinity . . . in simple things" ("VA," 50): fire in the streets, worry about the safety of her daughter, repudiation by the air marshal after seven short meetings, travel in Europe, the creation of her prose and verse epics. Then, she alludes to being prompted by news of the air marshal's remarriage (which stirs up an old betrayal). At this point "bitterness sets in," the old "fear of fear that runs within my veins, // the fear of helplessness, of being lost" ("VA," 52).

Finally, she adduces as the poem's deepest source of inspiration the emotional problem of "confinement," triggered this time by the broken hip that has incapacitated her in old age. This issue of confinement, redolent with a lifetime of painful associations, aroused her deepest fear, that she would "never write again" (*VA*, 53). In "rebellion" against this fear, she thought of the air marshal's heretical philosophy of "the *au-delà*," the next world, "Hell, Paradise" ("VA," 54). Hailing him (Luciferian "light-bearer") brought "the thought beyond the fear," first of writing a letter to him and then "this month, April" the miracle of her poem: "I seized my pencil / and my pencil wrote of the enchantment and the purple tent and how / following inexorable destiny, we met" ("VA," 58).

In this context of the poem's transcendent love match, H.D. shows how poetic language transforms the sexist meaning of the primal scene. She finds in Ambelain's *La Kabbale Practique* coequal feminine and masculine names of God (*"Alla"* and *"Teli"*), which she associates with the Spirit-ship that brought her messages from a host of recovered children. Superimposing the symbolic upon the literal, she then enacts a transformation. The perfect counterpart to the sinking of the *Lusitania*, the death of a child, the breakup of a marriage, this ship represents the womb as a life-bearing, message-

The Ship was what inspired us, what brought *Alla* and *Telli*
to the ultimate goal of their ambitions and their hopes,

> for it had come over and above the stresses and the fury and
>   the fear,
> bearing its priceless treasure

"O, so many," Alli said, "shouting and laughing";
the Ship was for you. ("VA," 61)

Further, H.D. asserts that her renewed sense of self, accomplished in and through the writing, makes the "almost unbearable story bearable" by providing a concept of eternity that is accessible ("VA," 62). Not a "vast conception of philosophy," eternity is a *"near extension of our own common time,"* wherein the re-created "Master of the Air" waits faithfully for her ("VA," 62). With sly humor she implies that the eternal spark flickers even when a bedridden old woman lights a cigarette—to tell a distant friend of the "anodyne" of "chestnut spires, so lovely in the dusk" ("VA," 62). No "high philosophy," eternity is in the telling.

At the end of "Vale Ave," when she tells us that "the secrets kept" by the air marshal (like Freud's) were greater than those he revealed, H.D.'s words themselves "seem suddenly to laugh" ("VA," 65). Instead of thwarting her, the air marshal's repudiation of the messages inspires the jouissance of the writer and the Nemesis of her poem: new words "to inaugurate a new age and a new mythology / a new Circe, Helen, Lilith" ("VA," 68). Finally, the poet prays that this "cloud of witnesses," her own words, may deliver her from "all iniquity, questioning and distrust," and she asks for "the blessing of the Ship, of the 'Parole' / in remembrance of the seven times we met" ("VA," 68).

In "Vale Ave" H.D. uses the childbirth metaphor to reconstruct the meaning of the primal scene by making the words of her poem, which she invests with life, the product of joyous intercourse between revised parental inner objects. In its sequel "Sagesse" she dramatizes the restorative effect of the preoedipal mother upon the imagination of the poet-daughter by showing how the inner colloquy of the poet reproduces the empathy between mother and child that is broken by an awareness of the father and the male order of language. In "Sagesse" the photograph of a captive "white-faced Scops owl from Sierre Leone" stares at the bedridden poet from the pages of *The Listener*, prompting a chain of associations that take her back into childhood and forward again to Küsnacht, associations that continue to play back and forth in time until they culminate in a present made joyous by the process of this exchange. H.D. celebrates the divinity of this "frantic" creature, bidding it to "stare out, glare out, live on."[11] Indeed, the rebellious old owl, Athene's bird, represents a suppressed aspect of her creativity, which she now acknowledges as sacred and life-giving: "May those who file before you feel / something of what you are—that God is kept within / the narrow confines of a cage, a pen" ("S," 59).

While she knows that most will probably laugh at this pathetic creature, the poet's thought that "some child may shudder," touched by its "majesty" ("S," 59) leads her to become that child again, standing with her father before the owl's cage at the zoo. Though she giggles at the bird like the others at first, when he points out its primitive power, she feels confused and threatened by the prospect of a world (and a God) that endorses its captivity: "He said, '*without your Father, no bird falls,*' / I don't know where or what it's all about; / I wish I could go home, get out of here" ("S," 60). Vulnerability and confusion, a child's response to the owl's hoot, causes the poet to call upon the angels Tara, "*Dieu fontaine de sagesse,*" and "Ptébiou" for comfort, for they are guardians and protectors who exist outside of the conventional Judeo-Christian script for men and women. Bolstered by meditation on these occult parental figures, her bones melt and her heart flames as she wishes for freedom to follow this mysterious voice, the voice of the child within, which has the power to change her mundane lake, the *Zürisee*, into "the haunted mere of *Märchen*": It is the means to wisdom ("S," 61).

In "Sagesse" when she speaks alternately as herself and as a child in wartime London, H.D. dramatizes a duality essential to the creation of poetry. She demonstrates what Denise Levertov has called the "inner colloquy" between the poet as maker and the poet as "reader within," that needy part of the self that comes to the poem innocently. H.D.'s sense of the creative process as an inner dialogue, as a means of communicating with others, and as a form of prayer, is shared by Levertov:

> The poet—when he is writing—is a priest; the poem is a temple; epiphanies and communion take place within it. The communion is triple: between the maker and the needer within the poet; between the maker and the needers outside him . . . ; and between the human and the divine in both poet and reader. By divine I mean something beyond both the making and the needing elements, vast, irreducible, a spirit summoned by the exercise of needing and making. When the poet converses with this god he has summoned into manifestation, he reveals to others the possibility of their own dialogue with the god in themselves.[12]

Communion with the child within, a sacred form of regression, enables the poet to experience the indwelling spirit of God in nature and to rephrase both temporal and eternal questions. H.D. dramatizes this childlike capacity for wonder and exaltation in one of her vivid imagist scenes; with a few deft strokes she shows how the little girl's confusion about the mysterious ways of God-the-Father is both heightened and mediated by love for her own father. As they move on to see the deer, she converses with an older boy, who helps her to climb up on the keeper's box to feed one while her father is not looking. Though she hops down when she is told, she imagines that the deer's tongue on her hand is a divine kiss, and she finds herself transported to an enchanted forest:

> —"now you hop down"—
>
> "yes, yes, I'm coming"—but I'm somewhere else,
> he kissed my hand, we're somewhere in the forest . . .
>
> I never thanked the boy, was he God, too. . . . ("S," 62)

Communion with the child within also affords the poet a measure of redemption through the recovery of a liberating discourse associated with the preoedipal mother. When she resumes her adult voice, H.D. associates God with "Goot—Goed"—such simple manifestations of goodness as the response of Sister Annie ("gut") who brings her coffee—and also with the (maternal) compassion of *"Dieu qui reçoit les pécheurs"* ("God who forgives sinners"; "S," 63). In all the languages of the world the divine contains a dimension of affirmation, of rejoicing—not only for "the simple people" who are "sinless," but for those (like herself) who "have known the desperate day of Cain" ("S," 63). In English also there is a linguistic association between God and "Good," but here H.D. turns again to Ambelain, to the invocation of divine powers through mystic names and formulas, for understanding and strength. For the thought of *"la droite de Dieu"* in her own tongue reminds her of the debilitating equation of divinity with male supremacy and authority.

Not only does the chain of word origins and word-sound associations afford H.D. a liberating departure from the male symbolic order, it also enables her to demonstrate the interpenetration of the sacred and the mundane in creativity. Meditation on the nature of God leads her to "Goth, the German, *Germain*," and to the connection between such everyday details as Germain's absence and her own creative power. (Heydt, her model for Germain, had sent her flowers before going off to America.) Just as she drew on the kabbalah for new imagery of the divine in "Vale Ave," H.D. compares the process in which she transforms Heydt's departure into poetry with the activity of the *En Sof* in the universe prior to creation. According to the kabbalist Isaac Luria, the infinite being, retreating from the arena of the universe, contracts into himself, thereby leaving an emptiness. "It is by the *En Sof's* retreat from infinite space into an infinitesimal monad of pure energy that the world comes into being."[13] Similarly, Germain's trip abroad, his temporary absence, causes a contraction of the poet's heart that produces, not spiritual death, but deeper vision and heightened creativity. She wonders,

Who will come back? a wandering flame,

a name, Goth, Gott, *Dieu admirable*, or another?
what Sun will rise, what darkness will unclose?

what spark, diastole, systole, compel, repel?
what counter-appeal contract the heart?

or not, what mystery? shall the winter-branch
be broken, fuel for another? or shall the branch,

prouder than spring, lordlier than summer,
strike deeper and grow higher to disclose

the last enchantment,
the white winter-rose? ("S," 65)

H.D. also draws upon other aspects of mysticism and the occult to explain the miracle of rejuvenation in sacred time and space that she enacts in her poetry. Referring to the idea that angels are guardians and interpreters in occult lore, she is "swept into a cycle of majestic spirits," into the company of the "seventy-two regents / of the great Temple of the *Oedipus Aegyptiacus*" in order to prove "the might / of the infinitely great to protect / the most minute" spark from the "extraneous chaos" ("S," 66). Here she alludes also to the kabbalistic aim of restoring the unity of a primordial, androgynous human (Adam Kadmon or Oedipus Aegyptiacus), prototype of the fully individuated self, whose female side is in exile. Her description of the divine as "a great tide that covers the rock pool" ("S," 67) and of cosmic consciousness as a state of dissolution is very like the mystic concept of "self-loss" that precedes unity with the Absolute.[14]

Finally, her designation of "Love" as a female spiritual force that generates the rebirth of the soul out of darkness is comparable to kabbalistic ideas about spiritual rebirth, which involve man's effort to redeem the exiled *Shekhinah*, the female *creatrix*.[15] She reassures Germain, who worries about her emotional health, that this state of vulnerability in which she is "shivering but inert" precedes the finding of female divinity in the self and the self in female divinity, and she

220

contrasts this moment of spiritual rebirth with the traditional birth of Christ:

> but *Dieu sauveur* last night was manifest,
> the attribute of Seket and her hour,
>
> 1.20 while we sleep;
> no infant in the straw,
>
> but simply Mary's flower,
> "Marah" the *Grande Mer*, patron and protectress,
>
> sword-lilies on their stalks,
> *Créatrice de la Foi.* . . . ("S," 73)

With more assurance than in *Trilogy*, H.D. refocuses our attention on the holy family, subordinating the importance of the divine son to that of the female creatrix whose power she (the daughter) inherits. She uses word origins to show how her tribute to Germain ("'german,' the near-relation") is simultaneously a tribute to her own "life-force":

> As Mary bowed before her Son, so I bow down,
> not to Germain, but in a way, to you, Germain;
>
> "german," the near-relation, "german," first;
> but that awaits the flower,
>
> seed that creates the fruit. ("S," 74)

Not only God-the-father but "*Sombre Mère Sterile* and *Brillante Mère Feconde* . . . hold the planets steady" in her universe; like the mundane mother who "spread the picture-book upon [her] bed," she is "always here"—the primary ground of her identity ("S," 75). The poem is composed when the poet recalls both "mother-father, Seket-Senciner"; the inner "child compassed it, / began and closed the circle" ("S," 76).

In order to close the circle of her poem, H.D. returns to the little girl in wartime London, picturing her dutifully helping her "mum" prepare dinner on a cold winter day. The protective mother, who has not fogotten last summer when her daughter was "took queer" at the zoo, attributes this unusual behavior to nervous strain from the war. When "Uncle Alf" begins to reminisce about "those buzz-bombs," she stops him from talking on in front of her daughter. In the following snippet of dialogue H.D. conveys the practical wisdom of the British working-class mother that transcends her humble social position:

> "how often must I tell you, Alf,
> that our ducks sees too much and hears too much
>
> and calls out in the night,
> maybe, she isn't bright or maybe, she's too bright,
>
> praying-like or singing-like, I wouldn't know;
> she screams or sings, *Father, Father*,
>
> then I shake her up and wake her up
> and call to Bert, and say,
>
> 'duckie, what is it dear?
> what is it now? dad's here.'" ("S," 78)

As Alf notes, it was the tireless compassion of such women that "kept us all going, kept the world . . . on its feet" during the war ("S," 79).

Thus the child's determination to be "a good girl," to do as mum says ("I water the geranium—is this being good?") leads the poet to self-determination and ultimately beyond the self. H.D. concludes by invoking the *Grande Mer*, by naming the names she shares with God. In an attitude of devotion, she prays all night for the strength "to serve your Power, / O *Leuké*-lily of this morning hour," and when "Venus 'strikes' at eight," she experiences the spiritual marriage that mystics associate with the highest stage of union with the divine.

H.D. begins the last lyric of "Sagesse" with lines from Psalm 18, a psalm that incarnates that sensation of unitive love. Then, she extends the imaginative field of the marriage image to include the existence of children. The laughter of these soul-children represents H.D.'s recovery of what Kristeva calls "the riant wellsprings of the imaginary" or "riant spaciousness," a joy without words that she will reinvest in the production of the new. [16] In lines that recall the vision she shared with Bryher at Corfu forty years earlier, she is instructed to "place [her] flowers" upon the shrine of those female angels who share the primal energy implicit in the divine name:

> *Dans le soleil, il a place sa tente,*
> *et c'est Lui-même qui s'avance,*
>
> *comme un Epoux hors de la couche nuptiale,*
> so Time and the Sun move on to the *Béthuliens*,
>
> when Venus "strikes" at 8;
> I don't know who they are or where,
>
> but laugh, they say, laugh, laugh, like children . . .
> laugh, they say, like simpletons, like idiots,
>
> fools and poets; laugh the world away,
> laugh, laugh and place your flowers
>
> on the shrine of Teut, Agad, Hana, Sila
> who share your name, *Soleil.* ("S," 84)

Just as mundane details of her confinement at Küsnacht enter into "Vale Ave" and "Sagesse," so the genesis of "Winter Love" and "Hermetic Definition" depends on similar interpolations and transformations. H.D.'s renewed contact with Ezra Pound inspired "Winter Love," and in the text of "Hermetic Definition" she re-created meetings with Lionel Durand and Saint-John Perse. In both, our knowledge of her personal experience literalizes the connection between creativity and procreation so that the childbirth metaphor reverberates in both directions, blurring the distinction between art and life. In both, the symbolic child or poem represents a linguistic triumph over the artist-mother's history of thwarted subjectivity.

H.D. felt that Erich Heydt had "re-injected" her with Pound at the Klinik when he inquired about the details of their early romance and then encouraged her to recall them for her memoir *End to Torment*. She had regained contact with Pound in the mid-1950s, when (like herself) he was confined to hospital. Appalled by his politics, she was loyal nevertheless, preferring to understand his current situation in the context of her own earlier knowledge of him. As she wrote to Norman Pearson when news of Pound's impending release from federal custody reached her:

> [Your letter] has given me back the early American scene, when almost everyone I knew in Philadelphia was against him, after that Wabash college *débacle*. Erich always said I was "hiding something." It was all *that*, my deep love for Ezra, complicated by family (and friends) lack of sympathy—my inner schism—outwardly I went on, after E. (1908) went to Venice. I have been writing of this and Erich has been helping me.[17]

An important aesthetic statement and a tribute to Pound, *End to Torment* is also the prologue to "Winter Love." Here H.D. articulates the "real content" of her relationship with her early fiancé, the first man to goad her ambition to write poetry. As in *Tribute to Freud*, she interweaves the present and the past, mingling the circumstances of recollection with memories themselves to create subtle harmonies that gradually accrete in meaning. Her memory of fiery first kisses in the snow, a moment in which she and Pound are eternally frozen, leads her to comment on the pathos of his current forced "confinement" and to consider his role in her own earlier confinements. Brilliant, magnetic, overbearing, the young Pound had once drawn H.D. out of the shadows; now he was like a caged lion in the zoo, having written his beautiful Pisan cantos in precisely such torment. The thought of his confinement reminds her of her own fear of being "caught, caged, confined—*a confinement*" (*ET*, 7), now at Hirslanden Klinik and long ago during her pregnancies. Pound's role then had been that of outrageous "directoire," gadfly, critic-competitor; she had given birth (in spite of him) the day after his visit:

> I did not see him at the time of my first confinement, 1915. I lost that child. The second was four years later, 1919. He hurtles

himself into the decorous St. Faith's Nursing Home, in Ealing, near London. Beard, black soft hat, ebony stick—something unbelievably operatic—directoire overcoat, Verdi. He stalked and stamped the length of the room. He coughed, choked or laughed, "You look like old Mrs. Grumpy" (or some such) "in Wyncote." Wyncote was where the Pounds had lived, outside Philadelphia. True, I wore a becoming (I thought) black lace cap. Naturally I looked no sylph. He seemed to beat with the ebony stick like a baton. I can't remember. Then, there is a sense of his pounding, pounding (*Pounding*) with the stick against the wall. He had banged that way, with a stick once before, in a taxi, at a grave crisis in my life. This was a grave crisis in my life. It was happening here. "But," he said, "my only real criticism is that this is not my child." (*ET*, 8)

"My only real criticism is that this is not my child." The full implications of Pound's comment, which so clearly reveals his sexual jealousy, leads H.D. to a central question: "The perfection of the fiery moment can not be sustained—or can it?" (*ET*, 11). Her demonstration of how the symbolic Child sustains this moment lies at the heart of her mature aesthetics. A manifestation of the preconscious mind, it compensates for or corrects the inevitable distortions of socially constructed consciousness.[18] When she remembers other times Pound interfered in her life, taking her away from friends and family, plying her with provocative books and ideas, H.D. recalls a favorite book, Balzac's mystical *Séraphita*. Connecting herself and Pound with the adolescent girl and boy in that story, whose mysterious androgynous lover eventually disappears or dies in the snow, H.D. considers the destructive self-images resulting from stereotypical sociosexual roles. Her memory of their being "caught in the act" by her disapproving father, who found them curled up together in an armchair, engenders a critique of typical courtship behavior in her day, during which the boy would become an animal and the girl, a madwoman. She insists, "Mr. Pound, it was all wrong. You turn into a Satyr, a Lynx, and the girl in your arms (Dryad, you called her), for all her fragile, not yet lost virginity, is *Maenad, bassarid*" (*ET*, 17).

225

Since no "act" afterward, though "biologically fulfilled," can have the significance of these "first *demi-vierge* embraces," if "the 'first love' is an uncoordinated entity, Angel-Devil—or Angel-Daemon or Daimon, Seraphitus-Seraphita—what then?" (*ET*, 19). She later found "a coordinated entity, Man-Hero" to "compensate and complete the picture," but any physical or intellectual perfection thereby achieved was merely reactive. What compensation had Pound achieved? His fate has been worse than hers. He exemplifies the poet's place in a noxious system: the poet "changed to Wolf or Panther, hunted down or captured" (*ET*, 19). Her memoir will contribute to the growing body of Pound literature by refracting this image.

H.D.'s desire to temper this grim picture of the Poet in the Iron Cage invites a cloud of memories, the emotional content of which she must clarify. She remembers feeling "enclosed in another dimension" when Erich Heydt took her hands as they huddled together on a bench in a crowded Zurich railway station. Heydt's tenderness drew into consciousness the vision of the Child that is "the 'fiery moment' incarnate" (*ET*, 33). Appearing from nowhere, a "small male child with short red-gold curls" poked into the market basket of the "typical *Hausfrau*" beside them, followed by "the inevitable [male] parent" moving tall and gaunt against the crowd (*ET*, 33). "Where did [the child] come from? How did he get there? It is only a moment" (*ET*, 21). Heydt's tenderness enables H.D. to realize an "existentialist dimension" of her affinity with Pound, to conceive of their spirit-child.

To convey the social significance of this moment, H.D. explains that she and Pound have been "through some Hell together, separately" (*ET*, 26). Reading Pound's "Canto 79" with its reiterated image of the lynx reminds her of his earlier fascination with the vidas of the troubadours, of his dramatization of the sadomasochism of a poet literally rabid for love in the early poem "Pierre Vidal Old." She had "developed along another line" involving a painfully perceived difference between herself, a fellow artist, and his wife, Dorothy, a type of self-effacing *"Leucothea"* who "'had pity' on ship-wrecked Odysseus" (*ET*, 31). Dorothy Pound's story could never have been H.D.'s, but it becomes hers "in retrospect"; though "the Achilles of [H.D.'s] fantasy . . . and the Odysseus of Ezra's" could never meet in life, "the two women, Helen (of [her] creative reconstruction) and the Penelope (a human actuality) *can* communicate," and their communication is a source of hope (italics mine; *ET*, 33).

Thinking about Pound from the perspective of her kinship with his wife Dorothy (whom she associates with the *Bona Dea*), H.D. considers Pound's fascism in a new light. Remembering that he wrote "Pierre Vidal Old" the same year that he complained that "this is not my child" and that he composed his *Pisan Cantos* while he lay confined on the floor of the Iron Cage, H.D. asks us to consider the impact of the process of reproduction on his and all human consciousness. Anticipating such contemporary feminist theorists as Mary O'Brien, she wonders how the problem of male alienation from key moments of the reproductive process has affected social institutions and political systems.[19] To what extent have ideologies of male supremacy been a product of strenuous masculine activity to negate the uncertainty of fatherhood? What "fearful effigies" from the past, what "ogres," what "dolls," have wrecked Pound and the modern world?

Considering her long *Helen* sequence from this perspective, H.D. realizes that she has been as victimized by the genderic differentiation of reproductive consciousness as he has. She had felt toward Pound the same "unconscious rivalry" she felt for her older brother, her mother's favorite, because "the mother is the Muse, the Creator, and in my case especially, as my mother's name is Helen" (*ET*, 41). The problems that Pound's situation presents are "the problems of our age," H.D. states, "consciously or unconsciously" we have all been bound up with him and his fate: "The prison . . . of the Self was dramatized or materialized by Ezra's incarceration" (*ET*, 56).

Fortunately, though we "put away childish things," there remains a reservoir of "dynamic or daemonic power" from which we may all draw: the vision of the child is H.D.'s symbol of a positive subversion of the old universe. As in Marcel Schwob's prose-poem "The Children's Crusade," it is as unarmed children that we will rescue the Holy Sepulchre. Contrasting Pound's magpielike method of historical collage with her own phoenixlike poetic process, she asserts that she gives birth to a new self out of the ashes of history. Finally, for H.D. to recall Ezra Pound is to recall her own childhood "hunger for music," her own wish to be a *wunderkind* like Van Cliburn, yet another "exact Séraphitus image" (*ET*, 50). This wish is both personal and cosmogonic; the Child that appeared at the Stadelhofen station is "Eros," a visible manifestation of her own (pro)creative strength: "The Idol that should have been, that could have been, that was somehow 'hidden,' was, is the *Wunderkind*. If I was not the Child (as a child), I would have the Child" (*ET*, 51).

Because she wished to commemorate the hidden dimensions of Pound's liberation, H.D. celebrated his "end to torment" by sending Dorothy, the devalued wife and mother, a yellow rose. Similarly, her poem "Winter Love" critiques the social institution of motherhood by expanding the childbirth metaphor to include a previously neglected moment of the procreative process: nurture. Subtitled "Espérance," the name of a symbolic child Helen nurses at the end of the poem, "Winter Love" demonstrates the woman poet's power to re-form herself and western culture through the medium of language. Here H.D. reprehends the operation of romantic thralldom depicted in *Helen in Egypt* and continues the dialogue with Pound implied in *End to Torment* by comparing Helen's failed romances of the past to the supreme satisfaction of "winter love." Having come to terms with the clamor and disillusionment of sexual warfare, she has achieved an inner harmony best expressed in the hush of silence:

> Now there is winter-love, a winter-lover
> who would take gladly — fondling the crisp leaves
> with a padded paw, sheathed — glad to find
>
> in the den, the sacred lair, no trap to entice,
> no rapacious loins, and sighs, not groans —
> no rain of arrows, no poisonous thrust of spears,
>
> no thundering on the stairs,
> no rasp of steel,
> only Taygetus' silence,

228

till a drift of snow
slides from a branch,
then silence more intense. ("WL," 88)

A meditation in three sections that are marked off by choric voices, "Winter Love" begins when the aged Helen breaks the silence of her mountain-top retreat to address her counterpart Odysseus-Pound, the archetypal poet-adventurer. Having resumed thought of him ten years after her dreamlike encounter with Achilles, after the securement of her own poetic myth, she compares the ways in which their art reflects their experience of procreativity. Though both she and Odysseus have been victims of sexual betrayal, this similarity is overshadowed by a more radical difference. For unlike her early suitor, whose intercourse with destructive or redemptive female avatars (Circe, Calypso) dominated his imagination, making anxiety about potency paramount, Helen locates her creative *agon* in pre- and postcoital parts of the reproductive process. While Calypso's cave is Odysseus' grotto, the scene of his adventure and the source of his return, Helen learned the sweetness of the honey-flower from "a child companion or old grandam" ("WL," 90). Beset by the repetition of "unsatisfied desire" (Achilles, Paris, Menelaus), she would have fallen but for that female voice calling her home, reminding her that "there was a Helen before there was a War" ("WL," 91). Adept now in the magic of word association ("The-tis — Sea-'tis"), she will employ that voice to heal the self-division she felt when Odysseus first departed after stealing her heart and "the future Helen / that wrecked citadels was born" ("WL," 92).

Dramatizing an inner dialectic between the constraints of social convention and the countervailing powers of the artist, the first choric sequence occurs after Helen remembers her earlier Idaean self. The chorus alternates between an attitude of despair at the damage done to women in history and one of hope based on the possibility of reweaving the pattern. The strophes carry the weight of doubt ("heavy, heavy the hand of Fate"), but the antistrophes have the last word, admonishing her to "dare to say Troy is forgotten," to sing a new song ("WL," 94).

If she refuses to heed "the hiss of death," the insatiable "thirst / of the moment un-mated" will "brighten the earth" and enable her to "recall first love and last" ("WL," 96). Having seen Odysseus off, she is now free to consider his significance.

The second section of "Winter Love" begins with Helen's rejection of the nurturing role Odysseus (and all of patriarchy) assigned to her. She refuses to be his muse, the holy grail of sustenance: "Helen's breasts, it was always Helen's breasts, / and the wine-cup that they wrought, / called Helen's breasts" ("WL," 97). Subtly alluding to Pound's "pomona, pomona," H.D.'s Helen would rather "wander in the Elysian-fields / and find the Tree" of life for herself ("WL," 97). Therefore she resists the temptation to let Odysseus rekindle the fire that would make her austere mountain hut the scene of a more conventional lovers' tryst; accepting meditation and art as her destiny, she asks him for a word of comfort instead: "I choose the spell, or enchantment" ("WL," 100). Perseverence in the lonely spiritual climb will bring memory of another world: "remembrance of narcissus buds to come, / buried now, under the snow" ("WL," 100). She will unravel the skein "of tangled memory and desire" with keen blades of thought, exchanging warmth and physical comfort for an icy crown of fresh snow:

> our hidden lair has sanctified *Virgo*,
> the lost, unsatisfied, the broken tryst,
> the half-attained;
>
> love built on dreams
> of the forgotten first unsatisfied embrace,
> is satisfied. ("WL," 103)

Afraid that Helen is in danger of being seduced once more, this time by her own fantasy of a tame, "true" Odysseus, the second choric sequence pulls her further inward, reminding her that he is also part of the world of surging armies and swaying masts, "the shifting scene" ("WL," 104). The chorus urges her to let him go — along with Paris and Achilles—all of whom are manifestations of "Apollo on the Walls," the proponents of a warrior ethos. To be self-sustaining, she must discount the patriarchal heterosexual romance in favor of a more archaic, feminized principle of creative energy:

> but it was from Song, you took the seed,
> the sun-seed from the Sun;
>
> none may turn back
> who know that last inseminating kiss;
> this is your world, Leuké,
>
> reality of the white sand,
> the meadow . . .
> *Parthenos.* ("WL," 105)

Adept in her craft, she must "conjure a magic circle of fruit trees" with roots to firmly embrace the "island-Helen" of her own legend ("WL," 106). She must leave conventional coupling to Paris and Oenone to invoke "the greater bliss / of Helios-Helen-Eros" ("WL," 106). Most courageously, she must "accept the accomplished fact" that she is "bereft," feel the pain of this "stark reality," and acknowledge her guilt:

> lift a stone
> and taste the salt of earth, the salt of sea
> and with the stone, strike at your breast and cry,
>
> "alas, alas, mine was the blame,
> mine was the guilt";
> down, down, down the path of glory,
>
> the Sun goes into the dark,
> the Gods decree
> that Helen is deserted utterly. ("WL," 108)

At this lowest point of desolate self-knowledge the poem's glorious final section begins. When she asserts that Helen is "blessed

231

anew" by wrapping herself in the "dark veils" of "the *femme noire*,"
H.D. adopts an animating relationship to guilt like that described by
Robert Jay Lifton, who distinguishes between the static guilt of
depression and "the ability to connect self-blame with imagery of
change and possibility, with imagery beyond guilt."[20] Helen knows
that "*l'isle blanche is l'isle noir*," that she will be restored by this
Egyptian ceremonial wrapping, her wound mystically cauterized, and
she is rewarded for daring to delve so deeply by the memory of gaiety
and harmony at "home" before the war and the company of her
childhood grandam:

> it was all over,
> I was wrapped in a tight shroud
> but you appear; the death-bands fall away;
>
> you have come, grandam, no toothless grin,
> no *corbeau sur une crâne*;
> "remember," you say, "Helen, remember." ("WL," 110)

The appearance of Helen's "grandam" is literally regenerative: it
generates all of the important women in the poet's life history. With this
single word H.D. subtly refers to herself (a hobbling old woman
whose crutch Helen carries), to her maternal grandmother "Mamalie"
from whom she inherited the "gift" of vision; and since she identifies
with her daughter Perdita who is about to give birth, she refers also to
her mother. Finally, by making this "grandam" the midwife to her
poem, she includes her relationship with Bryher. Helen's "*Grand
Dame*" takes her back before the "treachery or guilt or subterfuge" of
heterosexual encounter to a time of innocent laughter and enables her
to review her life from this recentered perspective. With increasing
excitement she answers her own haunting question, "There was a
Helen before there was a war, / but who remembers her?" by
assimilating all the broken pieces of her legend in a self-reflexive
emotional sweep ("WL," 110). "O grandam, you, you, you" is
followed by Menelaus, then Odysseus, then Achilles, and finally

Paris's "ultimate recognition," their departure, and "a moment of indecision" when she might have wavered, "fighting for her kingdom, / like a tiger" ("WL," 114).

Exorcising the effect of male myths of creativity with the aid of her grandam, Helen asks if "Helios-Helen-Eros," blissful self-realization, is the product of "golden first love, innocence," that is, "the Child before the Child was born" imagined as a divine son, the inheritance of the "golden Menelaus" ("WL," 112). She answers, no: "not Menelaus, but myself gazed up at me, // in the veiled glance of Helen-Hermione" ("WL," 112). In childbirth the powerful matrilineal bond reasserts itself, resulting in the mythical child Euphorion, in the memory of her historical child, Hermione, and in a new self-representation, the dream child "Espérance," who represents the hope of a utopian future:

> Hermione lived her life and lives in history;
> Euphorion, *Espérance*, the infinite bliss,
> lives in the hope of something that will be,
>
> the past made perfect;
> this is the tangible
> this is reality. ("WL," 112)

In the passage above, when H.D. examines the effect on consciousness of her own reproductive experience, she realizes that both sexual violence against women in patriarchy and traditional depictions of Eros (as the golden son) serve the male imagination's need to mediate the "alienation of the male seed in the copulative act" and the biological uncertainty of paternity.[21] She realizes also that woman's more extensive role in procreative process produces no such need: labor mediates the alienation of the fetus in the art of giving birth and guarantees that the child is hers. Therefore, when Helen associates the word "Child" with the Euphorion of received myth, with her historical daughter Hermione, and with Hope for the future, H.D. dilates that word's significance both materially and temporally. She simultaneously denotes an anterior literary corpus, a human being exterior to discourse, and a state of mind—thus creating an area of meaning in which the past, present, and future intersect. Through the medium of language the child and the poem become coextensive.

But the distinction between her historical daughter Hermione and the symbolic child "Euphorion, *Espérance*" bears a freight of pain as well as pleasure. "Did Paris remember her?" This last resonant question reminds Helen of "the guilt, the blame, the desolation" associated with Troy and triggers the searing irony of the final two additional lyrics ("WL," 114, 116). Here H.D. shows how public meanings shape the consciousness of individuals through metaphors that become embedded in ordinary speech, thus giving socially determined roles an immutable "natural" quality. With extraordinary lyric intensity she uncovers the fraught nexus of experience embedded in the childbirth metaphor by revealing that Helen is bound by the internalization of her role in procreation even at the very moment when she wishes to transcend it:

> grandam, midwife, *Sage-Femme*,
> I pray you, as with his last breath,
> a man might pray, keep *Espérance*,
>
> our darling from my sight,
> for bliss so great,
> the thought of that soft touch,
>
> would drag me back to life
> and I would rest. ("WL," 115)

Brought forth in darkness, the poem is placed in Helen's arms by a *Sage-Femme* who seems to her alternately wise and cruel because nurturance itself means renewed confrontation with potentially debilitating personal ghosts, with her "phantom self": invisiblity, hopelessness, fate. When Helen mentions the midwife's cruelty, surely H.D. was thinking of generations of women who died in childbirth or of the depleted bodies of prematurely old women given over to nursing.

Helen's cry "I die in agony whether I give or do not give" does not refer simply to biological fact; it also asks us to consider a social problem. For as Adrienne Rich has pointed out, the act of suckling a child, like a sexual act, "may be tense, physically painful, charged with cultural feelings of inadequacy and guilt; or, like a sexual act, it can be a physically delicious, elementally soothing experience, filled with a tender sexuality."[22] All depends on whether the woman's labor has been forced or not.

Though fraught with pain, the finale of the poem is also ecstatic: "I am delirious now and mean to be, / the whole earth shudders with my ecstasy" ("WL," 116). Here H.D. has in mind Heidegger's *"die drei Ekstasen der Zeitlichkeit"* ("the three ecstasies of temporality"); because it fuses the past, present, and future, the act of remembering "is an *ecstasy*, even if the thing remembered is as — 'some dull opiate to the brain'" (*ET*, 55). Chosen by the poet and therefore not an affliction, the nurture of Hope explodes the prison-house of language. With a compression reminiscent of metaphysical poetry, the last lines of "Winter Love" simultaneously convey both an intense conflict between self-preservation and maternal love and an ethical imperative derived from these very feelings. For when she speaks of nurture, H.D. speaks not only of motherhood but of the possibility of wider sociosexual relations motivated by concerns beyond dominance and control; and when she speaks of death, H.D. does not mean killing, but the handing over of a vitality that can then be recycled. Women's reproductive consciousness is also a consciousness that she herself was born of a woman's labor, a labor that links human beings with natural process and confirms genetic coherence and species continuity. Finally, Helen willingly sacrifices herself to Hope because what is sacrificed is the institution of motherhood, not the truth of female experience. By proclaiming the centrality of both the child and her words, H.D. reappropriates the "corporeal ground" (Rich's words) of her intelligence and her creativity:

> cruel, cruel, *Sage-Femme*,
>
> wiser than all the regents of God's throne,

235

why do you torture me?
come, come, O *Espérance*,

Espérance, O golden bee,
take life afresh and if you must,
so slay me. ("WL," 117)

If "Winter Love" concludes with a passage of surpassing lyrical intensity, H.D.'s last poem, "Hermetic Definition," is a masterpiece of elegant understatement. Having created a new mother-poet-self at the end of "Winter Love," H.D. dramatizes the operation of her new (pro)creative power more fully by basing the entire tripartite structure of her last poem on the trimesters of pregnancy and celebrating this double birthing power. Working within both contexts at once, she gives new life to a dead male admirer by immortalizing him in her poem; she differentiates her poetics from those of a male contemporary; and she takes her place in literary tradition on her own terms. This blurring of the distinction between art and life is evident even in the poem's title: at first glance it refers to the mythical Hermes, charlatan, magician, god of secrets, psychopomp, but a second look reveals his initials to be the poet's own. H.D.'s allusion to Hermes emphasizes the magical rather than the biological nature of the phallic symbol; as Norman O. Brown reports, historically the phallus does not signify the penis but craft itself.[23]

As if to lend credibility to the old wives' tale that women replicate the life cycle in the process of parturition, the three parts (or trimesters) of "Hermetic Definition" reflect back on three stages of the poet's life history (and three phases of her relationship with men) while referring simultaneously to the present. In part 1, "Red Rose and a Beggar" (which glances back at her book of poems *Red Roses for Bronze*), H.D. addresses Lionel Durand, the Haitian reporter who interviewed her for *Newsweek*, making him typify all the handsome young men in her past who were both attentive and undermining. In part 2, "Grove of Academe," her tribute to Saint-John Perse (who was honored with her by the American Academy of Arts and

236

Letters) also refers to such midlife mentors as Freud, and to the enlightened male literary tradition represented in her work by Shakespeare and William Morris. Similarly, part 3, "Star of Day," refers not only to the rebirth in the poem of the dead Durand but to her final self-representation as the poet-mother who bears the poem-child.

In part 1, though she appears to question why the young Durand came from Paris to "trouble [her] decline," H.D. quickly makes him the vehicle through which "the reddest rose unfolds," the rose of maternal love that she has equated with creative passion.[24] More like a son to her than a lover, he is associated with the Doge, chief magistrate of Venice, a city connected with her mother (Venice-Venus) and with female creative power. Though he mistakenly minimizes her verses in his review, his very arrival from Paris as "Bar-Isis . . . son of Isis" testifies to her power of naming, to her inheritance of the living Word. Though he cannot appreciate her hospitality (a heart condition prevents him from drinking her wine or eating salted food), she would enter his senses through the fragrance of incense, praying to him as to a youthful counterpart of the "Isis-self": "bid me not despair, / Child of the ancient hierarchy . . . / and you to-day" ("HD," 8).

H.D.'s association of Durand with "Bar-Isis" or Horus leads her to consult occult sources once more to convey his deepest significance. This time she refers to Robert Ambelain's *Dans l'ombre des cathédrales*, which claims that ancient Egyptian religious beliefs influenced Christian doctrine under cover of Christian nomenclature and iconography. Specifically, she employs Ambelain's idea that the Cathedral of Notre Dame in Paris is built on the site of an ancient temple of Isis, whose cult has endured among initiates through the centuries. Ambelain writes that the inscription on the cathedral is written in code: though it seems merely to mark the dedication of the building to the Virgin Mary in 1257, it actually expresses an alchemical formula for controlling the forces of *Mère-Nature*.[25] As Vincent Quinn has pointed out, these beliefs underlie H.D.'s conviction that the young man from Paris is related to her at a spiritual level beyond their external circumstances. Like Isis and Horus, "they are performers in the perennial drama of Creator and Creation. The awe and love she feels for the visitor is the love of parent for child and of the poet for his art."[26]

As Bar-Isis, Durand helps H.D. to recall once more "the rush, the fervour" of youthful enchantment and the "tremor, the earthquake" of her inevitable fall: "who can escape life, fever, / the darkness of the abyss?" ("HD," 9). Though she is "judged—prisoner" by her refusal to disregard her infatuation, a feeling prompted not only by his beauty and strength but also by his vulnerability, H.D. chooses to translate the Latin word "*Secondo*," from the inscription on Notre Dame, to clarify what he is to her: "*Seconde, aide, et favorise // l'action de la Nature*" ("HD," 12). Realizing that Durand's heart condition means that he "might go at any moment," she utilizes her own "condition," a fertile state of mind, to conceive of his importance. Referring first to Pound's line (from "Canto 106") "So slow is the rose to open," she turns to lines from her early poem "Red Roses for Bronze" to explain that the ideal of beauty that inspired her love and artistry then was an "abstraction," still unborn because she still connected sexuality with romantic love. Fusing Durand with Rafer Johnson, the U.S. decathlon star, she offers new lines to him, a "reality," in the hope that these new words, which celebrate maternal love, will outlive both of them:

> if it took 30 years for my *Red Roses for Bronze*
> to find the right image,
>
> perhaps in 30 years,
>
> life's whole complexity will be annulled,
> when this *reddest rose unfolds*. ("HD," 16)

Both H.D.'s ambitious claim of immortality and Pound's despairing questions about the value of his work invite a moment of uncertainty. What has *she* done with her life? What do her assortment of angels and devils amount to? Will they guide her "with dignity // into a known port" ("HD," 17), or do they invite reproof and mockery? Devotion to her craft is all that she is really certain of: "hours, minutes, days, years" spent to assemble "lines competent to praise" ("HD," 19). Rejecting the traditional stimulants used to get in touch with spiritual forces (hemp, sesame-seed, poppies), her litany requires only "the days' trial" and the "*hachish supérieur* / of dream": "I must keep my identity, / walk unfalteringly toward a Lover, / the *hachish supérieur* of dream" ("HD," 21).

H.D.'s devotion to poetry is rewarded in part 2, when she meets Saint-John Perse, whose work she has admired. For like the "Red Rose and a Beggar," "Grove of Academe" refers to not only her past but also a recent event, the ceremony on May 25, 1960, at the American Academy and National Institute of Arts and Letters, where H.D. received in person the Award of Merit Medal for Poetry. On that occasion, Perse, the French poet-diplomat who was the previous recipient of the award, was made an honorary member of the Academy. In a letter to Norman Pearson, H.D. writes that when she faltered while walking back from the podium, he reached out to steady her. She remembered "the gallant Léger Léger's gesture as [she] staggered—no swayed gracefully—from the reader's desk."[27] Perhaps because it evoked her vision at Corfu a lifetime earlier, H.D. makes this gesture the dramatic center of her poem. Perse's recognition of her, recognition by a male poet of her own age whom she admires, is her real reward for a life of devotion:

> it's that you write,
>
> even that I have written;
> what is miraculous? I don't know,
> it just happened,
>
> it wasn't that I was accepted
> by the State, the Office, the Assembly,
> but by you. ("HD," 24)

H.D. returns Perse's gallant gesture and differentiates her work from his by writing a duet with him. (She quotes from his work eighteen times in French and alludes repeatedly to his imagery.) Addressing him deferentially as "Seigneur," she praises the magnifi-

239

cence of his worship of the Muse, claiming that she is "swept away" in the "orgy" of his lush, tropical landscapes. Yet "the aloes, the acacia" of his remembrance of childhood do not detract from the stark rocks and "camomile-daisies" of hers; rather, her own "personal treasures" are enhanced by the contrast: their two bodies of work "meet in antithesis" ("HD," 31). Similarly, though she admires his "giant-concept / of deserts, the earth entire," she does not feel competitive in any destructive way; rather, he draws her out "to compete with [his] frenzy" on her own terms ("HD," 33). Referring simultaneously to her own early conflict around motherhood and authorship depicted in "Helios and Athene," and to Aeschylus' *The Libation Bearers* (where Clytemnestra dreams she gave birth to a serpent who will bite her — her son Orestes), H.D. writes of her new camaraderie with Perse:

> I am alive in your recognition;
> Athene stands guardian,
> and there is ecstasy and healing
>
> in her acceptance of the ποιηγησ [poet-maker] fantasy,
>
> her serpent feeding
> from a cup . . . . ("HD," 33)

A lover/son who incorporates the great mother in his speech, Perse's *Anabase* reveals the secret of his revitalizing power: *j'aviverai du sel / les bouches mortes du désir*" ("I will revive with salt the dead mouths of desire") ("HD," 34).

In the process of paying tribute to the extraordinary range and power of Perse's poetry, to his capacity for "*transhumance*," spiritual ascendancy or detachment, H.D. clarifies her own poetic values, which center instead on connection with nature and with other human beings, a moral by-product of female socialization.[28] If he would be "one with Time and the star cycle," then by antithesis she is an "ant or eel," a small snake who would dart "straight for the antithetical center" ("HD," 37). She knows that, though her "step is uncertain," she must "gain humanity again" ("HD," 39). Perse and the Grove are there as "the exact intellectual component / or the exact emotional opposite" of the "reddest rose" ("HD," 41). Refusing to step "over the horizon" with Perse, she returns to her "old habit" of "lighting candles" on Christmas Eve like her Moravian ancestors.

H.D. tells us that "Grove of Academe" was completed on Christmas Eve, and that she finished the abbreviated last part, "Star of Day," on February 19, just after Valentine's Day. (Her first grandson's name was Valentine.) Though she began her last poem just after Durand's death, the morality of connection she celebrates in this poetic rebirth gains in poignancy when we remember that H.D.'s father and brother died during her second pregnancy. (Her frame of reference may also include the fates of her male contemporaries: Aldington, sick and broke; Pound, certifiably insane; Lawrence, prematurely dead.) With the explicit intention of giving "him" new life, and the implicit one of representing an apocalyptic view of history that privileges regeneration, H.D. compares herself with Saïs, the Egyptian city where Isis reigned supreme and "brought forth the Star of Day, / at midnight when the shadows are most dense, / the nights longest and most desperate" ("HD," 45).

"What have you done?" she asks Saïs, "what has the word done?" ("HD," 46). H.D.'s answer draws on the experience of parturition from the perspective of both mother and poet: one carries another self inside oneself to which one gives birth. As she reviews the history of this poem's composition—her earlier "condition," the required period of separation, and now the delivery—H.D. frames her final contribution as a woman poet in terms that reinscribe the mother's undeniable virtue as a generator of new concepts as well as of human beings: "*générateur, générant,* / never to be gainsaid" ("HD," 50). The creation of a language that recovers the themes and values of female experience for the general good enables H.D. to triumph over male dismissal and rejection. Her words "*I want to light candles,*" reminiscent of her Moravian childhood, remind her that the angel Azrael, who seemed demonic, was not the angel of death "but of birth" ("HD," 51). Praying to him, she will revive both Durand and herself. Now that he is born in her poem, it does not matter whether Durand has "gone to archangels and lovers / or to infernal adventures" for they exist together inside the text she has created ("HD," 55).

The last lines of "Hermetic Definition" convey the quiet certainty of enlightenment, the peaceful homecoming of the imagination that H.D. wished for. With a simplicity achieved after a lifetime of endeavor, mourning becomes morning:

> there is always an end;
> now I draw my nun-grey about me
> and know adequately
>
> *the reddest rose*
> *the unalterable law* . . .
> Night brings the Day. ("HD," 55)

H.D.'s final image, "Star of Day," revokes both the frigid polestar of her early poem "Stars wheel in purple" and the flaming "star in the night" of *Helen in Egypt*. Instead, it suggests the star on top of her childhood Christmas tree and the sun, images of regeneration that transcend the human. Having lived through the devastation of two world wars, H.D. came to see her effort to create new symbolic forms — that incorporate female reproductive consciousness into the cultural mainstream — not only as a struggle for both women and an abstract humanism but also as a means of integrating the historical with the natural world. In her last poem she canonizes this effort, adding to the panoply of world literature and myth.

Notes

Introduction

(After the first full citation in notes, references to H.D.'s works are made parenthetically in the text.)

1. Adrienne Rich, *Of Woman Born: Motherhood as Experience and Institution* (New York: Bantam, 1974), 21.

2. "Advent," in *Tribute to Freud* (Boston: David R. Godine, 1974), 148; hereafter cited in the text as "Advent."

3. "*H.D. by Delia Alton* [Notes on Recent Writing]," *Iowa Review* 16 (Fall 1986): 184. H.D. writes: "I grew tired of hearing these poems referred to, as crystalline. Was there no other way of criticizing, of assessing them? But perhaps I did not see, did not dare see any further than my critics. Perhaps my annoyance with them was annoyance with myself."

4. Rich, *Of Woman Born*, chapter 2.

5. Barbara Johnson, "Apostrophe, Animation, and Abortion," *Diacritics* 16 (Spring 1986): 37.

6. J. David Sapir, "The Anatomy of Metaphor," in *The Social Use of Metaphor*, ed. J. David Sapir and J. Christopher Crocker (Philadelphia: University of Pennsylvania Press, 1977), 6.

7. Ibid., 10.

8. Susan Stanford Friedman, "Creativity and the Childbirth Metaphor: Gender Difference in Literary Discourse," *Feminist Studies* 13 (Spring 1987): 75.

9. Gregory Zilboorg, "Masculine and Feminine," *Psychiatry* 7 (1944): 257–96; Karen Horney, "The Dread of Woman," in *Feminine Psy-*

chology, ed. Harold Kelman (New York: W. W. Norton, 1967), 133–46.

10. Mary O'Brien, *The Politics of Reproduction* (Boston: Routledge and Kegan Paul, 1981), 20.

11. Ibid., 125.

12. Sandra Gilbert and Susan Gubar, *The Madwoman in the Attic: The Woman Writer and the Nineteenth-Century Literary Imagination* (New Haven: Yale University Press, 1979), 7.

13. Elizabeth Sacks, *Shakespeare's Images of Pregnancy* (London: Macmillan, 1980), 4.

14. Terry Castle, "Lab'ring Bards: Birth *Topoi* and English Poetics 1660–1820," *Journal of English and Germanic Philology* 78 (April 1978): 193–208.

15. Loralee MacPike, "The Fallen Woman's Sexuality: Childbirth and Censure," in *Sexuality and Victorian Literature*, ed. Don Richard Cox (Knoxville: University of Tennessee Press, 1984), 54–71.

16. Sandra Gilbert and Susan Gubar, *No Man's Land: The Place of the Woman Writer in the Twentieth Century*, vol. 1 (New Haven: Yale University Press, 1988), chapter 1.

17. William York Tindall, *A Reader's Guide to James Joyce* (New York: Farrar, Straus and Giroux, 1971), 199–200.

18. Jeannine Hensley, ed., *The Works of Ann Bradstreet* (Cambridge, Mass.: Harvard University Press, 1967), 221.

19. Quoted by Susan Gubar in "The Birth of the Artist as Heroine: (Re)Production, the Kunstler Tradition, and the Fiction of Katherine Mansfield," in *The Representation of Women in Fiction*, ed. Carolyn Heilbrun and Margaret R. Higgonet (Baltimore: John Hopkins University Press, 1983), 19.

20. Linda Gordon, *Woman's Body, Woman's Right: A Social History of Birth Control in America* (New York: Penguin, 1977), 189.

21. Christopher Crocker, "The Social Functions of Rhetorical Forms," in *The Social Use of Metaphor*, ed. J. David Sapir and J. Christopher Crocker, 50.

22. Gubar, "The Birth of the Artist as Heroine," 39.

23. Richard Coe, *When the Grass Was Taller: Autobiography and the Experience of Childhood* (New Haven: Yale University Press, 1984), 1–40.

24. Ibid., 9.

25. Peter Coveney, *Poor Monkey: The Child in Literature* (Suffolk,

England: Richard Clay, 1957), Introduction.

26. Carol Sklenicka, "Lawrence's Vision of the Child: Reimagining Character and Consciousness," *D.H. Lawrence Review* 18 (Summer/Fall 1985–86): 151–68.

27. Susan Stanford Friedman and Rachel Blau DuPlessis, "'Woman Is Perfect': H.D.'s Debate with Freud," *Feminist Studies* 7 (1981): 417–30.

28. Jessica Benjamin, "The Oedipal Riddle: Authority, Autonomy, and the New Narcissism," in *The Problem of Authority in America*, ed. John P. Diggins and Mark E. Kann (Philadelphia: Temple University Press, 1981), 196.

29. Rachel Blau Duplessis, *Writing beyond the Ending: Narrative Strategies of Twentieth-Century Women Writers* (Bloomington: Indiana University Press, 1985), chapter 5.

30. Adalaide Morris, "A Relay of Power and of Peace: H.D. and the Spirit of the Gift," *Contemporary Literature* 27 (Winter 1986): 493–524.

31. D. H. Lawrence, *Fantasia of the Unconscious* (New York: Viking, 1960), 179.

Chapter 1

1. *Tribute to Freud* (Boston: David R. Godine, 1974), 37; hereafter cited in the text as *TF*.

2. Nancy Chodorow, *The Reproduction of Mothering: Psychoanalysis and the Sociology of Gender* (Berkeley: University of California Press, 1978). Chodorow argues that children of both sexes develop core gender identity concomitantly with differentiation: the boy learns his gender identity as being not female, while the girl builds her gender identity on continuity and identification with mother. After the oedipal phase, when male power and cultural hegemony give sex differences a transformed value, girls may experience difficulties with feminine identity because of the male bias in favor of separation over relation.

3. *Notes on Thought and Vision & The Wise Sappho* (San Francisco: City Lights, 1982), 40; hereafter cited in the text as *NTV*.

4. Barbara Guest, *Herself Defined: The Poet H.D. and Her World* (New York: Doubleday, 1984), 111. For a more detailed account of the

relationship between H.D. and Aldington after Perdita's birth, see Caroline Zilboorg, "A New Chapter in the Lives of H.D. and Richard Aldington: Their Relationship with Clement Shorter," *Philological Quarterly* 68 (Spring 1989): 241–61.

5. Kenneth Fields, Introduction to *Tribute to Freud*, xxxiv.

6. Barbara Ehrenreich and Dierdre English, *For Her Own Good: 150 Years of the Experts' Advice to Women* (New York: Anchor, 1979), 127.

7. Havelock Ellis, *Studies in the Psychology of Sex* (New York: Random House, 1906), 2: 230. See also idem, *The Dance of Life* (Boston: Houghton Mifflin, 1923), 113.

8. Adalaide Morris, "Projected Pictures: H.D.'s Visionary Moments," *Contemporary Literature* 25 (Winter 1984).

9. In her article "The Oedipal Riddle," cited earlier, Jessica Benjamin summarizes Heinz Kohut's theories as follows:

> Kohut understands the narcissistic dilemma primarily in terms of a failure to receive positive responses to one's early narcissistic strivings. The more satisfied the early strivings for self-display and autonomy . . . the less likely the self-image will remain grandiose. In the preoedipal phase there are two types of experience needed: to merge with another's cohesive self and to be mirrored by an audience in one's autonomous performance. Given essentially positive experiences, the child can react to minor losses by developing a sense of self and providing these functions for itself (optimal frustrations). Appropriate gratification would allow narcissism to develop naturally from fantasies of omnipotence to real autonomy. (203)

10. Carl Kerenyi, *Eleusis: Archetypal Image of Mother and Daughter*, trans. Ralph Manheim (New York: Pantheon, 1967), 149.

11. Albert Gelpi, Introduction to *Notes on Thought and Vision*, 13.

12. *Magic Ring*, ms. at the Beinecke Library, 152ff.

13. Carl Kerenyi and C. G. Jung, *Essays on a Science of Mythology* (New York: Bollingen Foundation, 1949), 50.

14. Adalaide Morris, "Reading H.D.'s 'Helios and Athene,' " in *Extended Outlooks: The Iowa Review Collection of Contemporary Women*

Writers, ed. Jane Cooper et al. (New York: Collier, 1982), 157.

15. Ibid., 157.

16. "Helios and Athene," in *Extended Outlooks*, 150; hereafter cited in the text as "HA."

17. Barbara G. Walker, ed., *The Woman's Encyclopedia of Myths and Secrets* (San Francisco: Harper and Row, 1983), 833.

18. Philip Slater, *The Glory of Hera: Greek Mythology and the Greek Family* (Boston: Beacon Press, 1968), 95.

19. Carol C. Nadelson, " 'Normal' and 'Special' Aspects of Pregnancy: A Psychological Approach," in *The Woman Patient: Medical and Psychological Interfaces*, vol. 1, ed. Malkah Notman and Carol Nadelson (New York: Plenum, 1978), chapter 6.

20. Marianne Hirsch, *The Mother/Daughter Plot: Narrative, Psychoanalysis, Feminism* (Bloomington: Indiana University Press, 1989), 15.

21. Slater, *The Glory of Hera*, 95.

Chapter 2

1. Perdita Schaffner, "Sketch of H.D.: The Egyptian Cat," in H.D.'s *Hedylus* (Redding Ridge, Conn.: Black Swan Books, 1980), 142; hereafter cited in the text as "Sketch."

2. John Cournos, *Miranda Masters* (New York: Alfred A. Knopf, 1926).

3. H.D. to John Cournos, in Donna Krolik Hollenberg, ed., "Art and Ardour in World War One: Selected Letters from H.D. to John Cournos," *Iowa Review* 16 (Fall 1986): 148.

4. H.D.'s novel *HERmione* was published by New Directions in 1981; the first four chapters of *Paint It Today* were published in *Contemporary Literature* 27 (Winter 1986).

5. See Nadelson. " 'Normal' and 'Special' Aspects of Pregnancy."

6. *Fields of Asphodel*, unpublished ms. at the Beinecke Library, sec. I, p. 11; hereafter cited in the text as *FA*.

7. Larry G. Peppers and Ronald J. Knapp, *Motherhood and Mourning: Perinatal Death* (New York: Praeger, 1980), 56.

8. Marshall H. Klaus and John Kennell, *Maternal-Infant Bonding* (St. Louis: C. V. Mosby, 1976), 210. See also Nancy Chodorow, "Family

Structure and Feminine Personality," in *Women, Culture and Society*, ed. M. Rosaldo and L. Lamphere (Palo Alto, Calif.: Stanford University Press, 1974), 46.

9. *Compassionate Friendship*, unpublished ms. at the Beinecke Library, 51; hereafter cited in the text as *CF*.

10. Jill Betz Bloom, "The Effect of Parental Object Loss upon the Course of Female Psychosexual Development" (Ph.D. dissertation, Boston College, 1981), 19–20.

11. *Paint It Today*, unpublished ms. at the Beinecke Library, chap. 1, p. 6; hereafter cited in the text as *PIT*.

12. Chodorow, *The Reproduction of Mothering*.

13. *HERmione* (New York: New Directions, 1981), 4; hereafter cited in the text as *H*.

14. Susan Friedman and Rachel Blau DuPlessis, "'I Had Two Loves Separate': The Sexualities of H.D.'s *Her*," *Montemora* 8 (1981).

15. Helen K. Gediman, "Romanticism, Narcissism and Creativity," *Journal of the American Psychoanalytic Association* 23 (1975).

16. *Palimpsest* (Carbondale: Southern Illinois Press, 1968), title page; hereafter cited in the text as *P*.

17. Sharon K. Heybob, *The Cult of Isis in the Graeco-Roman World* (London: E. J. Brill, 1978), 73.

18. R. E. Witt, *Isis in the Graeco-Roman World* (Ithaca, N.Y.: Cornell University Press, 1971), 22.

19. Heybob, *The Cult of Isis*, 1.

20. Cyrena Pondrom, ed., "Selected Letters from H.D. to F. S. Flint: A Commentary on the Imagist Period," *Contemporary Literature* 10 (Autumn 1969): 593.

21. *Hedylus* (Redding Ridge, Conn.: Black Swan Books, 1980), 80: hereafter cited in the text as *Hed*.

22. M. Esther Harding, *Woman's Mysteries* (New York: Harper and Row, 1976), chapter 11.

23. Adrienne Rich, "Vesuvius at Home: The Power of Emily Dickinson," in *On Lies, Secrets and Silence: Selected Prose* (New York: W. W. Norton, 1979).

24. Chodorow, in Rosaldo and Lamphere, eds., *Women, Culture and Society*, 64.

Chapter 3

1. *Some Notes on Recent Writing*, excerpted in *Bid Me to Live* (Redding Ridge, Conn.: Black Swan Books, 1983), 204–11; hereafter cited in the text.

2. Jeanne Kammer, "The Art of Silence and the Forms of Women's Poetry," in *Shakespeare's Sisters*, ed. Sandra Gilbert and Susan Gubar (Bloomington: Indiana University Press, 1979), 153–64.

3. Alicia Ostriker, "No Rule of Procedure: H.D.'s Open Poetics," excerpted in *How(ever)* 5 (October 1989): 21.

4. Pound praises poetry that is "austere, direct, and free from emotional slither" in "A Retrospect," in *Literary Essays* (New York: New Directions, 1968), 12. He uses the phrase "mythopoetic sense" in a letter included in *Ezra Pound and Dorothy, Their Letters (1909–1940)*, ed. Omar Pound and A. Walton Litz (London: Faber and Faber, 1985), 343.

5. Kerenyi and Jung, *Essays on a Science of Mythology*, chapter 2.

6. *Collected Poems: 1912–1944*, ed. Louis Martz (New York: New Directions, 1983), 5–42; hereafter cited in the text as *CP*.

7. *Autobiographical Notes*, ms. at the Beinecke Library.

8. Rachel Blau DuPlessis, "Romantic Thralldom in H.D.," *Contemporary Literature* 20, no. 2 (1978): 178.

9. *Notes On Euripides, Pausanias, and Greek Lyric Poets*, ms. at the Beinecke Library, 6; hereafter cited in the text as "Notes on Greek Poets."

10. Susan Gubar, "Sapphistries," *Signs* 10, no. 1 (1984).

11. Letter to Bryher, February 14, 1919, ms. at the Beinecke Library.

12. Stephen Orgel, *The Illusion of Power: Political Theatre in the English Renaissance* (Berkeley: University of California Press, 1975).

13. Carl Kerenyi, *Athene: Virgin and Mother* (Zurich: Spring 1978) 77.

14. Lillian Faderman, *Surpassing the Love of Men* (New York: William Morrow, 1981).

15. Kerenyi, *Eleusis*, 64.

16. Ibid., 57.

17. Linda Clader, *Helen: The Evolution from Divine to Heroic in Greek Epic Tradition* (Amsterdam, The Netherlands: E. J. Brill, 1976), 2.

18. Susan Friedman, *Psyche Reborn: The Emergence of H.D.* (Bloomington: Indiana University Press, 1981), 234.

19. Robert Jay Lifton, *The Life of the Self* (New York: Simon and Schuster, 1976), 23.

20. Guest, *Herself Defined*, 194.

21. Susan Stanford Friedman, "Modernism of the 'Scattered Remnant': Race and Politics in the Development of H.D.'s Modernist Vision," in *H.D.: Woman and Poet*, ed. Michael King (Orono, Maine: National Poetry Foundation, 1986), 91–116.

22. For a more detailed discussion of the transpositions in *Red Roses for Bronze*, see Marilyn Authur, "Psychomythology: The Case of H.D.," in *Rhetoric, Literature, and Interpretation*, ed. Harry R. Garvin (Lewisburg, Pa.: Bucknell University Press, 1983), 65–71.

23. William Shakespeare, *The Winter's Tale*, ed. Frederick E. Pierce (New Haven: Yale University Press, 1955), 70.

Chapter 4

1. Guest, *Herself Defined*, 245.

2. H.D. to Bryher, November 1, 1935, quoted by Louis Martz in the introduction to *Collected Poems*, xxiv.

3. Friedman, *Psyche Reborn*, 12.

4. H.D. to Bryher, March 1, 1933, ms. at the Beinecke Library.

5. Ibid.

6. H.D. to Bryher, March 5, March 10, and March 23, 1933; mss. at the Beinecke Library. See also *Tribute to Freud*, 17, 44, and "Advent," 131.

7. H.D. to George Plank, May 1, 1935, ms. at the Beinecke Library.

8. Kerenyi and Jung, *Essays on a Science of Mythology*, 50.

9. *Magic Ring*, unpublished ms. at Beinecke Library, section II, p. 162; hereafter cited in the text as *MR*.

10. H.D. to Bryher, April 25, 1933, ms. at the Beinecke Library.

11. H.D. to Bryher, April 26, 1933, ms. at the Beinecke Library.

12. H.D. to Bryher, April 27, 1933, ms. at the Beinecke Library.

13. H.D. to Bryher, April 24 or 25, 1933, ms. at the Beinecke Library.

14. Ibid.

15. Ibid.

16. Ibid.

17. Ibid.

18. Chodorow, *The Reproduction of Mothering*, 147.

19. H.D. to Bryher, May 3, 1933, ms. at the Beinecke Library.

20. Ibid.

21. H.D. to Bryher, May 15, 1933, ms. at the Beinecke Library. "Uc-n" is H.D.'s idiosyncratic abbreviation for "the unconscious."

22. H.D. to Bryher, May 26, 1933, ms. at the Beinecke Library.

23. Ibid.

24. Harding, *Woman's Mysteries*, 125.

25. "The Master," in *Collected Poems*.

26. Rachel Blau DuPlessis and Susan Friedman, "'Woman Is Perfect': H.D.'s Debate with Freud," *Feminist Studies* 7 (Fall 1981): 420.

27. Ibid.

28. Sigmund Freud, *New Introductory Lectures on Psychoanalysis*, in *The Standard Edition of the Complete Psychological Works*, vol. 22 (London: Hogarth Press, 1950), 135.

29. Ibid.

30. Louis Martz, Introduction to *Collected Poems*, xxvi.

31. Ibid., xxxvii.

32. H.D. to Bryher, Wednesday, August 14, 1935, ms. at the Beinecke Library.

33. H.D. to Bryher, Saturday, August 24, 1935, ms. at the Beinecke Library.

34. Euripides, *Ion*, trans. with notes by H.D. (Boston: Houghton Mifflin, 1937), 6; hereafter cited in the text as *I*.

35. Guest, *Herself Defined*, 253.

36. *Thorn Thicket*, 13, ms. at the Beinecke Library.

37. *Trilogy* (New York: New Directions, 1973), 4; hereafter cited in the text as *T*.

38. H.D. to Norman Pearson, quoted in Foreword to *Trilogy*.

39. Ibid.

40. H.D., quoted by Guest, *Herself Defined*, 254.

41. H.D., *Within the Walls*, ms. at the Beinecke Library; hereafter cited in the text as *WW*.

42. H.D., *The Gift* (New York: New Directions, 1982), frontispiece; hereafter cited in the text as *G*.

43. Friedman, *Psyche Reborn*, 183.

44. John Jacob Sessler, *Communal Pieties among Early American Moravians* (New York: Henry Holt, 1933), 20.

45. Renee Neu Watkins, "Two Women Visionaries and Death," *Numen* 30, no. 2 (1983): 180.

46. *The Gift*, 10, typescript at the Beinecke Library.

47. Deborah Kelly Kloepfer, "Flesh Made Word: Maternal Inscription in H.D.," *Sagetrieb* 3 (Spring 1984): 27.

48. H.D. to Norman Holmes Pearson, August 9, 1943, ms. at the Beinecke Library.

49. Roy Schafer, "Action and Narration in Psychoanalysis," *New Literary History* 12, no. 1 (1980): 61–85.

50. "Fortune Teller," originally chapter 2 of *The Gift*, omitted from the New Directions publication but published subsequently in the *Iowa Review* 16, no. 3 (1986): 18–41.

51. Sandra Gilbert, "Soldier's Heart: Literary Men, Literary Women and the Great War," *Signs* 8 (Spring 1980).

52. "Fortune Teller," 31.

53. *The Gift*, notes (1959), 10, typescript at the Beinecke Library.

54. Michael Fixler, ed., *The Mentor Bible* (New York: New American Library, 1973), 111.

55. Friedman, *Psyche Reborn*, 76.

56. Susan Gubar, "The Echoing Spell of H.D.'s *Trilogy*," in *Shakespeare's Sisters*, ed. Sandra Gilbert and Susan Gubar (Bloomington: Indiana University Press, 1979), 204.

57. Ibid., 206.

58. Ibid., 206.

59. Ibid., 206.

60. Ibid., 204.

61. Morris, "Projected Pictures: H.D.'s Visionary Moments."

62. Gubar, "The Echoing Spell of H.D.'s Trilogy," 207.

63. Alicia Ostriker, *Writing Like a Woman* (Ann Arbor: University of Michigan Press, 1983), 33.

64. Gustav Davidson, *A Dictionary of Angels* (New York: Free Press, 1967), 33.

65. Herbert Lockyer, *The Women of the Bible* (Grand Rapids, Mich.: Zondervan, 1967), 94.

66. Friedman and DuPlessis, " 'Woman Is Perfect,' " 420.

67. Ibid.

68. Gubar, "The Echoing Spell of H.D.'s *Trilogy*," 211.

69. Ibid.

70. Barbara Walker, *The Woman's Encyclopedia of Myths and Secrets*, 703.

71. Gubar, "The Echoing Spell of H.D.'s *Trilogy*," 213.

Chapter 5

1. Winifred Bryher, *The Days of Mars: A Memoir, 1940–46* (New York: Harcourt Brace Jovanovich, 1972), 151.

2. Peter Coveney, "The Image of the Child in English Literature," in *Rethinking Childhood*, ed. Arlene Skolnick (Boston: Little, Brown, 1976), 62–66.

3. *Bid Me to Live [A Madrigal]* (Redding Ridge, Conn.: Black Swan Books, 1983), 62; hereafter cited in the text as *BML*.

4. *By Avon River* (New York: Macmillan, 1949), 6; hereafter cited in the text as *BAR*. For another reading of *By Avon River*, which also discusses H.D.'s use of the conventions of romance, see Susan Stanford Friedman, " 'Remembering Shakespeare Always, But Remembering Him Differently': H.D.'s *By Avon River*," *Sagetrieb* 2 (Summer/Fall 1983): 45–70. Friedman argues that H.D.'s tribute "moves the reader toward a vision of Shakespeare as an androgynous man and poet dedicated to the mystical Love at the center of the esoteric tradition" (46).

5. Denis de Rougemont, *Love in the Western World*, trans. Montgomery Belgion (New York: Harper & Row, 1974), book III.

6. Robert Langbaum, Introduction to William Shakespeare's *The Tempest*, in *The Signet Classic Shakespeare*, gen. ed. Sylvan Barnet (New York: New American Library, 1964), xxix.

7. Guest, *Herself Defined*, 278.

8. W. H. Auden, Introduction to Shakespeare's *Sonnets*, in *Signet Classic Shakespeare*, ed. William Burto, xxxii.

9. *The Sword Went Out to Sea*, part I, p. 21, ms. at the Beinecke

Library; hereafter cited in the text as *Sword*.

10. Peter E. Firchow, "Rico and Julia: The Hilda Doolittle—D. H. Lawrence Affair Reconsidered," *Journal of Modern Literature* 8, no. 1 (1980): 66.

11. Ibid.

12. David Cavitch, *D. H. Lawrence and the New World* (New York: Oxford University Press, 1969), 30.

13. John Walsh, Afterword to *Bid Me to Live*, 193.

14. Kloepfer, "Flesh Made Word," 48.

15. Walsh, "Afterword," 196.

16. Ibid.

17. H.D. to Bryher, August 28, 1949, ms. at the Beinecke Library.

18. Meyer Schapiro, "On a Painting of Van Gogh," in *Modern Art* (New York: George Braziller, 1978), 92.

19. *Hermetic Definition* (New York: New Directions, 1972), 45; hereafter cited in the text as *HD*.

Chapter 6

1. H.D. to Norman Pearson, November 19, 1960, ms. at the Beinecke Library.

2. H.D. to Norman Pearson, October 10, 1960, ms. at the Beinecke Library.

3. "Winter Love" in *Hermetic Definition*, 112; hereafter cited in the text as "WL."

4. Eliseo Vivas, Appendix on the "Constitutive School," in *D. H. Lawrence: The Failure and the Triumph of Art* (Evanston, Ill.: Northwestern University Press, 1960). See also Wayne C. Booth, *The Company We Keep: An Ethics of Fiction* (Berkeley: University of California Press, 1988), chapter 10.

5. *Helen in Egypt* (New York: New Directions, 1961); 1; hereafter cited in the text as *HE*.

6. William Prost, "The Eidolon of Helen: Diachronic Edition of a Myth" (Ph.D. diss., Catholic University of America, 1977), 19.

7. Albert Gelpi, "Hilda in Egypt," *Southern Review* 18 (Spring 1982): 236.

8. Horace Gregory, Introduction to *Helen in Egypt*, x.

9. Werner Jaeger, *Paideia: The Ideal of Greek Culture*, vol. I, 2nd ed., trans. Gilbert Highet (New York: Oxford University Press, 1945), 13.

10. Charles Rowan Beye, *The Iliad, the Odyssey and the Epic Tradition* (New York: Anchor Books, 1966), 120.

11. Ibid., 164.

12. Susan Friedman, "H.D.," in *Dictionary of Literary Biography 45: American Poets, 1880–1945*, First series ed. Peter Quartermain (Detroit: Dale Research Co., 1986), 54.

13. Homer, *The Odyssey*, trans. Albert Cook (New York: W. W. Norton, 1967), 47.

14. Jessica Benjamin, *The Bonds of Love: Psychoanalysis, Feminism, and the Problem of Domination* (New York: Pantheon, 1988), 79.

15. Susan Gubar, "Mother, Maiden and the Marriage of Death: Women Writers and an Ancient Myth," *Women's Studies* 6 (1979): 302.

16. Gelpi, "Hilda in Egypt,"; Friedman, *Psyche Reborn*, 264.

17. DuPlessis, *Writing beyond the Ending*, 82.

18. H.D. to Norman Pearson, January 17 [1954?], ms. at the Beinecke Library.

19. Friedman, *Psyche Reborn*, 63.

20. Gelpi, "Hilda in Egypt," 245.

21. Northrop Frye, *Anatomy of Criticism* (Princeton: Princeton University Press, 1951), 193.

22. Janice Radway, *Reading the Romance: Women, Patriarchy, and Popular Literature* (Chapel Hill: University of North Carolina Press, 1984), 138.

23. Friedman, *Psyche Reborn*, 292ff., and DuPlessis, *Writing beyond the Ending*.

24. Prost, "The Eidolon of Helen," 323.

Chapter 7

1. Denise Levertov, *The Poet in the World* (New York: New Directions, 1960), 246.

2. Peter L. Berger and Thomas Luckmann, *The Social Construction of Reality: A Treatise in the Sociology of Knowledge* (New York: Anchor, 1967), 40.

3. Julia Kristeva, *Revolution in Poetic Language* (New York: Columbia University Press, 1984), 7.

4. H.D. to Viola Jordan, quoted by Guest, *Herself Defined*, 307.

5. Susan Suleiman, "Writing and Motherhood," in *The (M)other Tongue: Essays in Feminist Psychoanalytic Interpretation* (Ithaca: Cornell University Press, 1985), 352–77.

6. *Thorn Thicket*, 8, ms. at the Beinecke Library; hereafter cited in the text as *TT*.

7. *Hirslanden Notebooks*, I, 1, ms. at the Beinecke Library.

8. Sigmund Freud, *Three Essays on the Theory of Sexuality* (1905), quoted in Harold P. Blum, "On the Concept and Consequences of the Primal Scene," *Psychoanalytic Quarterly* 47, no. 1 (1979): 29–47.

9. Friedman, *Psyche Reborn*, 179.

10. "Vale Ave," in *New Directions 44*, ed. James Laughlin (New York: New Directions, 1982), 18; hereafter cited in the text as "VA."

11. "Sagesse," in *Hermetic Definition* (New York: New Directions, 1972), 58; hereafter cited in the text as "S."

12. Denise Levertov, "Origins of a Poem," in *The Poet in the World*, 45.

13. Charles Poncé, *The Kabbalah* (Wheaton, Ill.: Theosophical Publishing House, 1978), 98.

14. John Ferguson, *Encyclopedia of Mysticism and Mystery Religions* (New York: Crossroad, 1982), 127.

15. Ponce, *The Kabbalah*, 256.

16. Julia Kristeva, *Desire in Language* (New York: Columbia University Press, 1984), 283.

17. H.D. to Norman Holmes Pearson, June 3, 1958, quoted by Michael King in the Introduction to *End to Torment: A Memoir of Ezra Pound* (New York: New Directions, 1979), 6; hereafter cited in the text as *ET*.

18. Kerenyi and Jung, *Essays on a Science of Mythology*, 79.

19. O'Brien, *The Politics of Reproduction*, 49.

20. Robert Jay Lifton, *The Broken Connection: On Death and the Continuity of Life* (New York: Simon and Schuster, 1979), 193.

21. O'Brien, *The Politics of Reproduction*, 29–30.

22. Rich, *Of Woman Born*, 151.

23. Norman O. Brown, *Hermes the Thief*, quoted by Ramascar Shaktini in "Displacing the Phallic Subject: Wittig's Lesbian Writing," *Signs* 8 (Autumn 1982): 34.

24. "Hermetic Definition," in *Hermetic Definition*, 3; hereafter cited in the text as "HD."

25. Robert Ambelain, *Dans l'ombre des cathédrales*, quoted by Vincent Quinn in "H.D.'s 'Hermetic Definition': The Poet as Archetypal Mother," *Contemporary Literature* 18 (Winter 1977): 53.

26. Ibid.

27. H.D. to Norman Pearson, quoted in the Foreword to *Hermetic Definition*.

28. Carol Gilligan, *In a Different Voice: Psychological Theory and Woman's Development* (Cambridge, Mass.: Harvard University Press, 1982), chapter 2.

Bibliography

BOOKS AND PARTS OF BOOKS

Bid Me to Live [A Madrigal]. Redding Ridge, Conn.: Black Swan Books, 1983.

By Avon River. New York: Macmillan, 1949.

Collected Poems, 1912–1944, ed. Louis L. Martz. New York: New Directions, 1983.

End to Torment: A Memoir of Ezra Pound. New York: New Directions, 1979.

Euripides. *Ion*, trans. with notes by H.D. Boston: Houghton Mifflin, 1937.

The Gift. New York: New Directions, 1982.

"*H.D. by Delia Alton* [Notes on Recent Writing]," *Iowa Review* 16 (Fall 1986).

The Hedgehog. London: Brendin, 1936.

Hedylus. Redding Ridge, Conn.: Black Swan Books, 1980.

Helen in Egypt. New York: New Directions, 1961.

"Helios and Athene." In *Extended Outlooks: The Iowa Review Collection of Contemporary Writers*, ed. Jane Cooper *et al*. New York: Macmillan, 1982.

Hermetic Definition. New York: New Directions, 1972.

HERmione. New York: New Directions, 1981.

Notes on Thought and Vision & The Wise Sappho. San Francisco: City Lights, 1982.

259

Palimpsest. Carbondale, Ill.: Southern Illinois University Press, 1968.
Tribute to Freud (including "Advent"). Boston: David R. Godine, 1974.
Trilogy. New York: New Directions, 1973.
The Usual Star. Dijon, France: Imprimerie Darentiere, 1934.
"Vale Ave" (poem). In *New Directions 44*, ed. James Laughlin. New York: New Directions, 1982.

UNPUBLISHED MANUSCRIPTS
(WITH DATES OF COMPOSITION)

Autobiographical Notes (notes), 1949?.
Compassionate Friendship (memoir), 1955.
Fields of Asphodel (novel), 1921–22.
Hirslanden Notebooks (journal), 1957.
Magic Mirror (novel), 1955.
Magic Ring (novel), 1944, 1954.
The Mystery (novel), 1949–51.
Notes on Euripides, Pausanias, and Greek Lyric Poets (essays), 1916? 1918? 1919, 1920.
Paint It Today (novel), 1921.
Pilate's Wife (novel), 1924, 1929, 1934.
The Sword Went Out to Sea (novel), 1946–47.
Thorn Thicket (notes), 1960–61.
The White Rose and the Red (novel), 1948.
Within the Walls (sketches), 1941.

Secondary Sources

Agenda 25 (Autumn/Winter 1987). Special issue devoted to H.D. Aldington, Richard. *Death of a Hero*. London: Penguin Books, 1936.
———. *Life for Life's Sake*. London: Casell, 1968.
Ambelain, Robert. *Dans l'ombre des cathédrales*. Paris: Editions Adyar, 1939.
———. *La Kabbale practique*. Paris: Editions Niclaus, 1931.
Arthur, Marilyn. "Psychomythology: The Case of H.D." In *Rhetoric, Literature, and Interpretation*, ed. Harry R. Garvin. Lewisburg, Pa.:

Bucknell University Press, 1983.

Auden, D. H. Introduction to Shakespeare's *Sonnets*, ed. William Burto. In *The Signet Classic Shakespeare*, gen. ed. Sylvan Barnet. New York: New American Library, 1964.

Benjamin, Jessica. *The Bonds of Love: Psychoanalysis, Feminism, and the Problem of Domination*. New York: Pantheon, 1988.

———. "The Oedipal Riddle: Authority, Autonomy, and the New Narcissism." In *The Problem of Authority in America*, ed. John P. Diggins and Mark E. Kann. Philadelphia: Temple University Press, 1981.

Berger, Peter, and Thomas Luckmann. *The Social Construction of Reality: A Treatise in the Sociology of Knowledge*. New York: Anchor, 1967.

Bernikow, Louise. *Among Women*. New York: Harper and Row, 1980.

Beye, Charles Rowan. *The Iliad, The Odyssey and the Epic Tradition*. New York: Anchor Books, 1966.

Bloom, Jill Betz. "The Effect of Parental Object Loss upon the Course of Female Psychosexual Development." Ph.D. dissertation, Boston College, 1981.

Blum, Harold P. "On the Concept and Consequences of the Primal Scene." *Psychoanalytic Quarterly* 47, no. 1 (1979).

Booth, Wayne C. *The Company We Keep: An Ethics of Fiction*. Berkeley: University of California Press, 1988.

Burnett, Gary. *H.D. Between Image and Epic: The Mysteries of Her Poetics*. Ann Arbor, Mich.: UMI Research Press, 1990.

Bush, Douglas. *Mythology and the Romantic Tradition in English Poetry*. New York: W. W. Norton, 1963.

Bryer, Jackson R., and Pamela Roblyer. "H.D.: A Preliminary Checklist." *Contemporary Literature* 10 (Autumn 1969).

Bryher, Winifred. *The Days of Mars: A Memoir, 1940–46*. New York: Harcourt Brace Jovanovich, 1972.

———. *The Heart to Artemis: A Writer's Memoirs*. New York: Harcourt, Brace and World, 1962.

Camboni, Marina. "H.D.'s Trilogy, Or the Secret Language of Change." *Littérature d'America* 6 (Spring 1985).

Castle, Terry. "Lab'ring Bards: Birth *Topoi* and English Poetics 1660–1820." *Journal of English and Germanic Philology* 78 (April 1978).

Cavitch, David. *D. H. Lawrence and the New World*. New York: Oxford University Press, 1969.

Chaboseau, Jean. *Le Tarot*. Paris: Editions Niclaus, 1946.

Chisholm, Dianne. "H.D.'s Auto*hetero*graphy." *Tulsa Studies in Women's Literature* 9 (Spring 1990).

Chodorow, Nancy, "Family Structure and Feminine Personality." In *Women, Culture, and Society* ed. M. Rosaldo and L. Lamphere. Palo Alto, Calif.: Stanford University Press, 1974.

———. *The Reproduction of Mothering: Psychoanalysis and the Sociology of Gender*. Berkeley: University of California Press, 1978.

Clader, Linda. *Helen: The Evolution from Divine to Heroic in Greek Epic Tradition*. The Netherlands: E. J. Brill, 1976.

Coe, Richard. *When the Grass Was Taller: Autobiography and the Experience of Childhood*. New Haven: Yale University Press, 1984.

Collecott, Diana. "Mass Observation Results." *Line* 13 (Spring 1989).

———. "Remembering Oneself: The Reputation and Later Poetry of H.D." *Critical Quarterly* 27, no. 1.

———. "What Is Not Said: A Study in Textual Inversion." *Textual Practice* 4 (Summer 1990).

Contemporary Literature 10 (Autumn 1969). Special number on H.D.

Contemporary Literature 27 (Winter 1986). Special number on H.D.

Collecott, Diana. "Mass Observation Results." *Line* 13 (Spring 1989).

Cournos, John. *Autobiography*. New York: Alfred A. Knopf, 1935.

———. *Miranda Masters*. New York: Alfred A. Knopf, 1926.

Coveney, Peter. "The Image of the Child in English Literature." In *Rethinking Childhood*, ed. Arlene Skolnick. Boston: Little Brown, 1976.

———. *Poor Monkey: The Child in Literature*. Suffolk: Richard Clay, 1957.

Crocker, Christopher. "The Social Functions of Rhetorical Forms." In *The Social Use of Metaphor*, ed. J. David Sapir and J. Christopher Crocker. Philadelphia: University of Pennsylvania Press, 1977.

Davidson, Gustav. *A Dictionary of Angels*. New York: Free Press, 1967.

de Rougement, Denis. *Love in the Western World*, trans. Montgomery Belgion. New York: Harper and Row, 1974.

Downing, Christine. *The Goddess: Mythological Images of the Feminine*. New York: Crossword, 1981.

DuPlessis, Rachel Blau. *H.D.: The Career of That Struggle*. Bloomington: Indiana University Press, 1986.

———. "Romantic Thralldom in H.D." *Contemporary Literature* 20, no. 2

————. *Writing beyond the Ending: Narrative Strategies of Twentieth-Century Women Writers*. Bloomington: Indiana University Press, 1985.

Ehrenreich, Barbara, and Dierdre English. *For Her Own Good: 150 Years of the Experts' Advice to Women*. New York: Anchor, 1979.

Ellis, Havelock. *The Dance of Life*. Boston: Houghton Mifflin, 1923.

————. *Studies in the Psychology of Sex*. 2 vols. New York: Random House, 1906.

Faderman, Lillian. *Surpassing the Love of Men*. New York: William Morrow, 1981.

Ferguson, John. *Encyclopedia of Mysticism and Mystery Religions*. New York: Crossroad, 1982.

Firchow, Peter. "Rico and Julia: The Hilda Doolittle–D. H. Lawrence Affair Reconsidered." *Journal of Modern Literature* 8, no. 1 (1980).

Fixler, Michael, ed. *The Mentor Bible*. New York: New American Library, 1973.

Freud, Sigmund. *New Introductory Lectures on Psychoanalysis*. In *The Standard Edition of the Complete Psychological Works*. London: Hogarth Press, 1950.

Friedberg, Anne. "Approaching Borderline." *Millenium Film Journal*, nos. 7/8/9 (Fall–Winter 1980–81).

Friedman, Susan. "Against Discipleship: Collaboration and Intimacy in the Relationship of H.D. and Freud." *Literature and Psychology* 33 (1987).

————. "Creativity and the Childbirth Metaphor: Gender Difference in Literary Discourse." *Feminist Studies* 13 (Spring 1987).

————. "H.D." In *Dictionary of Literary Biography 45: American Poets, 1880–1945*. First Series, ed. Peter Quartermaine. Detroit, Michigan: Gale Research Co., 1986.

————. "Modernism of the 'Scattered Remnant': Race and Politics in the Development of H.D.'s Modernist Vision." In *H.D.: Woman and Poet*, ed. Michael King. Orono, Maine: National Poetry Foundation, 1986.

————. *Psyche Reborn: The Emergence of H.D.* Bloomington: Indiana University Press, 1981.

————. "'Remembering Shakespeare Always, But Remembering Him Differently': H.D.'s *By Avon River*." *Sagetrieb* 2 (Summer/Fall 1983).

263

Differently': H.D.'s *By Avon River*." *Sagetrieb* 2 (Summer/Fall 1983).

Friedman, Susan, and Rachel Blau DuPlessis. "'I Had Two Loves Separate': The Sexualities of H.D.'s *Her*." *Montemora* 8 (1981).

————. "'Woman is Perfect': H.D.'s Debate with Freud." *Feminist Studies* 7 (1981).

Frye, Northrop. *Anatomy of Criticism*. Princeton: Princeton University Press, 1951.

Gediman, Helen K. "Romanticism, Narcissism and Creativity." *Journal of the American Psychoanalytical Association* 23 (1975).

Gelpi, Albert. "Hilda in Egypt." *Southern Review* 18 (Spring 1982).

Gilbert, Sandra. "Soldier's Heart: Literary Men, Literary Women and the Great War." *Signs* 8 (Spring 1980).

Gilbert, Sandra, and Susan Gubar. *The Madwoman in the Attic: The Woman Writer and the Nineteenth-Century Literary Imagination*. New Haven: Yale University Press, 1979.

————. *No Man's Land: The Place of the Woman Writer in the Twentieth Century*. New Haven: Yale University Press, 1988.

Gilligan, Carol. *In a Different Voice: Psychological Theory and Woman's Development*. Cambridge, Mass.: Harvard University Press, 1982.

Gordon, Linda. *Woman's Body, Woman's Right: A Social History of Birth Control in America*. New York: Penguin, 1977.

Gubar, Susan. "Mother, Maiden and the Marriage of Death: Women Writers and an Ancient Myth." *Women's Studies* 6 (1979).

————. "'The Blank Page' and the Issues of Female Creativity." In *Writing and Sexual Difference*, ed. Elizabeth Abel. Chicago: University of Chicago Press, 1982.

————. "The Birth of the Artist as Heroine: (Re)Production, the Kunstler Tradition, and the Fiction of Katherine Mansfield." In *The Representation of Women in Fiction*, ed. Carolyn Heilbrun and Margaret R. Higgonet. Baltimore: John Hopkins University Press, 1983.

————. "Sapphistries." *Signs* 10, no. 1 (1984).

————. "The Echoing Spell of H.D.'s *Trilogy*," in *Shakespeare's Sisters*, ed. Sandra Gilbert and Susan Gubar. Bloomington: Indiana University Press, 1979.

Guest, Barbara. *Herself Defined: The Poet H.D. and Her World*. New York: Doubleday, 1984.

Hanscombe, Gillian, and Virginia Smyers. *Writing for Their Lives: The Mod-*

ernist Women 1910–1940. Boston: Northeastern University Press, 1988.

Harding, Esther. *Woman's Mysteries*. New York: Harper & Row, 1976.

Hensley, Jeannine, ed. *The Works of Ann Bradstreet*. Cambridge: Harvard University Press, 1967.

Heybob, Sharon K. *The Cult of Isis in the Graeco-Roman World*. London: E. J. Brill, 1978.

Hirsch, Marianne. *The Mother/Daughter Plot: Narrative, Psychoanalysis, Feminism*. Bloomington: Indiana University Press, 1989.

Hirsh, Elizabeth. " 'New Eyes': H.D., Modernism, and the Psychoanalysis of Seeing." *Literature and Psychology* 32, no. 1 (1986).

Hollenberg, Donna Krolik, ed. "Art and Ardour in World War One: Selected Letters from H.D. to John Cournos." *Iowa Review* 16 (Fall 1986).

Homer. *The Odyssey*, trans. Albert Cook. New York: W. W. Norton, 1967.

Horney, Karen. "The Dread of Woman." In *Feminine Psychology*, ed. Harold Kelman. New York: W. W. Norton, 1967.

How(ever) 3 (October 1986). Special issue on H.D.

Hughes, Glenn. *Imagism and the Imagists: A Study in Modern Poetry*. Stanford: Stanford University Press, 1931.

Iowa Review 16 (Fall 1986). Special issue on H.D.

Jaeger, Werner. *Paideia: The Ideal of Greek Culture*. Vol. 1, 2d ed., trans. Gilbert Highet. New York: Oxford University Press, 1945.

Jaffe, Nora Crow. " 'She Herself Is the Writing': Language and Sexual Identity in H.D." In *Literature and Medicine* 4 (1985).

Johnson, Barbara. "Apostrophe, Animation, and Abortion." *Diacritics* 16 (Spring 1986).

Kammer, Jeanne. "The Art of Silence and the Forms of Women's Poetry." In *Shakespeare's Sisters*, ed. Sandra Gilbert and Susan Gubar. Bloomington: University of Indiana Press, 1979.

Kerenyi, Carl. *Athene: Virgin and Mother*. Zurich: Spring, 1978.

———. *Eleusis: Archetypal Image of Mother and Daughter*, trans. Ralph Manheim. New York: Pantheon, 1967.

Kerenyi, Carl, and C. G. Jung. *Essays on a Science of Mythology*. New York: Bollingen Foundation, 1949.

Klaus, Marshall H., and John Kennell. *Maternal-Infant Bonding*. St. Louis: C. V. Mosby, 1976.

Kloepfer, Deborah Kelly. "Flesh Made Word: Maternal Inscription in

————. *The Unspeakable Mother: Forbidden Discourse in Jean Rhys and H.D.* Ithaca: Cornell University Press, 1989.

Kohut, Heinz. "Forms and Transformations of Narcissism." *Journal of the American Psychoanalytical Association* 14 (April 1966).

Kristeva, Julia. *Desire in Language.* New York: Columbia University Press, 1984.

————. *Revolution in Poetic Language.* New York: Columbia University Press, 1984.

Laity, Cassandra. "H.D. and A. C. Swinburne: Decadence and Modernist Women's Writing." *Feminist Studies* 15 (1989).

Langbaum, Robert. Introduction to William Shakespeare's *The Tempest.* In *Signet Classic Shakespeare*, gen. ed. Sylvan Barnet. New York: New American Library, 1964.

Larsen, Jeanne. "Text and Matrix: Dickinson, H.D., and Women's Voice." In *Engendering the World: Feminist Essays in Psychosexual Poetics*, ed. Tamma Berg et al. Chicago: University of Illinois Press, 1989.

Lawrence, D. H. *Fantasia of the Unconscious.* New York: Viking, 1960.

Levertov, Denise. *The Poet in the World.* New York: New Directions, 1960.

Lifton, Robert J. *The Broken Connection: On Death and the Continuity of Life.* New York: Simon and Schuster, 1979.

————. *The Life of the Self.* New York: Simon and Schuster, 1976.

Lockyer, Herbert. *The Women of the Bible.* Grand Rapids, Mich.: Zondervan, 1967.

MacPike, Loralee. "The Fallen Woman's Sexuality: Childbirth and Censure." In *Sexuality and Victorian Literature*, ed. Richard Cox. Knoxville: University of Tennessee Press, 1984.

Morris, Adalaide. "Projected Pictures: H.D.'s Visionary Moments." *Contemporary Literature* 25 (Winter 1984).

————. "Reading H.D.'s 'Helios and Athene.'" In *Extended Outlooks: The Iowa Review Collection of Contemporary Women Writers*, ed. Jane Cooper et al. New York: Macmillan, 1982.

————. "A Relay of Power and of Peace: H.D. and the Spirit of the Gift." *Contemporary Literature* 27 (Winter 1986).

————. "Science and the Mythopoeic Mind: The Case of H.D." In *Chaos and Order: Complex Dynamics in Literature and Science*, ed. N. Katherine Hayles. Chicago: University of Chicago Press, 1991.

Nadelson, Carol. "'Normal' and 'Special' Aspects of Pregnancy: A Psychological Approach." In *The Woman Patient: Medical and Psychological Interfaces*, vol. 1, Malkah Notman and Carol Nadelson. New York: Plenum, 1978.

O'Brien, Mary. *The Politics of Reproduction*. Boston: Routledge and Kegan Paul, 1981.

Orgel, Stephen. *The Illusion of Power: Political Theatre in the English Renaissance*. Berkeley: University of California Press, 1975.

Ostriker, Alicia. "No Rule of Procedure: H.D. and Open Poetics." Excerpted in *How(ever)* 5 (October 1989).

————. *Writing Like a Woman*. Ann Arbor: University of Michigan Press, 1983.

Peppers, Larry G., and Ronald J. Knapp. *Motherhood and Mourning: Perinatal Death*. New York: Praeger, 1980.

Poesis: A Journal of Criticism 6, nos. 3/4 (1985). Special issue on H.D.

Ponce, Charles. *The Kabbalah*. Wheaton, Ill.: Theosophical Publishing House, 1978.

Pondrom, Cyrena, ed. *The Road to Paris: French Influences on English Poetry, 1900–1920*. Cambridge, England: Cambridge University Press, 1974.

————. "Selected Letters from H.D. to F. S. Flint: A Commentary on the Imagist Period." *Contemporary Literature* 10 (Autumn 1969).

Pound, Ezra. *Ezra Pound and Dorothy, Their Letters (1909–1940)*, ed. Omar Pound and A. Walton Litz. London: Faber and Faber, 1985.

————. *Literary Essays*. New York: New Directions, 1968.

Prost, William. "The Eidolon of Helen: Diachronic Edition of a Myth." Ph.D. dissertation, Catholic University of America, 1977.

Quinn, Vincent. "H.D.'s 'Hermetic Definition': The Poet as Archetypal Mother." *Contemporary Literature* 18 (Winter 1977).

Radway, Janice. *Reading the Romance: Women, Patriarchy, and Popular Literature*. Chapel Hill: University of North Carolina Press, 1984.

Rich, Adrienne. *Of Woman Born: Motherhood as Experience and Institution*. New York: Bantam, 1974.

————. *On Lies, Secrets and Silence: Selected Prose*. New York: W. W. Norton, 1979.

Roche, Judith. "Myrrh: A Study of Persona in H.D.'s *Trilogy*." *Line* 12 (Fall 1988).

Rosaldo, M., and L. Lamphere, eds. *Women, Culture, and Society.* Stanford: Stanford University Press, 1974.

Sacks, Elizabeth. *Shakespeare's Images of Pregnancy.* London: Macmillan, 1980.

Sagetrieb 6 (Fall 1987). Special issue on H.D.

San José Studies 13 (Fall 1987). Special issue on Emily Dickinson and H.D.

Sapir, J. David. "The Anatomy of Metaphor." In *The Social Use of Metaphor*, ed. J. David Sapir and J. Christopher Crocker. Philadelphia: University of Pennsylvania Press, 1977.

Schafer, Roy. "Action and Narration in Psychoanalysis." *New Literary History* 12, no. 1 (1980).

Schaffner, Perdita, "Sketch of H.D.: The Egyptian Cat." In H.D.'s *Hedylus*. Redding Ridge, Conn.: Black Swan Books, 1980.

Schapiro, Meyer. "On a Painting of Van Gogh." In *Modern Art.* New York: George Braziller, 1979.

Sessler, John Jacob. *Communal Pieties among Early American Moravians.* New York: Henry Holt, 1933.

Shaktini, Ramascar. "Displacing the Phallic Subject: Wittig's Lesbian Writing." *Signs* 8 (Autumn 1982).

Sklenicka, Carol. "Lawrence's Vision of the Child: Reimagining Character and Consciousness." *D. H. Lawrence Review* 18 (Summer/Fall 1985–86).

Slater, Philip. *The Glory of Hera: Greek Mythology and the Greek Family.* Boston: Beacon Press, 1968.

Suleiman, Susan. "Writing and Motherhood." In *The (M)other Tongue: Essays in Feminist Psychoanalytic Interpretation.* Ithaca: Cornell University Press, 1985.

Sutherland, Donald, and Hazel Barnes. *"Hippolytus" in Myth and Drama.* Nebraska: University of Nebraska Press, 1960.

Sword, Helen. "Orpheus and Eurydice in the Twentieth Century: Lawrence, H.D., and the Poetics of the Turn." *Twentieth Century Literature* 35 (Winter 1989).

Tindall, William York. *A Reader's Guide to James Joyce.* New York: Farrar, Straus and Giroux, 1971.

Vivas, Eliseo. *D. H. Lawrence: The Failure and the Triumph of Art.* Evanston, Ill.: Northwestern University Press, 1960.

Walker, Barbara G., ed. *The Woman's Encyclopedia of Myths and Secrets.* San Francisco: Harper and Row, 1983.

Walker, Cheryl. "H.D. and Time." In *Taking Our Time: Feminist Perspectives on Temporality*, ed. Frieda Forman. New York: Pergamon Press, 1989.

Watkins, Renee Neu. "Two Women Visionaries and Death." *Numen* 30, no. 2 (1983).

Witt, R. E. *Isis in the Graeco-Roman World*. Ithaca, New York: Cornell University Press, 1971.

Zilboorg, Caroline. "A New Chapter in the Lives of H.D. and Richard Aldington: Their Relationship with Clement Shorter." *Philological Quarterly* 68 (Spring 1989).

Zilboorg, Gregory. "Masculine and Feminine." *Psychiatry* 7 (1944).

Index

Swinburne, Algernon: "Itylus," 48

"*Sword* cycle" (H.D.), 159–60; visions of Viking ship described in, 160. *See also entries for individual novels*

Sword Went Out to Sea, The (H.D.), 159, 160, 161

Tarot, Le (Chaboseau), 209–10

"Tempest, The" (H.D.), 143–45

Theseus, 179, 192–96

Thetis: as depicted by H.D., 183, 184, 186, 190–93, 197, 202; as important subject to H.D., 84–85

"Thetis" (H.D.), motherhood as threat in, 84–85, 88

Thorn Thicket (H.D.), as diary of reaction to Heydt's engagement, 208–9

Timaeus (Plato), 8

"To Anthea" (Herrick), 163

Tolstoy, Leo: *Anna Karenina*, 10

"Tribute to the Angels" (H.D.), 98, 110; as account of psychic modification, 129–33; revelations quoted in, 129–30; symbolism of alchemy in, 129, 130–31

Tribute to Freud (H.D.), 17–19, 101, 170; compared to "The Flowering of the Rod," 134–

35. *See also Writing on the Wall*

Trilogy (H.D.), 13, 14, 98; anticipated in "The Master," 114; child as symbol in, 142; dreams recapitulated in, 109, 126–27, 131–33, 136–37; "family romance" in, 126–27; foreshadowed in *Within the Walls*, 119; H.D.'s analysis reenacted in, 125, 133, 135; related to *The Gift*, 13–14; retelling of scriptures in, 125, 126, 129–34, 135–38; shell and pearl imagery in, 44, 127–28; spiritual transformation as theme of, 125, 126, 129, 133. *See also entries for individual poems*

"Triplex" (H.D.), 92, 94

Troubadours, 143, 154–55; Pound's interest in, 226

Ulysses (Joyce), 10

"Vale Ave" (H.D.), 205, 208, 209, 210–16; "confinement" as source of inspiration, 215; kabbalah as source of divine imagery in, 219; "primal scene" re-created in, 210, 216; "processus" of lovers in, 210–15; renewed sense of self revealed in, 215–16

Van der Leeuw, J. J., 99

Van Gogh, Vincent. *See*
Gogh, Vincent Van
Veronese: *Marriage of Cana*,
171
Viking ship: H.D.'s visions of,
160, 161; as symbolic of
womb, 215–16
Voyance, La (Chaboseau), 209

"Walls Do Not Fall, The"
(H.D.), 98, 126–29; symbolism of shellfish in 127–28
Walsh, John, on *Madrigal*, 173
"Wash of Cold River" (H.D.),
88
"What Do I Love?" (H.D.),
98
"When I Am a Cup" (H.D.),
92, 94
White Rose and the Red, The
(H.D.), life of Siddall as
basis of, 159, 162
"White World" (H.D.), 82
"Winter Love" (H.D.), 228–
36; aged Helen depicted in,
229–30; connection to *Helen
in Egypt*, 175–78, 202; as
continuation of dialogue with
Pound, 226, 228–29; as critique of social institution of

motherhood, 228–35; *End to
Torment* a prologue to, 224,
228; women in H.D.'s life
depicted in, 232
Within the Walls (H.D.), 98,
119–20
Wolle, "Mamalie" (grand-
mother), 13, 121, 122, 124,
162
Women in Love (Lawrence), 10
World War I, 5, 19, 20, 33,
106, 118, 160, 161, 162–63,
207
World War II, 6, 15, 19, 98,
162; effect on H.D., 118–19,
122, 160, 161, 206–7
Writing on the Wall (H.D.):
"Advent" as postlude to, 101,
102–4; as memoir of H.D.'s
analysis with Freud, 98–99,
111, 133, 134, 138. *See also
Tribute to Freud*

Yorke, Dorothy: Aldington's
liaison with, 163, 208; por-
trayed in *Bid Me to Live*,
163

Zinzendorf, Count, 121, 122,
162